ADVANCE PRAISE FOR

# cubanology

"Welcoming as the *guenmai* soup whose making recurs throughout this journal, *Cubanology* carries the flavors of zen intensives, languages, and housecleaning; Greek retsina and Dutch beer; murmured conversations with books, friends, strangers, cultures, countries, and conditions. Omar Pérez is equally home-leaver and home-maker wherever he travels. Language is his pillow; *zazen* his backpack; music and imagination's freedoms his left and right shoes."

JANE HIRSHFIELD

"I'm quite taken by *Cubanology*, a book of the quotidian that rises to the universal. In morning we have *zazen*, in the afternoon we have language(s) and poetry, then later there is *guenmai* for 70 people (recipe included: carrots, onions, turnips, celery) but usually just for three or four or one. Are we in Amsterdam, or Athens, Munich? Yes. It is *Cubanology*, after all, and 'He proposed realviciousization,/seated at the deskritorio' is the way poems are written when you are Omar Pérez. Part Pound, part Bolaño, add a Brechtian play, mix in some Hart Crane, spiced with Marianne Moore, Larry Eigner and Paul Hoover (Paul Hoover!), this is a global 24 hours that stretches time to eternity, consolidates place, and with a polyglot sensibility that seems bent on unifying all languages. Reading *Cubanology* is more like meditating than reading. Which is to say the ritual of the day. Which stays with you, and is tomorrow, the eternal day."

BOB HOLMAN

"Omar Pérez's *Cubanology* is a Book of Days for the new century, a clear-eyed account of his travels in Europe, in the form of journal entries, essays, poems, translations, and meditations dating from 2002–2005. 'To one seeking the truth,' he writes (translating the 'Sandokai'), 'I offer only this: don't waste any time.' Hence he schools his readers in the art of making and measuring time according to the precepts of his Buddhist faith, the practice of which provides the scaffolding for this fascinating journey, which suggests that even if, as he writes, 'travel intoxicates,' it also reveals the heart and soul of one of the most important artists of our time."

CHRISTOPHER MERRILL

"To read *Cubanology* is to experience body/mind/spirit as a visceral materiality of time. Interweaving nomad with perpetual lesson, Omar Pérez threads poem to diary to essay to lyric as a function of the orbital rhizome; to align traveler with song / *and from there to the sky*. Pérez embodies the hybrid form as storyteller before language. The diaspora is in the zazen, the culture we're seeking is there, inside—among our interpersonal planes, within the synesthesia of these pages—allowing us to fire up chronology's vehicle beyond 'ology to become 'the potential immigrant,' as translator Kristin Dykstra situates in her expansive afterword. Fueled by the daily global / *reality is a field of signs, a force field* / awakening the steps that give back what the body aspires to be. *Cubanology* ignites mobility as the ability to create / *from chromosome* / *to Revolución*."

EDWIN TORRES

# cubanology

## OMAR PÉREZ

Translated and with an Afterword by
**Kristin Dykstra**

Station Hill Press
BARRYTOWN, NEW YORK

Published by Station Hill of Barrytown, the publishing project of the Institute for Publishing Arts, Inc., 120 Station Hill Road, Barrytown, NY 12507, New York, a not-for-profit, tax-exempt organization [501(c)(3)].

Online catalogue: www.stationhill.org
e-mail: publishers@stationhill.org

Cover and interior design by Susan Quasha.
Cover image: "Seated Portrait," engraving on linoleum, 2016. © Omar Pérez

Station Hill acknowledges all rights to photographs remain with their photographers as identified in List of Images.

Library of Congress Cataloging-in-Publication Data

Names: Pérez, Omar, 1964- author. | Dykstra, Kristin, translator.
Title: Cubanology / Omar Pérez; translated with an afterword by Kristin Dykstra.
Description: Barrytown, NY : Station Hill Press, 2018.
Identifiers: LCCN 2018024322 | ISBN 9781581771756 (pbk.)
Subjects: LCSH: Pérez, Omar—Travel—Europe. | Pérez, Omar—Diaries. | Europe—Description and travel.
Classification: LCC PQ7390.P432 C8313 2018 | DDC 861/.64—dc23
LC record available at https://lccn.loc.gov/2018024322

Manufactured in the United States of America.

*To Kris Dykstra,*

*the translatress*
*who has made a tribute*
*to lingua franca*

—OMAR PÉREZ


*Translation is an element in cultural crossings, including*
*migration, an important phenomenon in our ongoing human*
*history. I would like to dedicate the translation of this book*
*to all migrants in recognition of their dignity, knowledge,*
*contributions, and human rights.*

—KRISTIN DYKSTRA

# CONTENTS

# 1. A CUBAN SEEKS HIS ROOTS IN THE ICE

One fall night in the year 2001 in Havana, I find myself in a kitchen with an Argentine Zen monk, known as The Turk, scheming up a ritual soup. *Guenmai*, Cuban style, for twenty people.

Two bowls of rice, or a half pound.

A similar quantity of fruits of the earth: Onion, chive, celery, carrot and squash. It's the squash that adds a Cuban touch. The recipe also calls for radish. He substitutes turnip. I wouldn't know what to suggest as a substitute for the squash.

Rinse the rice, brown it lightly in the frying pan. In the meantime …

In the meantime, dice the fruits of the earth into squared Japanese centimeters—*guenmai* is of Japanese origin—, cook the cubes in a saucepan, barely covered with water.

When the water in the large saucepan begins to boil, *si butta* the rice, as the Italians say.

When the rice opens, you put in the cubed vegetables. *Guenmai* cooks over high heat until it arrives at its famous consistency: sperm, yin and yang in the stew. A little longer. Something else: The Turk and I discuss our travel plans. I tell him about my sister in Milan; about the university where my friend has invited me to teach for a brief time; and about the Rotterdam Poetry Festival, where I'll be a featured reader.

"Doesn't matter," says The Turk, and lights a cigarette. "Once you're in Milan, it will be a gateway into Europe and you'll be closer to the master. Let's go to bed, since we have to get up at six tomorrow."

*Amsterdam Dojo*

# ZERO (2002)

I arrived in Amsterdam one summer day at noon. I had left Milan Central by train, sleeper coach, awakened at three in the morning in the Rhine Valley: *Guten morgen*, the police want to see your documents. At five it's already daytime in Mannheim, *Frankfurt am Main*: dark forests, pointed houses: OPEL. The landscape peaceful, a great river.

And then Cologne. Gothic cathedral where I pray to the Virgin Mary, and naturally I buy a vial for my sister in one of the boutiques stocked with bottled waters from Cologne. At 10:16 we continue en route to Amsterdam. The direct train route doesn't exist nowadays, says a Milanese friend based in Amsterdam: the greed of rail companies and airlines deleted it from the program. A shame, a lost landscape of cows and rice growers, forests, windmills.

Finally Bauhaus, crystal, steel, and Centraal Station in Amsterdam.

At 1:30 I stop in front of the door of the zen *dojo*. It's closed. Following a strange and trusting impulse, I leave all of my luggage next to the glass doors and go down to the corner to sample a beer. When I return, someone has taken my luggage inside and closed up again. I go off in search of a coffeeshop and find it around the other corner: *Het Ballonetje*, The Little Balloon. Typical neighborhood enclave, peaceable, almost as if arranged in harmony with what awaits us tomorrow: *sesshin* with Master Stephane "Kosen" Thibaut, a day and a half of intensive practice.

Upon my return to the *dojo*, dinner is ready, Spanish wine on the table. As we wait for the master, tomorrow's *guenmai* cooks. Kosen arrives, we eat; the master talks about Cuba and his next *sesshin* there. The first *zazen* will be at 7:30 am. I sleep in the *dojo*.

Up at 5 a.m.; after cleaning, first *zazen* at 8, first *guenmai*.

*Zazen*, 11:30 a.m., lunch and we go to Ooster Park, on the east side, to enjoy the sun. *Zazen*, 4pm.

Dinner. *Zazen*, 8 p.m. I go to the corner for beers with Christophe Demeure, calligrapher monk of Lyon.

## SUNDAY 2

Up at 5; *zazen* 8 a.m. and again at 11. There are *mondos*, or questions and answers between disciple and master, from *buddha* to *buddha*. Then a party. I dance with Alga de Mar, the Colombian woman whose name translates as "seaweed." Kosen plans his next *sesshin* in Havana from December 10 to 20. He leaves.

Those of us who stay are invited to continue the symposium at the home of monk Paul Loomans, in a place I figure to be northeast of the *dojo*. *Il'y a du monde* and three children. The neighbors upstairs, Moroccans, offer couscous that we share on the patio under cherry trees. At dawn we survivors return to the *dojo*.

## MONDAY 3 JUNE

When the last foreigners leave, I stay alone in the *dojo* with a key loaned to me by the person in charge, Paul. Rules for occupying the *dojo* are simple: do all my *zazen* and make a small monetary contribution, or *fuse*, upon the conclusion of my stay.

I arrange my personal effects and head out for the *Centrum* in search of an Internet Point. I find it not far from a Chinese market where I buy oranges, apples, carrots, and lemons: *viva* revolution without paroxysms: Amsterdam obliges.

At three I find myself alone sitting *zazen* in the *dojo*. I wait for the Introduction to Zen class that takes place on Mondays. At 6 p.m. various monks and students arrive: Buddha in Dutch seems pleasant. "Easy does it." Here English is a true *lingua franca*, although many immigrants speak the local language. When the course ends, we prepare *gomasio*, toasted sesame seeds ground with salt, to accompany the week's *guenmai*.

### TUESDAY 4

Up at 7. The German musican monk Florian wakes me up, *Guenmai*. I go to Internet Point; the world is round and empty, the writing melancholy. At 3 p.m. I return to the *dojo* after a stroll for viewing boats and canals. I take a bath and, listening to Camarón, an idea slips out of me: *sangue non mente*. These days, reading the anthology of essays *Cuba, La isla del día después* (*Cuba: The Island the Day After*) and the polemic that it unleashed, I've confronted the idea of Che Guevara as a mass murderer, as E.H. Bustos characterized him. Master Deshimaru, who was in the Asia-Pacific War and had to have witnessed more than one massacre, clarifies the precept of not killing, saying that what must never be killed is the spirit of Buddha in the others.

As an everyday individual, I never experienced Guevara as anyone capable of killing the spirit of Buddha in others—the spirit of freedom, awakening for all, and the hope of victory over ignorance. An attempt to resemble those people who take their lives toward the ultimate consequences, like an arrow flying directly toward the mark or a comet shooting across space, affords the emotion of already living in the future. Or perhaps in that far corner of the universe where time doesn't exist and the dream of happiness comes true.

At least that was, during childhood, my case and I met nobody among my contemporaries who feared the prospect of transformation making us like *el Che*, not in the sense of being a warrior for hatred. I'm speaking here of one experience. It's nothing that would stand up to a detailed intellectual analysis, nor does it need one.

Of course, I'm not asking for the canonization of Ernesto *Che* Guevara; not even that of Father Varela. Of saints there are too many, and they need no endorsements. Saint Francis and Gandhi, who wouldn't kill a fly, correspond to the image of man given over to a never-ending mission. And Martí, architect of a war without hatreds; and David, for whom it isn't abhorrent to remark on his hatred of the enemy in his psalms.

But who, looking over his shoulder at Che Guevara, can say, "I am free of all hatreds"? Free of all desire to kill the spirit of awakening in myself and in others, purified of any internal violence separating me from all other lives?

With some beings, it's advisable to look them in the eye, not to look upwards from one's knees like a devotee, or to stand like a tourist looking up at a monument. Much less looking down from the height of a moral construct that turns you, in the end, into the conscious or unconscious accomplice of a system and civilization erected over all manner of crimes, commonly written off today as accidents or necessary evils.

### WEDNESDAY 5 JUNE

This is oasis. Up at 6 a.m., I continue my reading of Scholem's book, *Histoire d'une amitié*, which I picked up in Barcelona from the hands of my friend César Mora. Reading begun in the corner bar, where an Israeli waitress presides. She is lovely as an actress from the silent screen; her name is Ruth.

*Zazen* at 7:30; there are six people, and I serve *guenmai*. After the ceremony I give myself the job of placing herbs in the doorway and clearing the tables. It's mid-morning, *Kind of Blue* can be heard, and the White Widow comes looking for me.

… nor from the heights of a doctrine that would be intellectual, not biological, one that won't look at itself in the mirror of existence and consequently becomes incoherent even within its own terms. A morality of this kind deserves to be relegated to libraries and academies, and even then it could tell itself that it wasted the plant matter.

While a Zen monk, I don't take my personal victory over stupidity for granted. Nonetheless I can try not to hinder others in their own victory; this is how I've understood Taisen Deshimaru's idea about not killing Buddha's spirit. From that perspective, "the call to follow principles of the absolutely pure spirit" is attainable for me. Or the relation between Martí and Buddha. Or Lezama, his presence of a point of contact between writing and breathing. But it's not about promoting some Zen-Guevarism here or any other new category designed to shock conventional people and conquer the market. We poets don't write in order to produce *literature*.

At noon it rains, and the bar is a wonderful refuge. Alga del Mar has invited me to her house; but first we take a walk through the Gasperplas with its lake, its swans. At the house there is talking and cooking: rice, codfish, potatoes, fried banana chips. Salad and good red wine from Chile, which Mo Veld brought. Alga gives me a photo of Master Stephane—Kosen is his name as a monk—with tobacco and a Zapatista Movement t-shirt. I leave on transportation arranged by Alga: an old green bicycle. Arriving at the *dojo*, I can't sleep.

### THURSDAY 6TH

Up at 5, I put the altar in its place and spill the water for the flowers. A good start to the day. Yesterday I promised to get Che's diaries from the Congo for Alga.

*Zazen* for four cats. And females: one of them, Cristina, invites me on a bike ride to the Faculty of Philosophy. Waiting for us there is a friend who makes photocopies and color prints for students. His hobby or *liefhebberij*: sailboat, pipe, guitar. And a bicycle he rides, reclining. His name is Han. We talk about ayahuasca, Zen, political parties in Holland and the new right, ecology, and the wealthy people who destroy nature here to build highways and then buy a house in Provence.

From there we go on to Vondel Park, Amsterdam's legendary lung. I rush back for *zazen* at a run, and at night I walk through Ooster Park; the night is cool. Miles Davis on the way back, Coltrane and all the rest who blow through horns.

FRIDAY 7TH

Up at 5:30. I go through the altar, *bain rituel*, Miles and Scholem. *Zazen*: six people arrive under rain that intensifies as the bell rings. We finish, have a *cafecinho*; the boy who speaks Italian, Johan, is present.

Cristina with another invitation, to the *Troppen Museum* or Museum of the Tropics. It displays objects such as metal marimbas from Indonesia, the *gamelan*; feathered ornaments from Amazonia; domestic implements from Ghana; and among all these other things, Ifá's board. There are typical foods from Asia, Africa and Latin America.

On the way back to the *dojo* I get lost, as is my habit. It's not hard to get lost following canals. Amsterdam doesn't follow the rectilinear grid pattern of Central Havana, for example. The canals impede it; the bridges restore it. But water moves in curves, and the bicycle too.

I ring the doorbell at the *dojo*. The Yoga teacher opens the door for me. She's Italian, and her name is Barbara.

Before I go to sleep I hear *Kind of Blue* again, "Flamenco Sketches."

DOMENICA 9

Up at 9:30 a.m. Arnaud is the first to arrive. He speaks perfect Spanish with a Castilian accent. *Zazen*, 11 a.m. There are faces new to me alongside the regulars.

I go to Vondel Park with Cristina; the Blue Tea House, *Het Blauwe Thee-huis*, by architects H.A.J. and J. Baanders. 1936, exemplary of the *Nieuwe Bouwen*, or new Dutch construction, with basic geometries. Anyway, the teahouse is full: there are skaters, dogs, children, elderly people, wandering acrobats and maybe even a clown. Then we walk across the gallery. Passing the Rijksmuseum, it opens toward Museum Park. Mongolian musicians earn their living playing here: an ensemble of string instruments, accompanying a single singer. He uses harmonic vibration, imitating a cricket on the savannah or in an early morning breeze across the steppe. At the same time, he wiggles his hips slightly, his eyes half-closed. His whole body is a sounding board, a robust one. They're dressed in typical costumes and an air of solemnity—which doesn't prevent them, between songs, from making calls on cell phones.

Up to this point Cristina has acted as a guide for me in the city. She's younger than I am, and taller. Behind employee eyeglasses she has amber eyes, daughter of the waterfall. And her hair is like those drawings by Leonardo representing water, its tresses.

### MARTEDI 11

Up at 5:45 a.m. *Zazen*, I serve *guenmai*.

Then I go to Paul's house to watch the soccer match between France and Denmark. Counter to predictions, France loses 2 to 0. Paul calls the master to offer his condolences: Master is not very happy and doesn't appreciate the joke. Paul Loomans is an actor and mime and, like many Dutchmen, very diplomatic. But in this case, it does nothing for him. Master orders him off to hell.

### MERCOLEDI 12

Up at 5:45 a.m. *Zazen*. I ring the bell. I go to the little company where The Glamorous Mo Veld works using email. Invites me to lunch at a snack bar on the corner. The weather is good, and we eat outside at tables, quasi-picnic style.

In the afternoon I meet Cristina at Vondel Park again: *overmacht*. Dutch for *force majeure*.

Up at 5:45 a.m. *Zazen*, then ready to leave. I go off to Rotterdam for Poetry International, arriving at 2:30. A smiling young woman meets me at the station and takes me to the hotel.

After resting I meet up with Antonio José Ponte. I eat with Tatjana Daan and Erick Menkveld, organizers; also the Egyptian poet Girgis Shoukri and another from Zimbabwe, Titus Moetsabi. With Titus and Ponte, I go out for a walk. Ponte disappears into one of those alleys straight out of Fritz Lang. Titus and I end up in a Surinamese discoteque. At 5, *buona notte*, or *buon giorno*.

Rotterdam is quite different. It was bombed during the war, and little remains of the city Erasmus knew. Here towers are tall and the streets symmetrical. And still there are canals. *Nieuwe Bouwen*? Could be. Although according to the official timeline the new style of construction occurs, as a movement, only from 1915 to 1940, its influence extends to the present day, like *Bauhaus* and the *Nieuwe Zakelijkheid*. Even in its ultramodern expressions. Anyway, a more extroverted city than Amsterdam.

There are many markets with foodstuffs: yucca, *malanga*, *plátano macho*, beans, coconut. The city is lively in its science-fiction architecture. In older zones, the Dutch know how to be rustic.

There are poets of all styles and figures in the festival, from a rapper like Umar Bin Hassan, accompanied by a guitar player from Detroit, to Jacques Roubaud, who presents a "Defense of Poetry." His questions are:

> Is poetry still possible?
> Is poetry elsewhere?
> Modern poetry, why so obscure?
> What is poetry?

We take a boat ride through the port of Rotterdam, said to be the largest in the world. And it does seem infinite.

The festival makes space for minority languages like K'iche and Maya, as well as Welsh, Latvian, Corsican, Sursilvan, and Milanese. There are two translation workshops dedicated to the Chinese poet Shang Ch'in and the Dutch poet J. Eijkelboom, where poems are translated from one tongue into another, another, another ... until arriving back at the original tongue. There's a place for Cuban poetry, which Damaris Calderón joins, and a tribute to Cesare Pavese, the loner. Many poets get together to read their favorite Pavese poems. I read "Atlantic Oil."

The poets are invited to the Keith Haring exhibition at the Boijmans Van Beuiningen Museum. I attend with Cristina, who has come from Amsterdam. Haring has humor, a sense of ancient symmetry ("fearful symmetry"), and color that goes straight to basic emotions, almost flatly. Who knows why, but Joseph Fleury Crepin comes to mind for me, with his pagan icons, his touches of voodoo, Byzantine light. They say that Crepin, plumber and medium, received an order in a vision to paint three hundred canvases invoking the end of the second World War: when he completed the designated amount, the Holocaust came to a close. But he kept on painting until his death. Haring too.

With Titus Moetsabi I work on an English version of a poem by the Dutch writer Remco Campert (1929):

> There is a deep shuddering
> in the blush of the ashamed body
> for the burning caress
> of the sun & the strong wind
>
> soaked in sweet rain
> I am
> in the soft of the ear
> till love becomes skin on me
> like a fable you tore the heart
> of tenderness in me
> now you are my earth quaking

the woods are in flames
we open the house
to the fire of the unfamiliar men

which I translate into Spanish afterwards:

*En el rubor del cuerpo avergonzado*
*hay un profundo temblor por la caricia*
*ardiente del sol y el viento fuerte*

*así estoy empapado de la dulce lluvia*
*en lo suave de las orejas*
*hasta que el amor se me hace piel*
*como una fábula me heriste*
*el corazón*
*de la juventud*
*y ahora haces temblar mi tierra*
*y arden los bosques*
*y abrimos la casa a los fuegos*
*de los hombres extranjeros*

Poetry International, well organized and generous, concludes on the 22nd, and "felt no distance between people," says a poet from Holland. Before we depart Cristina, Titus and I eat lunch in a café not far from the hotel, to watch the match between Senegal and Turkey. The Africans lose 1-0, to our despair, but Turks at the neighboring table drink a victory beer.

### SUNDAY 23

The eternal walk through Vondel Park. Christa invites me to see the outstanding film *The Matrix* at her house.

The essential part, *special effects & martial arts* aside, is probably the master-disciple relationship. *Here we are, in the machine.*

### LUNEDI 24

Up at 8:32 a.m. *Zazen*. Market. Honey. *Buona notte.*

### MARTEDI 25

Walking through the neighborhood of Jordaan. The way to travel to a Paris that no longer exists.

### GIOVEDI 27

At 8 p.m. I fly out to Milan. Thanks to the iron bird, you can drink your coffee in Amsterdam *Oud West* and eat your *pasta asciutta* in Piazza Piola. Or vice versa. I didn't come to Milan this time for *l' especulation prescient-ifica* but to help my sister, who's giving birth: *el niño la mira, mira, el niño la esta mirando*. That's Lorca: the child is looking, look / the child is looking at her. For a forty-year-old woman who has already suffered one Cesarean, the birth seems like it might involve complications. Let's see, Milan, if your miasmas bring good health this time.

The city empties out in the summer. The Milanese flee, and in the streets, you see only ghostly automobiles. You can jog through the streets without so much danger of asphyxiation. As contamination lessens, the mosquitos multiply, specters surging out of the canals that Mussolini filled. I shuttle from Corso Buenos Aires, where they make the best pizza and my very own slice, to the Internet Point overseen by an Arab, to the *palazzo* where my sister is waiting: *l'anima semplicetta volentier torna a quel che la trastulla* (Purgatory, Dante). My pastime. At times I go to the public pool with my nephew, and we come back, soaked in chlorine, to cheer up the expectant mother. At last it's time to admit her. The hospital is a popular beauty: a fascist-style classic, its *Mater Voluminosa* of art deco stone next to the entry ramp.

At the *fondazione* Elvira Baldaracco, Marina Zancan and Emmanuela Favoino want to hire me to do a Spanish translation of *il romanzo Nessuno torna indietro* by the illustrious Alba de Céspedes. The pay is minimal and the deadline for the printer pressing, but the project is interesting, an adventure. I accept, receiving the original edition and an earlier translation rendered in a noble tone. That one was published in Spain during Franco's rule.

**WEDNESDAY 17 OF JULY. GANESHA'S DAY.**

My nephew Dario has spent one day on earth. They still have him in the hospital fishbowl, where we visitors squeeze together like tourists in front of the glazed Pietá of San Pietro. But the Cuban-Milanese angel is already promising. Love, in its own particularity, has "given birth." At one in the morning I consult the *I Ching* about the upcoming trip to Cuba and it answers:

> *Fu, Il Ritorno.* 24
> End of one cycle, beginning of another.
> Good health! Rest, respite.
> Winter solstice. November—December.

What more is there to say. Will we see each other in Cuba? At any rate, we continue the conversation this way.

As August begins, I leave Milan on a train for Ancona, then continue by boat to Patras after a short stopover in Igoumenitsa. The wonder of the Greek sea silences this journal, and in any case, Durrell is accurate in his opening to *Prospero's Cell*: "But once you strike out from the flat and desolate Calabrian mainland towards the sea, you are aware of a change in the heart of things: aware of the horizon beginning to stain at the rim of the world: aware of islands coming out of the darkness to meet you." And he goes deeper:

> You enter Greece as one might enter a dark crystal; the form of things becomes irregular, refracted. Mirages suddenly swallow islands, and wherever you look the trembling curtain of the

atmosphere deceives. Other countries may offer you discoveries in manners or lore or landscape; Greece offers you something harder—the discovery of yourself.

Through this *discovery*, and envisioning myself in front of Cristina again, this time in her country of birth, I take a risk in Pireas. I pawn my passport for 17 euros to a girl from Eloudas: if she defrays the cost of my travel to Crete, I'll also give her a bottle of Chianti. About Crete I'll say no more right now save that the transaction went through. I remember the eagle on the crag and the Victor, called *Ligariá* here, potent and flowering next to dusty highways.

*Crete*

After the ships and airplanes that return me to Europe (let's just say it openly here: Greece is not Europe), I'm back on a train, this time going to Kosen Thibaut's summer camp in Cataluña.

Here there isn't much space for carrying journals around either. I'm a novice, I'm in the kitchen. On August 22 I write on a piece of bread wrapper:

First day of preparation. Rain at sunrise; we're in Mas Silvestre, in the Catalan Pyrenees. The tent Cristina and I are sharing is soaking wet.

There's El Turco, The Turk, whom I haven't seen since that night in Havana. We drink *mate* with Pierre Leroux, the monk from Barcelona's *dojo*.

In the kitchen, which is a blessing, an international team of eight people. María Teresa Vuillemin, the *tenzo* or chief cook, explains the conditions. Each person, according to his or her situation, makes *guenmai*, takes leftovers away from the meal, taps the metal, and places incense on the master's table. For the others, kitchen and more kitchen. There's enough kitchen for the entire day. Plus the *zazen* that completes it. Some days we have enough time to walk through the forest or swim in the pool. Swimming, I catch a cold. During *zazen* drops of snot drain out of me and onto the *kesa* Pierre loaned to me. During the *kusen* (teaching), Stephane talks about a return to silence.

### SATURDAY 16 NOVEMBER, AMSTERDAM

*Oh, Cubanology*! I pick up this journal like a vice. Somehow it extends a thing that was interrupted by the ocean in Greece. Why am I starting up this book of days again? Because I believe in human betterment!

Therefore, Yoga with Barbara in the *dojo*; approximately one hour. Iyengaar system: good for the body-spirit and for *zazen* posture. In the first few minutes I relax too much and nearly fall asleep. I finish reading Scholem's *Histoire d'une Amitie*, where he tells his memories of Walter Benjamin.

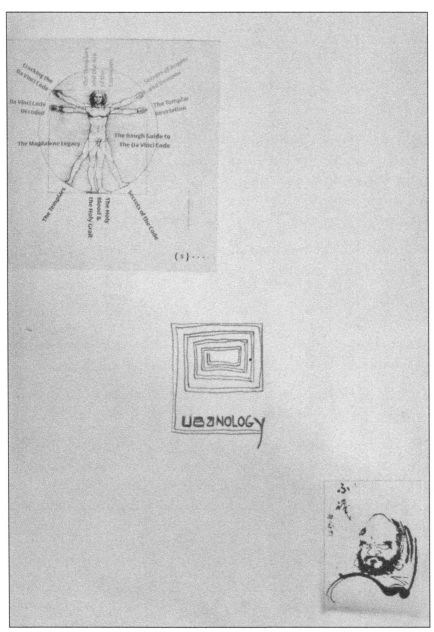

*"Cubanology" journal opening page*

I lead the morning's *zazen*. Recap: dinner with Cristina's family was a success, the people friendly and the food not bad at all. As for the rest, I've purchased a drill in Praxis with other tools for making bookcases and furniture to hold books and records, etcetera.

Cuba? I still have doubts. Above all, after the failure I suffered on October 10 when I had to return from the airport to my house, melancholic, because I didn't have a Cuban permit in my passport. My forgetfulness and other bureaucratic delays caused me to miss the *sesshin* with Kosen in Havana, but: *I feel pretty, o so pretty, it's alarming how pretty I feel*

Yesterday I tried to work on my translation of the novel, but I couldn't concentrate. Regardless, the laptop is smooth as silk.

Vespers at a *sesshin* led by Pierre Leroux after his ad hoc arrival from Barcelona.

*Een cadeautje*, a little gift, as they say here. A day and a half of practice, you eat in the *dojo* and work as a spiritual exercise.

I finally reserved a return flight to Cuba for Wednesday the 27th. Recently I haven't managed to sew my *kesa* or work on the translation of *Nessuno torna indietro*. Stories about women in Fascist Rome. Still, I advance somewhat in my study of Deshimaru; César Mora says it might be picked up for publication in a Barcelona literary review, *El Ciervo* something.

In *sesshin* I'm responsible for the coffee service: *koffee*, cookies, sugar, *melk* & steaming *thee*.

Amsterdam Schiphol airport—to Milano Malpensa—to Havana's Jose Marti.

My son Mariano is waiting for me at the airport with my mother. Populating my dreams: a rapid visit to Havana, forays, running around. Sea, coast, reef. Hastily going on to Mexico.

Guadalajara, Mexico, from November 29 to December 9: International Book Fair with a group of poets, artists, dancers, musicians, etc. The Brigade, as we're known. We're staying at an old Sheraton fallen on hard times, with a nice pool. In the middle you can stand up. Jorge Luis Arcos invites me for beer one night and we go to a little bar, well-stocked and colorful. Two girls make advances without letting up until the owner throws them out, indignant: "This is no place for that kind of business; you can leave." The next morning, we visit a neighboring market. Arcos presents me with a little chess game. I use it to experiment with *Lerne Kombinieren*, a book of offensive situations loaned to me by Paul Loomans, my adversary from the Low Countries: *ain't got no problems, only solutions*, John Lennon used to say. But in these cases, there aren't any solutions without their own problems.

I do *zazen* in the hotel room with nice carpet, which I share with the peaceable Edel Morales. Of activities there aren't many, of course, if I choose to focus only on the ones that directly involve me and take walks around this warm city. I have a coffee with Emilio García Montiel, whom I hadn't seen since an afternoon on the Hill, and José Manuel Prieto, who gives me an interesting Russian-Cuban novel. I read straight through it in my hotel room without stopping. As for the rest of the time—including some rum with Sigfredo Ariel—I read a few poems in public, and when they invite me to lecture about contemporary Cuban poetry, I present "Martí and Buddha." Some ask: And what does that have to do with anything?

I remember the flights, vulgar and loud. Not at all like a European airline, aside from the international style of the food.

Havana again. I'm already saying goodbye to Mariano on the corner of Belascoaín and San Lázaro. "Papa, I want you to buy me a Batman suit."

L'Italia é una reppublica
fondata sull'equilibrio
fra piacere e dovere.

*Se propeonía darse cruenta,*
*sentado en el escretorio*
*se asombaba de ver pasar los días;*
*en un esfuerzo matremático*
*incendió su propio cigarrillio*
*con las manos unidas en plagaria.*
*El apegarse y el apegrase*
*se rebellan expontaneamente*
*en una etrica, per fecula feculorum*
*Amen.*

[*L'Italia é una reppublica*
*fondata sull'equilibrium*
*fra piacere e dovere.*

He proposied realviciousization,
seated at the deskritorio
he was amazed to see days going by;
hands united in prayer
in a mathematical exertion
he lit his own cigarette.
Attachment and agreasement
spontaneously rebel each other
right into splenethics, *per fecula feculorum.*
Amen.]

# 2003

Kosen's winter camp at Mas Gircos, Cataluña, has ended. Our return trip takes us through Lyon: Paul, Cristina, María from Catalonia, and a *bodhisattva* from Eindhoven, named Saskia like the wife of Rembrandt Van Rijn.

Right here I pick up the book of days, *compresso il diario scrivere e tradurre. O fado s'asculta, lavoro sodo nella prima versione di Nessuno torna indietro* by Alba de Cespedes. At 4:45 I've finished one page. Number 88. I've already managed to send the first third of the text to the editors in Havana, even though I haven't always gotten comments back from them.

### TUESDAY 7

0 degrees Celsius in the *dojo*. I forget my gloves; I get the bell wrong for the ceremony. I tell Paul, I'm sorry, I made a mistake. Yes, he tells me, you go too fast. First you have to do *sampai*, the threefold prostration, with everybody and then the *Hannya Shingyo*, the Heart Sutra. I've learned how to say sorry.

> *esclarecida desde el exterior*
> *a la luz del contacto con los demás*
> *la verdadera fisionomía*

> [clarified from without
> through the light of contact with others:
> the true physiognomy]

At 10 a.m. I start translating. At 7:30 p.m. I finish.

*On mange.* I want to read you this story I received from Sigfredo Ariel. Writing about the Year of Ifá: Elegguá reigns, divinity of merchants and service personnel; his companion is Oshún, goddess of maternity. *Ogundá*

29

*Ogbe*: Ogunda wraps the head that has received the blessing; Ogún makes a clean cut with the sword.

It's best to pay off your debts to the saints. Speaking without argument gives clarity / honesty is the best politics; here I have the Dutch political ideal incarnated by Spinoza. As long as the world exists, the vulture will eat no grass. *Mayimbe.*

*Olofi Onire Oniche Ekó.* God gives us what is good and asks for nothing in return.

**WEDNESDAY 8TH**

I begin another session of translation: 10:20 a.m., page 100. No comments so far from the editors, since they're not rushing it into print.

> *Me sentiré*
> *contento e inútil*
>
> [I'll feel
> contented and useless]

At 5pm, ten pages. Spaced but promising.

At night we go to a building that once belonged to squatters. Now cultural transactions happen there. Afterwards, a café and Tarkovsky's *Solaris*.

**THURSDAY**

*Zazen* at home. I start translating at 9 a.m. I finish ten pages by 4 and go out to run errands. The market at *Ten Kate Straat* is crowded. There are five hundred very different people in one 150-meter stretch of road. Smoke from incense, cannabis, Vietnamese spring rolls, kebabs; fresh fruit, oranges from Morocco. *Bruin* bread, meaning brown, and French baguettes, Amsterdam cheese, and Israeli tubers, the ones we know as *malangas*.

*Ken* above, the stationary one, mountain
*Sun* below, the smooth one, wind
Ku ("Decay"), 18
Report:

> The work on A Rotten Thing represents a noble success.
> The moment is favorable for crossing great waters.
> Three days before the beginning,
> after beginning, three days.

That which is lost because of humans can be restored through the effort of humans.

First you must know the causes of corruption, after which you must be alert, during the period just prior to the beginning. Then you have to be drafted, in the best of ways; have to acknowledge the idea that *men goed in het nieuwe gareel komt*; you then put the collar and harnesses back on, so you don't relapse: then, the importance of being alert again during the period just after the beginning: three days.

In place of *onverschilligheid*, indifference, and *traagheid*, slowness, is *vastberadenheid*, resolution and energy. Classic theme of the *I Ching*: perseverance.

I get an email from Kris Dykstra about the Buffalo anthology:

> Hola O. I was emailing back and forth with Bob Creeley about
> the anthology, and I included your translator-poem. He wrote
> back:
>
> Dear Kristin, That's a beautiful poem—even in my humble
> Spanish, etc.
> Best as ever,
> Bob

It was enough to take phrases from Creeley himself, from the prologue to his *Selected Poems* from 1996, and organize them "into the form of a poem." Which is not hard with Creeley.

*Humanamente hablando, pero como*
*el lenguaje piensa decirlo, de su propia*
*mente y sentimiento, siempre provocativo.*
*Hubiera preferido escribir prosa.*

*Poesía? Sus materiales,*
*tan constantes, simples,*
*esquivos, específicos.*

*Cuesta tan poco y tanto.*
*Toda la vida ocupa,*
*pero sólo encuentra la vida*
*Viviendo.*

*Música,*
*última palabra y comunion*
*sin dueno*
*sin más razon ni error*
*que nosotros mismos*
*la palabra sufre nuestras presunciones.*
*Silencio el resto.*

[No doubt it is all a dream: Humanly speaking, but / how language thinks to say it, of its / own mind and feeling, always provocative. / I would have preferred to write prose. / Poetry? Its materials, / so constant, simple, / aloof, specific. / It costs so little and so much. / It occupies all of life, / but finds life only / in living. / Music, / last word and communion / having no owner / having no greater reason or error / than we ourselves / the word suffers our pretensions. / The rest, silence.]

*Dojo*, bell. At 10 I'm already seated; Hitachi temperament. *Tradurre*, and Da Vinci? Looking for his *autorritratto* I find *La Scapiliata* from 1508; I show it to Cristina. No one has drawn a woman's hair like Leonardo, who studied water, its currents, and compared them to curls. Cristina's hair looks like that. *Donna in piedi presso un corso d'acqua*, from 1518, one of the last drawings in Amboise, guest of Francis I …

If you think about Leonardo's writings and the drawings of Victor Hugo … What is a hobby, what is a profession, is labor? Leonardo, *"diluviale, clandestino e frammentario"* as a writer, according to *il Baldinoi* in his introduction to *Aforismi, novelle e profezie*. 100 pages, a thousand *lire*. What times those were, one might say. Leonardo's lyre no longer exists. And who could play it?

I cook garbanzos, sauté rice. Election night: Christian Democrats triumph!

*Zazen*: 3 people. Afterwards we go to the corner café.

Mariano replies:

> Papa, I like your poems a lot. take care of the louse, the big old
>     bird, and the frog.
> dress warm, warm, warm, put on a hat that covers your ears.
> I'm sending you the story of the enchanted frog.
> I'll do some drawings for you and a letter for ileana to send you.
> take good care of dario, diego, amor and josué.
> I still haven't figured out how to walk like chaplin.
> bring me a bottle of soda and everything because I need to stick
>     this here.
> and bring me two pens, a felt-tip and a soldier doll so it can look
>     like it's on stilts.

I follow his instructions for dressing warmly to the letter.

At 7 p.m. I go out, crossing the bridge at Kinker Straat, to my dance lesson from Lamine, the Yoloff dancer. An hour of *djembe* drumming. Lamine teaches me the foundation with the *dum dum*, the drums serious: *Hey, you, I'm talking to you*, the *dum dum* should say. Yet the response from the *djembe* is unpredictable, very syncopated. So is Lamine: aerial, taking off in order to be able to land, his arms flexible branches. The Dutch students follow it as best they can. Who said that Dutchmen can't dance? Or rather, Dutch women. In the wintertime you have to sweat to invoke the sun.

### MONDAY 27

Good day! I meet up with Nanne Timmer, a friend of Atilio Caballero, who serves as professor of Cuban literature in the University of Leyden: *Café De Jaren*, Of The Years, near Waterloo Plein. I identify myself with a Brazilian cap: world champion.

Alga calls: "Aren't you coming over to sew?" Okay.

At night I start editing the article about Deshimaru and his books. Thorny ascent up the mountain, *ma con Amore*, mountain of the Troubadours.

### TUESDAY 28 JANUARY

I'm going to the *dojo* to celebrate
the birth of Martí

I want to write Mariano a letter beginning this way

> *Voy a una casita*
> *Que tengo en el viento ...*

> [I'm going to a little house
> I have in the air ...]

34

It makes me very happy that you answered and remember Lilita, Josue, Diego and Dario. I'm in Amsterdam, where there are a lot of canals and seagulls. In the morning I go to the *dojo* and then I work on the computer. It's very pretty, but I haven't given it a name yet. Cristina sends you a kiss. So now: learning how to walk like Chaplin.

*Voy a una casita*
*que tengo en el viento*
*y lo que suceda*
*después te lo cuento*

[I'm going to a little house
I have in the air
and later I will tell you
whatever happens there]

### THE FURTIVE FUTURE. FRIDAY 31

Marathon completed with the final pages of the Alba de Céspedes book. And yet I haven't received a single bit of information from the editors regarding the nature of the text. Are they planning to pay me back with collaboration? It remains to be seen. They may not offer collaboration as payment.

In the afternoon I start on the *kesa* again!

### THE FUTURE DRAWING NEAR: TODAY IS SATURDAY, FEBRUARY 1

What time is it? 5:21 in the afternoon: Chinese New Year breaks out, and Cristina invites me to the *Nieuwe Markt,* located in the Chinese community. We see the Dragon Dance; they play drums and cymbals. Shop owners hang cabbages tied in red wrapping at the doorways: it's a favor for the Dragon, the musicians and dancers. Others put out oranges and scallions. The Dragon gobbles it all up. Happy New Year!

*Livre du Kesa*: A study of the *kesa*, and how to sew it.

I'm cold.

### MONDAY 3

I start translating Dennis Tedlock for the Buffalo Anthology: *Lo que dice la sangre*, a story of shamans. *A little yoga. Kitchen*: beans and rice. *Buona notte.*

### TUESDAY 4

As agreed I go to Haarlem to lend a hand with Barbara and Ken's move: from Orange Street to Acacia: from citrus to psychotropic thorns.

### WEDNESDAY 5

> *Y sé que has abjurado,* O Firenze
> *patria* di poco amore
> *sin perder la ternura, Dante*
>
> [And I know you've reneged, *O Firenze*
> homeland *di poco amore*
> without losing tenderness, Dante]

*Dojo.* I return home and finish the *kesa*'s long panels. Very long ones. Still need the short ones. Very short ones. It's seven, a smoke? Deshimaru, fourth page. At night Cristina reads stories, very well, in Dutch: Roald Dahl and his gory versions of Little Red Riding Hood & Family.

*Parlando cose que* holding silence is beautiful.

From *Zen and Cerebellum* by Master Deshimaru:

In Zen the consciousness of existence is the true content: here and now. Now is the present instant, no more than a point in time. And consciousness, country of thought, is man's own.

Three domains of consciousness, then, can be delineated.

The first is the subject: the ego, self.
The second is the object.
The third, the only true domain, is the setting, the place of current and final existence.

The true religious problem is located in this third domain. The first two domains do not exist except as categories: one, as subjective existence, without noumenon, not real; the other, as objective existence, not real. True existence is located in the third domain, in the quality of interdependence expressing a relation between the first two. In its capacity as a method, interdependence can be explained through a developmental process. But in Zen, it's given through the contraction of this domain into a point in time, a transcendental process occurring within a relative world.

With respect to this third domain we can give no verbal explanation.

So much for quantum physics, Deshimaru.

**WEDNESDAY 12**

(*La canzone* set aside.) 6:45 a.m. *Zazen* at home. The first sewing of panels for the *kesa* is finished. I cook and finish a short essay, "Deshimaru and His Books":

The question, "What is *Zen*?" has left us a legacy of innumerable responses.

But "Zen is *zazen*." This definition from the master Dogen, which honors the abruptness of his method and object of study, leaves little margin for lengthy explanations or pleasurable speculation. *Zen*, and especially the Soto school to whose dissemination Dogen as much as Taisen Deshimaru contributed so notably, doesn't put much emphasis on cognitive experience—so appreciated in the West—if it depends on books and readings.

Why write about Zen, then?—Maybe discussing Deshimaru's books can be another way to study his practice. Moreover, we have access to numerous texts: the ones that he put together, such as *Autobiography of a Zen Monk*, or others compiled by his disciples from their notes about the teachings Deshimaru imparted during *zazen*, his oral teachings or *kusen*. The fundamental legacy of a Zen master like Deshimaru, and the most direct way to interpret his mission, is precisely in the practice of *zazen*, a recurrent theme in these books. They further testify to a venture of the greatest human and intellectual interest: creating an exchange between two cultures.

Even when the magnitude of Deshimaru's teaching may be far from exhausting itself in philosophical examination, and when it may be impossible to fit the span of his teaching inside the world of books and categories, the act of relating ourselves to a work surpassing all that is written offers us the chance to analyze its repercussions for life itself, its intimate relation with experience as such. The importance of this experience for arriving at real knowledge of the world around us and intuiting the unknown is a topic in Deshimaru's books. It's also a topic, or a passion, that runs through Plato's *Dialogues* and Leonardo's *Treatise on Painting*, to name other examples. In Deshimaru, in fact, we find the simplicity and expositive refinement of the thinker who has conquered the practical privilege of "knowing yourself."

As a result, it can be hard to remember that this reflection doesn't deal with a philosopher or thinker customarily cited in our Western culture but with a Zen monk, with the meanings that this word, *Zen*, takes from the Eastern tradition. He preferred to translate it as concentration, intimacy with one's own body-spirit. This paradox widens the perspective we bring to the work he wrote and published in the West. We can enjoy his work also as a journal recording an adventure, the transmission of Zen Buddhism in our contemporary moment.

The history of Zen exists as a crossing: out of the unity of body and spirit, whose lived image is the very posture of *zazen,* a silent meditation. We're not dealing with an element that can be debated merely at an intellectual level. It involves thinking with the body, a spiritual journey undertaken out of one's own matter. And though the posture is one of stillness, it doesn't contradict the vitality expressed through the displacement from one town to another, from one culture to another. In the seventh century Bodhidharma travels from Ceylon to China. There, in 1223, he helps the monk Dogen to return to Japan with a clear idea: *shikantaza,* simply sitting: *zazen* and awakening are identical. In 1967 Deshimaru arrives in Paris with his *zafú,* or meditation cushion, and the teachings of his master Kodo Sawaki, a revolutionary who liked to repeat: "*Zazen* is useful for nothing."

The evidence of an intercultural contact of the greatest intensity, as recounted in Deshimaru's books, helps to understand culture. Culture is the collection of actions that humans undertake in order to resolve and understand their passages through the universe. For a Zen monk, this coexistence with that which is eternal, expressed in the realization of the simple things in life, comes with a surprising consideration: the impermanence of all phenomena and their mutual interdependence. In the quantum century, therefore, Deshimaru upholds the necessary intersection of science with religion; in various texts, as in the cases of *Zen and Cerebellum* and *Zen and Self-Control,* he compares the magnitude of *zazen* to the magnitude of scientific discovery.

When I talk about these books, I'm not alluding to some new possibility for accumulating and consuming pieces of wisdom, ideologies, philosophies, etcetera. I refer to a process of de-accumulation that leads us to to give ourselves over, naked, to the nakedness of reality, such as it is. In his books Deshimaru frequently speaks of *mushotoku*: a lack of benefit. The human gesture that goes beyond individual effort. This gesture, isolated, sets roots in human experience for the act of renunciation, abandonment to the cosmic order not only during *zazen* but also in the most humble tasks of existence: "To have a goal, not only in *zazen* but in daily life, wanting to obtain or catch something, is a mental illness." *Zazen* without an objective, without the hope of attaining some benefit or merit, whatever this may be, is, according to Deshimaru, the basis of a *mushotoku* vision and attitude. And he concludes: "*Satori* (sudden Buddhist enlightenment) is nothing more than making oneself *mushotoku*. This single term negates all doctrine, all ideas, all concepts, all Buddhism and all theologies."

"I'm not trying to critique European civilization—Eastern civilization isn't so great either," Deshimaru says in *The Valley's Voice*. However, he continues to offer keen observations about the Western tradition, in which he emphasizes its dualities of mind and body, matter and spirit, God and man. He disapproves of its determinist view of human destiny, and above all, he points to its division of reality into categories as a method of apprehension. Coming into contact with Zen, this model of knowledge confronts a task that escapes the habitual strategies of the intellect: "Intellectuals always see Zen in an objective way, but if we want to know fire we have to touch it." The same mode in which many of his books were compiled reveals an unusual formula in the dissemination of thought.

Like the previously cited *Valley's Voice*—collected teachings imparted by the master during a retreat at Val d'Isere in 1977—the bulk of his books gather and translate his oral transmissions whose root is in *zazen*, enacted through bodily posture. It's about a true *lingua franca* of philosophy. Here one must understand the term as a direct and daily contact with the process of coming to knowledge. The *kusen* (from *ku*, the mouth, and *sen*, the teaching) was originally delivered in an English peculiar to Deshimaru, called *Zenglish*, rich with expressions from Sanskrit, Chinese, and Japanese, plus French or German. The *kusen* transmits the lived experience of man in light of eternity "from my spirit to your spirit":

> The fundamental power of the cosmos has neither beginning nor end. It is beyond time and space. It has nothing to do with personal choice, since this power guides man from outside. Even if we believe we're totally free thanks to our power of will, we aren't. We can never separate ourselves from the system of the cosmos. Will itself occurs inside this fundamental power of the cosmos.

Then, interspersed with the silence:

"Tuck in your chins," or "Push against the earth with your knees, and against the sky with your head." Or remarks on Nietzsche and Jesus, Socrates, Buddha and Bergson. In Bergson, who said he wanted to "remain among those who will be persecuted tomorrow," he finds a kind of empathy. He compares Bergson's method of thought to meditation, and his language to "perfume from a white orchid in the dark, primitive jungle."

In *The Book of the Kesa*, discussing the *Shobogenzo Kesa Kudoku* of master Dogen, Deshimaru reflects, "Throughout the history of Hinayana and Mahayana Buddhism all teachers, all the great monks abandoned their work in order to devote themselves to reading, to writing and translating the *sutras*. But acting in these terms is not achievement of the most elevated attitude. In the end, they studied the true transmission of the *kesa*, abandoning their misguided *kesas* in order to put on the true *kesa*." The *kesa*, from *kasaya* in the Sanskrit, is the robe the Zen monk sews for himself. He uses a cloth, in Deshimaru's words, "of unlimited color."

It's worth noting that without ever abandoning the *kesa* or *zazen*, Deshimaru also wrote books. His autobiography, a paradigmatic example, recalls travel notebooks or stories about rites of passage that offer the savor of a new myth. Just before boarding a ship to depart for war, Deshimaru takes leave of his teacher, Kodo Sawaki. With the attitude of someone delivering a great gift and a prophecy, his teacher spits out, "You will be like a hero blown by the winds of fortune." With the spirit of inquiry and faith in the unknown, Deshimaru translates his practice to the West without hesitating to subject it to scientific examination—for example measuring brainwaves during *zazen* or, more generally, the physiological and neurological dimensions of meditation in a seated posture.

Perhaps a greater importance obtains to his translation and commentaries, as well as *kusen*, addressing the fundamental texts of Zen Buddhism. From the *Shin Jin Mei* of the Chinese patriarch Sosan to Dogen's foundational work—and this is not to ignore his poems in *Eiheikoroku*, whose secret beauty Dogen marks with simplicity and emotion—volumes all accompanied by his calligraphy and drawings, impregnated with the blend of strength and delicacy from the school of Basho or the inkwash tradition: "Taking from the pine that which belongs to the pine, from bamboo that which belongs to the bamboo."

"If one lives as one writes, in what bookstore will we find those poems?" So goes one of the favored apothegms of Dada. In Deshimaru, with the peculiar disagreement between word, thought, and action being resolved, we find poems. Then their life, so far as we can view it from afar through writing, is the poem of a seabird flying through infinity, of the fish swimming in the ocean: *mushotoku*, simply flying, continuing. "Our spirit's motion is, itself, our life's motion and an awakening. Our spirit is a principle of creation. It is self-understanding, self-creating." This is Deshimaru. In his books, he narrates the magnificent task of changing ourselves into what we already and truly are.

**THURSDAY 13**

*Zazen.* Visit to a Refugee Assistance Center to learn about the current immigration procedures in Holland. For example, it's usually complicated for an Algerian married to a Dutch woman to gain access to Fortress Europe—even when they have children. *Insha'Allah*!

Preparations for the Amsterdam *sesshin* this weekend. First purchases:

> Yogurt, lentils, ginger, garbanzos, nuts for the salad.
> Rice and pasta, feta cheese and parmesan.
> Bananas, oranges, melon, strawberries, apples.
> Yucca, sweet potato, potato, green plantain, squash, pepper.
> Lettuce, tomato, leek, onion, cucumber, hot pepper.
> Basil, mint.
> Mushrooms, broccoli.

Three meals, ten people. I'm cooking.

To: habana_zen@yahoo.com
Subject: Recipes for flan and bread pudding

Flan: a can of condensed milk; water measured with the same
can; five eggs gently beaten; a pinch of salt and a teaspoon of
vanilla.

Mix all ingredients together and pour into a mold, previously
coated with caramel. Put the filled mold into a bain-marie.

To make the caramel used to coat the mold, bring a little bit of
sugar in water to boil. And watch carefully so that the caramel
doesn't burn. It should be done inside the mold itself. Swirl the
syrup in the mold until everything is coated, then let it harden.

Bread pudding: For three loaves of bread, you use one can of
milk. Moisten the bread until it turns to paste. It needs three
eggs, cinnamon, vanilla, sugar to taste, a pinch of salt. You can
sprinkle it with almond, peanut, grated coconut, etc.

The mixture should not be very soft or very hard, just slightly
doughy. The consistency of the finished pudding depends on it.

Follow the same process with the caramel-coated mold, and it
goes into the bain-marie.

Watch very carefully to see that the pot always has water in it,
to prevent sticking. If it comes out well, enjoy! And if not, may
you enjoy it that way too.

Love,
Lilia Rosa

After recycling paper in the containers on *Jan Pieter Heijn Straat*, yes, here I am. The Kashmir Lounge is the typical coffee shop with an Eastern air, though the music may be techno. One part tourist establishment and one part neighborhood hangout, it has its quietest hours in the morning. Decorated with Hindu-Buddhist-Tibetan styles, *de rigueur* cushions where chance visitors recline for a photo. I'll take some of myself someday too. Niches, Ganeshes, Hashish: are you here to stay for a while? No, I'm not recyclable, I keep burning papers and don't love the music.

SATURDAY 22

I receive a dictation from Mariano:

> Oiuyte22qopOy4ro—a
> zoomar
> omar
> mariano
> buo
> vile
> motorcycle

SUNDAY 23 FEBRUARY

Probably the day when Rita, Cristina's mother, passed away. When she doesn't answer the telephone we go to her house on Amstelveen to make sure she's safe, and she's dead. As we prepare for the funeral, Uncle Yura arrives from Greece. In the cemetery at Zorgvlied we sing the *Hannya Shingyo* and burn incense. I write a poem in English & Dutch.

DEATH OF A HUMAN BEING

"In the last couple of days," says the neighbour
"no life signs in the kitchen."
Life signs, the kitchen: *miteramu.*

The corpse translated by the police, efficiently
"It's a sad day," yet the sun shines
outrageous.
sit by the water and the little girl
waves at the ducks:
*kwek, kwek, kwek,*
*ik ben goed maar ik ben niet gek.*
I am good but I'm not stupid.

O Milky Way, homeland
it's night sunflower:
now you can go everywhere

Then a version in Spanish.

## DEATH OF A HUMAN BEING

"In the last couple of days", *dice el vecino*
"no life signs in the kitchen".
*Signos vitales, la cocina:* miteramu.
*El cadáver traducido por la policía,* efficiently.
"It's a sad day", *sin embargo el sol brilla*
*desaforado.*
*Siéntate junto al agua y la niñita*
*saluda a los patos:*
"Kwek, kwek, kwek
ik ben wel goed mar ik ben niet gek!"
Oh, *Vía Láctea*
*es noche, girasol*
*ahora puedes ir adonde quieras.*

Secret revelation here & now, out of time's cradle: the deceased must be moved out of the house.

A piano, two bottles of Greek wine and one Portuguese rosé, two bicycles, books of paintings: Van Gogh, Brueghel & Co., oils for painting, canvases, an African head, romance novels, roses (dried up), plants, excrement from many many doves who are going on to live somewhere else. Rita, fugitive rose whom I met only over the phone, I'm cleaning out your house, to learn how to recognize you, and so that a real estate agent can rent it out again. But you, Rosa, no one can rent you out. No one ever could.

TUESDAY

The temple part over, the highway begins, the marvelous routine. Cristina and I go out to walk through A'dam. Cristina's boss comes to visit us. He brings us a CD by Silvio Rodríguez as a gift! I pick up the *"Lingua Franca"* manuscript again, my notebook filling with disconnected sonnets.

TUESDAY 15TH

*Zazen.* Lunch on the grass in Vondel Park with Jurryt van de Vooren, who gives us his book about the epic ordeal of Dutch ice skating. During some winters, the truly severe ones, the Dutch go even farther north in the country to celebrate their skating marathon. They have their own rules and the person who wins there is as great as Cruyff, which is saying a lot. Jurryt's book deals with that epic tradition. He's a sportswriter whose birthday we're celebrating today in the Dutch way. As if nothing mattered.

Singing and sewing, sometimes muttering in silence.

THURSDAY 17TH

Up: *zazen.*

La Boheme: I read *Europe After 1870.*

I cook *stampot*, a Dutch type of mashed potatoes. Butter, potatoes, milk, onion, carrots.

When the water boils you add the diced potatoes, onion and carrot. Mix the puree with milk and butter.

> nibelungo dichter *anivela la perla*
> *guardián de la cuerda* dichter
> nibelungo, *verdad?*
> *estrofa, soneto, cuerda,*
> *tela por donde cortar,*
> *ladrido? para qué*
> dichter nibelungo *la tela,*
> *la perla, la cuerda no da más*
> dichter *nibelungo*
> *amigo* underground *del más allá*

> [*Nibelung dichter* levels pearl
> guardian of *dichter* string
> *Nibelung,* right?
> strophe, sonnet, string,
> fabric out of which to cut,
> barking? what for?
> *dichter Nibelung* the fabric,
> pearl, string gives nothing else
> *dichter Nibelung*
> underground friend from the beyond]

Punctuation marks, exclamations, etc. originate inside writing, and not the other way around: done backwards equals done straight.

## SUNDAY 20TH

*Zazen,* some fifteen people. Alga leads. Cristina, emotional, rings the bell. "It's the weight of all the patriarchs coming down on you," Alga says.

21 degrees in the shade. Rosendaal, and we come back home late. At roughly 9:30 p.m. I start to make *guenmai*; Cristina helps me. Finished at midnight,

> *A medianoche comienza la vida*
> *A medianoche comienza el amor*
> *Goce compadre, tómese un trago*
> *Viva la vida y olvide el dolor.*

> [At midnight life begins
> At midnight love begins
> Enjoy, my friend, have yourself a drink
> Live life and forget your pain.]

Looks like Khayyam, but it's from a song by Beny Moré.

*Zazen*, Paul leads. *Guenmai*, coffee and croissants: *printemps*.

> *escribir? para qué*
> *si mientras tanto*
> *los cubanos sentimentales beben su sueldo en risas*
> *y sonrisas*
> *los cubanos sentimentales son yo*
> *invito a los otros para consolarles*
> *consuélate como yo que he invitado a los otros*
> *cubanos sentimentales.*

> [writing? for what?
> if in the meantime
> the sentimental Cubans drink their salary in laughter
> and smiles
> these sentimental Cubans are
> I invite the others to console them

console yourself like me, the one who invited the other sentimental Cubans.]

In a music store on Utrechtstraat, I found Carlos Embale for just 9 euros.

## WOENSDAG 23 APRIL

Finish *History of Europe from 1870*, from the Franco-German war between Keyser and the Republique to the Cold War between good guys and bad guys. A continuity: war. A "politically correct" book, as history should be.

Ajax vs A.C. Milan, as night falls. But in spite of playing their best game in years, Ajax falls to Milan 3 to 2.

Crafty moves from Pippo Inzaghi. It's the Champions League.

Before going to sleep I read *Life and Meaning*, an anthology; Tolstoy, Schopenhauer, etc.

Ecclesiastes: Christ. *Amplificatio: nel mezzo del camin della sua vita*, Tolstoy ended up without Life, or Meaning

## SUNDAY

*Zazen*. Caroline leads. Victor the Portuguese musician is there, as well as Tharn the English lover, and another ten people tossed up here onto this shore …

## WOENSDAG 30 APRIL

Cristina's birthday and *Koninginen Dag*, or the Queen's Day. But we don't celebrate in A'dam. Up at 6:30 a.m., we celebrate it on the road to Burgundy. After 1000 kms in the car, with Johan from Utrecht and Victor the Portuguese musician as our drivers, we touch down. Christian Morales proposes work in the kitchen for me. I take care of the luggage and go off to cook. Dinner with master Stephane. To sleep: *minuit*.

Up at 6:30 a.m., shower and to the kitchen.

Light meal 9 a.m.

10:00 *Zazen* and a ceremony for Cristina's mother: *choko* (altar), *Hannya Shingyo*.

Kitchen: Lunch at 1:30.

After lunch Kosen holds an intense, spontaneous *mondo*, a question and answer session with a disciple. He cries, laughs, talks about justice, the earth, and karma. He believes in the importance of rage, if it is just. Birds sing in the vineyards. The church raises its cross in the wind. The burro gets its member some air.

Poetry is the *materia prima* of happiness (after Aristotle).

I share room 35 with Paul Loomans: *Bon jour*! And reflection returns, about the relations between Zen and French culture, European culture, Western culture. Since the arrival of Deshimaru in Paris, since Stephane's arrival in Cuba, something has happened inside me, inside the world, inside everything and everyone linking the two. We'll see each other in the kitchen. Delirium.

That which is weak is strong. Our father! The repugnant task o' writing. I'll look up the etymology of repugnant: *suscitare avversione o disgusto*. From Lat. *Re, contro y pugnare, combattere. Garzanti*.

At 3:15 I go back to the kitchen. The kitchen people arrive before 3:30 p.m, the designated hour for *samu*, our meditative work for the community. They stay after the allotted time ends, depending on what the *tenzo* may need. An hour of *samu*, at any rate: cutting and peeling tubers and vegetables for dinner and tomorrow's *guenmai*; cleaning, shopping, sewing, etc.

The *zazen* begins at five. A distinctive event: Stephane speaks dramatically about Zen theater, a tradition he attributes to Deshimaru, as well as Sawaki.

He shares anecdotes about his master: *Allumez vous votre cigarette, Stéphane*. At the same time he comments on Sekito's *San Do Kai*. Another distinctive twist: three *zazen*, two *kin hin* or walking meditations.

In the kitchen again, then dinner and at 9 p.m., *zazen*. He continues the commentary on the *San Do Kai*: That which is known, that which is unknown, that which is unknowable: this is *zazen* (I'm smoking, now, an intellectual in the room). According to Kosen, *zazen* grants us the responsibility to enter the unknowable without dying, without burning, without losing our minds.

"*Pas de problemes pendant zazen*", *il dit*.

It's eleven o'clock, time for bed.

**MAY 2**

*Zazen* 7:30. Stephane continues with *San Do Kai*. Kitchen.

But the kitchen goes more smoothly for me this spring, compared to the summer camp; after lunch I go to the forest, *boscaiolo*. We'll see …

5 p.m. *zazen*.

Kitchen—dinner. Final *zazen*, 9 p.m.

Beer, cheerfulness. I talk with Stephane: "Havana is so warm and friendly. And Cubans like to create poems, it comes naturally for them. Not like here in Europe."

I cross words with Christophe Demeure, calligrapher monk from Lyon. He too has written poems and translated Chinese poems, the one on *Shin Jin Mei* (faith-mind), etc. And then I talk with Christian, small-town hairstylist turned urban monk.

I myself am I myself

*Zazen* 7:30.

*Promenade*
*Guenmai*

*Zazen* 11 a.m. The *San Do Kai* continues: "The step forward is not possible without the step backwards. Light is not possible without darkness." And, "Master Keisan said it in that *mondo*: No one exists who is not someone. That is to say, Buddha isn't God."

A *balade*, a two-hour hike at 4.

From the highest point of our ascent you see Mont Blanc. Then we descend to the camp, *dojo*, temple.

These days I've remembered Creeley: while arriving in the car, looking out the window, seeing a horse grazing behind a fence, hanging up my towel.

Dinner at circa 7:30 pm.

*Zazen* 9 p.m. *Fukanzazengi*, a *sutra* created by Dogen.

Continued with the *guenmai*.

"Loving persons is loving God, because it's not possible to love God without loving people," Stephane said.

> *recojo del bosque la hierba*
> > *y ella me dice:*
> > *el costado mediterráneo de la muerte*
> > *qué sofrosinia!*
>
> *el café sosegado, el arroz*
> *desgranado*

*y todas las muchachas se han enamorado*
*de aquel que dió su bendición a a la montaña*

[I bring grass from the forest
    *and she tells me:*
    *the Mediterranean side of death,*
    *such sophrosyne!*

the coffee quieted, rice
shelled
        *and all the girls have fallen in love*
        *with the man who blessed the mountain]*


## DIMANCHE 4 MAI

Up at 6 a.m. Bathroom. To *la cuisine avec* Christian Morales. *Bon jour, bon jour, guenmai* begins again: back to tossing ingredients into the large casserole dish. Commodious, its mouth some 80 centimeters from the floor. Making herbal tea: melissa, mint, etc. And the *guenmai* tea. Coffee is made too, but that's done by the workers.

After the walk one must lie prostrate outdoors in front of an altar improvised for this purpose. Sing the *Hannya*, the short *Eko, Ji Ho San*. There are nine prostrations or *pai*.

This *guenmai* for 70 people was made with

    2 kg brown rice
    1 kg carrots
    2 kg green onions
    1 kg turnips
    Half a bunch of celery
    3 onions

When the water boils you put in the rice. When the rice opens, *eclate*, add the vegetables. Stir and stir. Christian explains why letting it stick to the bottom means destroying the whole thing. Impressive explanation based on the laws of physics.

After the *guenmai* ceremony, you set incense on the master's table and sing the *Bussho Kapila*. *Zazen*, the last one, at eleven. I return to the kitchen *avec respect*. *Zazen*, then, and *Mondo*. I raise my hand.

> *Question*: Last year there was a *sesshin* in Cuba and I didn't go. I want to ask forgiveness for that. Also, I came to Europe in hopes of practicing more often with you, with the *sangha*. Up to this point my hope has been realized, but I never had the opportunity to ask you whether it's better for me to stay here in Europe or go back to Cuba.

> *Answer*: In other words, is it always the same—that which is best, and that which is worst? Where do I need to be? What is it that must be practiced? What is the Way, where is the Way? Effectively, one need not think in an indirect way. It's not that we are thinking in an indirect way, it depends on dimension. Where is our location, really?

> Sometimes I don't go to *zazen* because something is more important to me in that moment. Yet I always say: "*Zazen* is the most important thing in existence, it is the essence." But there are moments when one has to know how to say: "No, now this other thing is more important." For example, the most important thing right now for the *Tenzo* is cooking.

> Clearly it's different for each person, but knowing what it is, that's up to you. No one else can know what the most important thing is for you. I have no criteria for saying: "This is more important than that."

And then he talks about Cuba. He tends to refer to Cuba and Cubans with respect and sympathy: "A very pure *sangha*. We Europeans are rich in *argent*, but the Cubans are rich in love." After the *mondo*, lunch and goodbyes.

Christian questions me in the kitchen with a glass of red Burgundy in hand. According to him I have maintained an attitude "*de distance et respect avec la cuisine. Je veux te remercier particulairement.*" Is that an ironic remark?

Ill-timed hug for Stephane, another for Pierre, and off I go with the Hollanders. Always in a hurry, the Dutch.

### AMSTERDAM, MAY 6

Call the lawyer, call my sister, call my mother. Papers are papers. Lying benefits an honest man. Truth is a crook's gift.

### MAY 8

My first baby-sitting job: the child is 5 months old. His parents, a Dutch woman and a Surinamese man. Their *jabáo*, or blond mulatto, is named Noah. *Noé*.

Received over email: "Interior Revolution," in an English rendition by Jesse Haas. Overall it needs revision. The translation is nearly done. Additionally, at Alga's request, I begin a translation of the *Sandokai*, from a macaronic English, from one of those editions made in pasta: "Let's see what comes out of you."

### MONDAY

Lawyer specializing in immigrants. Famous because he managed to save the Dutch right of residence for a Surinamese man ruled guilty of trafficking cocaine. A brave exception, *The Utrecht Lawyer*. Film title.

I complete a version of the *Sandokai*. I use verses from Master Stephane's *kusen*.

I order the Zorro outfit for my son at a costume store on Rozengracht. I sew my own suit: *quadre de longueur!* 205 cms.

### *SANDOKAI*

*El espíritu del gran sabio de la India, se ha transmitido*
*del este al oeste, invisible, en toda su pureza de agua clara.*
*En cada humano la inteligencia y la sensibilidad es diferente*
*pero en la Vía sur y norte no existen.*
*Al nacer nos aferramos a las cosas,*
*creamos ilusión siguiendo un ideal,*
*cada uno de los sentidos y su objeto*
*entran en mutua relación y sin embargo son*
*en si mismo únicos:*
*de ahi la dependencia y la no dependencia. Cada cosa,*
*en forma y sentimiento, es diferente*
*y cada voz, en su singularidad, es dulce o áspera.*
*Palabras: "alto", "mediano",*
*son oscuras como lo que definen;*
*la luz separa lo turbio de lo transparente.*
*Asi como el niño regresa a la madre,*
*las propiedades de los cuatro elementos marchan juntas:*
*el fuego es calor, el aire movimiento, el agua moja,*
*la tierra es compacta; los ojos para ver, los oidos escuchan,*
*se huelen los olores, y en la lengua lo agrio y lo salado.*
*Y sin embargo en cada cosa en interrelación, como las hojas*
*que vienen de la raíz, el principio y el fin*
*regresan a la fuente.*
*Se habla entonces de lo alto y lo bajo:*
*la fuente espiritual brilla en la luz,*
*los afluentes van en la oscuridad, así,*

*apegarse a los fenomenos es causa de ilusión,*
*pero ir encontrando la verdad interior*
*no es aún verdadero* satori.
*El paso d'alante depende del paso d'atrás,*
*la luz no es posible sin lo oscuro. Todo lo que vive*
*tiene conciencia y lleva en sí*
*reposo y movimiento. He aquí que lo ideal*
*y lo real van juntos, como caja con su tapa.*
*Como dos flechas se encuentran en el aire*
*así van juntos lo ideal y lo real.*
*Comprendan la verdad fundamental de estas palabras:*
*no vale la pena formular categorías,*
*si al seguir tus sentidos no realizas la verdad fundamental*
*como podrías, por mucho que camines, hallar la via recta?*
*Al caminar se pierde la distincion de cerca y lejos*
*y si tu llegaras a perderte, como montanas,*
*como rios, nuevos obstaculos ante ti surgirian.*
*A quien busca la verdad solo esto ofrezco:*
*no pierdas tiempo.*

[SANDOKAI

The spirit of India's great sage has been transmitted
from East to West, invisible, in all its purity, clean as water.
In every human, intelligence and sensibility differ
but South and North don't exist along the Way.
After our birth we clutch at things,
create hope by pursuing an ideal,
every one of the senses and its object
enters into mutual relation and nonetheless are
unique in and of themselves:
from this fact, dependence, and non-dependence. Each thing,
in form and feeling, is distinct
and each voice, in its singularity, is sweet or harsh.

Words: "high," "medium,"
are obscure as the thing they define;
light separates murkiness from transparency.
So as the child returns to its mother,
properties of the four elements work together:
fire is heat; air is movement; water, moist;
earth, compact. Eyes to see, ears to hear;
the nose picks up scents, the tongue, bitter and salty turns.
Nonetheless, within every thing in interrelation, as from some root
came leaves, beginning and end
return to the source.
Then someone speaks of that which is elevated and that which is low:
a spiritual source shines within the light,
tributaries move into obscurity; thus a
gradual attachment to phenomena creates hope,
but moving forward, finding interior truth,
is not yet true *satori*.
The step forward relies on the step backwards,
light is impossible without the dark. All that lives
has consciousness and carries within itself
repose and motion. Herein, that the ideal
and the real move together, as a box with its cover.
As two arrows meet in the air,
so the ideal and real move together.
Understand the fundamental truth of these words:
formulating categories is worthless,
if by following your senses you don't create a fundamental truth,
walking so long, how could you find a straight path?
As you walk, the distinction between near and far gets lost
and if you too should get lost: then as mountains and
rivers, new obstacles may surge before you.
To the person seeking truth I offer only this:
don't waste any time.]

Z. 22 people, eight monks and four or five new faces. The little bell? I make a mistake. Such moderation, exactitude: *sophrosyne*.

In the afternoon, with Cristina, to the home of Sandra from Bahia for an *acarajé*. Among Brazilians. Sandra, a dance teacher, celebrates her departure from A'dam after many long years of her stay in the cold. Now she's returning to Bahia and does so by cooking. Foods of the orishas; she fries, serves, fries, serves. The music is lovely but not live; and that, in the end, is what brings me warmth or not. *Bon viagem*, Sandra, those of us who will hibernate salute you.

> Breathing is my saxophone

Cristina gave me a book by Kazantzakis of Crete: *Captain Mikhalis*. The reading is slow, steep. The landscape he describes, no less so. Take your time. Mikhalis is strong, but blind. Freedom or Death is something you know, from age, from birth. Mikhalis is no different than the heroes from Latin America's jungles; colossal and human, *too human*, his life is a camp. With family. Relax, Mikhalis. The battle is long and the landscape beautiful. But he seems not to look at it, except as a lookout. He's waiting for ships, reinforcements, to arrive. In the meantime one must force the invader to show respect: the Turks. *Mama, gli turchi!* I remember Cavafy's problem: Barbarians, are they back again? Will they ever arrive? We are barbarians. We are the Turks.

Sewing the *kesa* is simple and complicated. Sometimes I take heart in thinking that it's only about a fisherman repairing his nets at sundown. He breathes in, breathes out, needle in, needle out. Now it's about fishing for men! Christ says. Well, you go fish for them. I have enough already.

> *Et l'envers doit etre aussi joli*
> *que l'endroit. Caramba!*

Cristina teaches me how to fold the *kesa*.

After the Z., in Kriterion, we find the monk Christophe de la Porte, his wife Barbara and son Eliah. And we go *chez eux* to dream. Christophe is a great conversationalist, one could even say an actor. *Comedie Francaise*; I'm afraid to tell him so, because he might take my admiration as an insult. But admiration is not always, in some way, an insult. Insult to our "image and resemblance," divine nature.

## MERCREDI

*Zazen*. Return to house. And, from the old East to the new North: *Buik-slotermeer Plein*, to care for Noah. His father returns from work, and we talk about Cuba's commercial potential: agriculture and telephones, for example. Like all businessmen, Guno has unpredictable ideas.

In the first case, it's about buying from the locals, hotel management and catering, fresh fruit: melon pears, lemon, mango, papaya, guava, loquat, garlic, watermelon and cantaloupe and, maybe, passionfruit. The fruit of passion: *maracuyá*.

The boxes are made in Cuba, as well as the crates and other aspects of the loading and unloading done through communal businesses. A type of cooperative that allows for collective income, bank accounts and communal credit for the purchase of machinery and materials.

Tax or percentage to the state. Pay in convertible money: Euros or dollars. Same thing, the dollar is descended from the *thaler*.

As for the telephone, a Cuban access number: 0800, for example. Locals pay according to the national price and currency, with the code for the card purchased in Europe. In this case Holland, though also in Italy, Spain, etc. An equal percentage for utilities goes to the state in which, for example, 500,000 monthly minutes are purchased. Interesting, and you pick up the jargon. We have pizza for dinner, with beer and cigars.

*Zazen.*

The last great change of Uranus, before it departs forever from our short lives, predicts still another formidable change for year's end.

Inaugurated in the *dojo*: exhibition of the paintings of the monk Reikai Vendetti, color portraits of monks and patriarchs.

With Monica we go to Dimos' place, the Greek restaurant on Clerqstraat. Good wine, better foods. And Dimos is a good *antropologos*.

I'm preparing to depart for Milan, land of Ludovico the Moor. A premonition for a city that is filling, discreetly or not, with South Americans. *Sono tanti. Ma tanti quanti? Tutti quanti?* It's the start of the trip to Cuba. Origin of the word *Milano*: *mediolanum*. A land in the middle, not Mediterranean.

## TUESDAY 15 JULY, AMSTERDAM

I come and go from Havana, passing through Madrid's Barajas airport. Description of Barajas: *degoutant*. Yesterday I accompanied Cristina to VROM. The Universal Ministry: Housing and Environment. Located at the center (or so it seems) of Den Hague, *gotterdamerung* for employees.

While I'm waiting for her outside the nearly transparent monolith, I walk alone through forest. There is no God greater than God, the Muslim's happy certainty.

## THURSDAY 24

Perfect. At 8:30 we turn in the request for the residency permit, or *Verblijfsbergunning*, at the mailbox of the Immigration Police, the one that shall be valid until ... Then we take a ride on our bicycles through the....

Paul calls: tomorrow I lead at the *dojo*. "He has to be up to what is comin' on," he says.

Up at 6:05 a.m. I go to the *dojo*. Paul left for the Pyrenees and went on from there to the *Campo de Verano, Zommerkamp*.

To northern Amsterdam, Buikslotermeerplein; by the market, plaza with fountain, and post office. Noah lives there. His parents work and leave him in my care: two hours. While he's sleeping, I take advantage of the time to clean the terrace. It's sunny. If he wakes up, I take him out for a drive, and he falls asleep again. And so our two hours pass. I return home on a bus.

> *Araña, no te aprisiones en tu tela*
> *ni te caigas de la pared!*

> [Spider, don't get trapped in your own web
> or fall from the wall!]

*Zazen*. At night we go to *To Ouzeri*, the Greek restaurant across from the one belonging to Dimos. Two Greek locations on the same street seems like a lot of activity. In fact, *To Ouzeri* is full. We stop at the bar and drink retsina, the white wine from Greece: *Malamatina*. Good. The music alternates with a particular, intentional modern effect, which the young bartender exemplifies. A sort of *disco-bouzukia*, Mediterranean salsa with features of *rai*. Here I imagine a work for theater:

### Bertold Brecht

A young actor returns to his region to stage a play about Bertold Brecht. It includes a discussion of "The Five Devices for Telling the Truth," five difficulties. People understand.

The effect of *vergreemdung*, or distancing, is executed by the actors in a rural setting. There they appear as fugitives on the run, in the manner of *As You Like It*.

All wear a mouse head and lion tail.

They move freely through the space of the restaurant, carrying the tables. Every once in a while, they interrupt this movement in order to enunciate a poem.

Important conversation between the author and his mother, in which both remove the mask and put it back on; the rumba is important *aussi*. The mother messily rearranges the "Five Devices" into the musical structure of rumba's *son*.

> *Todos somos ratas y leones*
> *Yo quiero reencarnar en esta vida*
> *Para morirme tranquila.*
>
> *[We're all mice and lions*
> *I want reincarnation in this life*
> *so I can pass away in peace.]*

The protagonist abandons the rural setting and returns to the city to invest his lion's tail in a real estate company. The mother remains with her son's mouse head, which she uses in a theater workshop for children. The poets interrupt the rumba to serve food on the tables.

### MAANDAG 28. PERFECT.

Coming back to the Brecht thing: it allows for a *prima scena* with people who come and go, putting masks on and taking them off. As props. International airport. Extemporaneous speaker. He can be called Socrates.

> *La religione del mio tempo*, by Passolini.
>
> *Pur sopravivendo, in una lunga appendice*
> *di inesausta, inesauribile passione*
> *che quasi in un altro tempo ha la radice-*

*so che una luce, nel caos, di religione,*
*una luce di bene, mi redime*

and here he speaks of the Mother. Then, in *Ai letterati contemporanei,*

*Non possiamo piú realmente essere d'accordo: ne tremo,*
*ma é in noi che il mondo é nemico al mondo.*

reversing the distich by Silesius,

He who in hell cannot without hell live
has not given himself fully to the infinite.

### DINSDAG 29

First conversation with my son since my return to A'dam.

### FRIDAY 1 AUGUST

Getting up when the sun takes off means, here and at this point in the summer: 5:25 a.m. I go out to run. *Zazen* at 8 a.m. The *dojo* is closed during the summer camp. I practice in my room. From there to paradise.

In reality, I make myself *cafecinho* and go to the *dojo* to pick up the García Márquez memoir that his compatriot Alga is loaning to me. A windbag, as usual, but not devoid of interest. These days you have to protect yourself from excessive motifs. *These days, no absolution is possible for man …* They happen, let's say—fantasies. *Sophrosyne.*

I begin to translate Paul Hoover.

*Sin verbo*
*en la eternidad,*

*la ciudad es*
*un guión de cine*

*en el que tú*
*puedes escuchar*

*la voz*
*de la distancia*

etc.

I go to the Vondelpark, where tango can be heard. An international orchestra: piano, acoustic bass, electric guitar, two violins, two Argentine accordions, and many dance pairs. The Dutch people can also be heard. They let the music take them, improvising the tango. I meet up with Nina, the German woman, and her little Killian; we communicate in French. She invites me to the Gay Parade, celebrated down the entire length of the Prinsengracht, or prince's canal: *Amateurisme*, Nina says, giving an artist's opinion. She herself is a painter and notes, as well, the importance of the atmosphere in the street. Summary: people cluster on the stairways and balconies, and in the French windows or *balkondeur*. The music is monotonous, more of the same, techno without much *tekne*: gay men enjoying themselves on the floats moving past, as if they were aboard ships fitted out for the purpose. A Roman carnival at a Northern latitude: *verfreemdung*.

And in general, the carnival is a grand idea. Dancing and being free from restraint. The procession continues all the way to Amstel. I go home. I read more of *Living to Tell the Tale*, by García Márquez. Food, white rice with vegetables, Chinese style.

### DIMANCHE 3

Third poem by Hoover completed.

> *En aforismos de verano,*
> *el gato lustroso se estira en prolífica maravilla ...*

Lezama already said it, ... *se estira como un gato para dejarse definir...*: stretches like a cat, allowing definition.

Midnight *zazen* and off to sleep.

*Dicen que el gerundio es malo*
*ando yendo, acaballando*
*Es tango un gerundio?*
*Y mambo? La envolvencia resolviendo*
*suave que me estás matando*
*En el intento: inventando*
*Desestimo amaneciendo?*
*quiero amanecer cantando*
*lelo matando canalla,*
*cómo está el niño? Acabando!*

[They say gerund is no good
going walking, mounting mare
Is tango a gerund?
Or mambo? The embrace resolving
smoothly you're killing me
In the attempt: devising
Disrespect dawning?
I want to wake up singing
Impish in motion
dopey killing it all,
how's the boy? Alive and kicking!]

It's 3:30 p.m. I make myself a Greek coffee and continue with the García Márquez. In the sun. I go to the *dojo* to water the plants.

Translations of all four poems by Hoover completed.

*la cálida mente amortajada*
*ocurrente y astuta*
*cargamos con rumores*

*quienes no podemos soportar*
*silencio o medida*
*la breve articulación*
*del infinito.*

Japanese tea. The world rushes past: fire, hunger, violence. I go out to run errands. This is a good example of the prices at Dirk van der Broek, the chain claiming to be Holland's cheapest market.

> One canvas bag 1.35 Euros
> 2 rice crackers 0.58
> 2 wheat crackers 1.30
> 2 orange juices 1.30
> 1 kilo rice 1.85
> 2 penne rigate 0.98
> 1 table wine 2.89
> 1 ice cream 1.89
> 2 lemons 1.38.
> TOTAAL 13.62

To this add one bunch of Colombian bananas: 1.90.

Cristina returns from Spain. *Voilà! Diz que* we're going to the beach with Nina: *Zandvoort aan Zee*, the large beach. And like a canvas from Seurat, rich in pointillisms, the punctilious Dutchman who brings special accessories for throwing a ball with his dog, the punctilious girls who go topless. We play *pétanque* with Jean Luc and a friend, an African painter: Saliou, who is from Burkina Faso. *Pétanque* on the sand. I'm playing for the first time and notice that the sand is deceptive. Poetry is prophesy. The Rimbaud democracy.

We go to the Amsterdam *bosque*, or forest. From *bos*, the *bosque* is not very thick. The canal holds rowboats and canoes. Cyclists move past, next to the canal. Some who have megaphones call out questions to the oarsmen and canoeists. At the Pancake House, or *Pannekoekenhuis*, there are ginger pancakes and peacocks who jump off the roof to walk about on the gravel.

On the way back my bike gets a flat tire. Again! It's an old black bicycle in the *oma fiets* style, a "grandma bike," noisy and beaten up. I'll have to light candles for saints to get it some help. And swap out the bike. For now we walk home after a nice conversation: bicycles! Then we rent a Chinese film, *The Swordsman*, with Jet Li. Terrific.

### SATURDAY 16

I eat lunch and go to the *dojo*. "Pretty bike you've got!" Arnaud says by way of greeting us at the entrance. It's a Gazelle that Cristina inherited from her mother and is loaning to me. *Zazen*: there's a girl who came from Argentina, named Luna. *San Pai*. The *san pai* is effective.

Email from the Havana *dojo* to specify the days for the *sesshin*, the intense meditation period, running December 1-5. Camping at El Taburete in Pinar del Río. Community of Las Terrazas. The distance from the capital will have to be written out clearly, in kilometers, as well as the way to get there from the highway.

Continue with trans. of Deborah Meadows. Poetics ...

### TUESDAY 19

6:30 a.m. *Zazen* at the *dojo*. I needed it recently. These three cats sitting in silence, together but not scrambled.

The poetics of de-industrialization, of de-dualization. Writing can't be a purely intellectual chore. Maestro of music: whoever said intuition cannot be contradictory? Long conversation with Christophe de la Porte in a coffeeshop at the *Centrum*. The Breton apocalyptic, with his comedian's manner of picking up and dropping the subject of the Way. If Christophe were Moliére, I would be his disciple. We take the opportunity to go together to the Vondelpark, where you can dance salsa. Maybe in A'dam Mokum there are more Cubans than one imagines.

I dream about grandmother Eloina: we're flying around like ninjas inside the house on the Malecon. It's an energetic movement, like bicycling, which allows the body to ascend in defiance of the law of gravity.

> *Flotar, volar*
> *el pájaro inmóvil sobre la chimenea.*

> [Floating, flying
> bird unmoving above the chimney.]

### Tuesday 26th

Up at 6 a.m. *Zazen* with *quatre chats. Cafecinho et croissants.*

Shopping for a Better World, and on the terrace of the café Alverna I run into Lamine. We talk about dance and music. He invites me to come to his classes again.

### Thursday 28th

*Zazen.* Baby-sitting with Noah from 12 to 4. I go back to my neighborhood, Lamine's lesson.

Description: playing the combination of three African drums, *dum dum* and two *djembes.* My hands blister. But the *balafon* sounds right. The pain is worth it.

### Saturday 30th

Is there modern dance in Paradise, or it contemporary? The Dutch improvise mechanically, the contradiction of a civilization with no *joie de vivre.*

Outside on the museum plaza are a Van Gogh and the *flamencos,* the flaming flamingos. The Rosenberg Trio is playing there, with their gypsy jazz, and the party is in the street. You dance salsa on the corner of Van Gogh & Co.

*Zazen* in the *dojo*. I go out in search of a cable for the modem; bingo on Kinkerstraat. I drink a coffee in the corner space recently inaugurated as the Coffee Company. Good cappuccino, a lot of chrome, as it should be. They'll call this moment an ancient one, as Alighieri would say.

I keep hunting for a curtain for my work station. The African Shop, so named for the heterogeneity of its content and form. Stroke of genius for 38 e. in Kitsch Kitchen. Here and now, kitsch is not necessarily cheaper than chic.

Walking toward the *Centrum*, I visit The *Tempel* of African Art. *Tempel* must be a Dutch spelling, but in this district, mixing is the norm.

I'm not carrying anything. I just ask if they repair drums. They do, and I take this opportunity to poke around among the instruments. The rattling staff, the gourd-marimba, and a larger marimba which the African called *bongó*. Things like that.

The workspace is ready, with its curtain to deaden air currents and the modem to facilitate the other kind of current, "going forth into the world." Cristina arrives from Den Hague and we go out for soup. On the way back, an unplanned detour. We're surrounded by squatters from the barrio. Bleak, empty, as if from a season come too late, the barman is the commissioner of the occasion: smoking, smoking, not thinking. Premiere of workspace, translating Chris Alexander. *Vado a letto* at dawn.

## MONDAY

Early. Baby-sitting: Noah. Three hours, twenty euros.

## TUESDAY

*Zazen*. What is the name of this plump woman, with the face of an actress and a nervous cigarette, who comes so often lately. I'll ask another *amsterdammer*.

*Papiamiento* Phrase Du Jour

Sunday: Every move anticipated: Chess.

Maandag: The world is full of polyglots.

Tuesday: Going out into the world, make yourself comfortable.

Woensdag: If my grandmother had wheels, she'd be a bicycle.

Jueves: A menthol cigarette doesn't cure a cold.

Friday: Let Juana shake everything up with her moves.

Sábado: *On peut tout critiquer.*

TBC. In the prostitutes' neighborhood I get a tuberculosis vaccination.

### WEDNESDAY 10

*Zazen.* I go out for a walk. As I leave the *dojo* I ask Paul, "What kind of weather is this, Paul?" "A Dutch writer says: It's everybody's weather."

### *Zazen* 6. 30 P. M: CAROLINE, VERO, ME.

I make time, if it can be said this way, in the Kashmir Lounge. It's a genteel smoking room for stray widower tourists, for faithless assassins, for wanderers without a way, the waitress dressed in an Asian costume, the *toilette boutique tibetaans* …

I go to play music with Lamine. Class over, he recommends construction of the box drum. I take his recommendation into account and also take into account, from Jan van Sleeuwen,

> Al reizend ervaart men het leven vreemder
> overal anders en overal eender.

Zen in Cuba is so new in light of the cosmic transit of the original, historic Buddhism that it's possible to say it doesn't exist. It doesn't exist, but it does exist.

Martí: a current of spiritual intensity passes through him, one that he transports from the Buddha to the island of Cuba.

*paseo por la tierra de los anamitas*
*con qué si el gallo no pone huevos*
*pá qué tú me llamas budismo Trasatlántico*

[walking through mushroomland I
with what, if the rooster lays no eggs
why'd you call me, Transatlantic Buddhism]

FRIDAY 12

For the first time, instead of going to the Buikslotermeerplein by bus, I bike, crossing the bay on ferries. Which even nowadays are free, though some would like ... It's about half an hour faster. And cheaper! Nice day with Noah, who is learning how to walk. On my way back, I meet Lamine on his way to Belgium: dancing. I've met up with the African in this city of concomitances so many times. But it's only with him that I talk, in the middle of the street, at the top of my voice like Africans, about our lives. The others are more reserved. Me too.

Pass by, or drop into, Dimos' place for a take-away *pikillia* & *kalamarakia*, breaded calamari, and retsina. He offers red wine and a cigarrette: "Go home, the *kalamarakia* gets *frío*!", he says. So much for *Lingua Franca*.

On the radio we listen to music by Yusa.

*Erisi Baluande, Erisi Baluande*
*Congo Duwé, Congo Duwé*
*Ay cunián gangulé!*
*Ay cunián gangulé!*
*Erisi ta mío*
*Oh, erisi Baluande!*

SUNDAY 14

Big party for a child, Killiam, in Erasmus Park. Erasmus, how many birthdays are celebrated in your name? Among others attending the party are Saliou Traore, the painter from Burkina Faso, and Christophe de Bretagne, with whom I play *pétanque*. The African wins. The great party ends in Dimos's place.

I continue with work for Book Light, publisher of *La revolution interieure* in a translation by Jesse Hasse. It has to be corrected and expanded, *amplificatio*.

### TUESDAY 16

*Zazen*. Then back home. *Jointje*. I begin the box drum on the balcony. Around 4 p.m. Nina interrupts me: *on va a jouer pétanque ancore avec Saliou*, she and Christophe by the *Melkhuis*, the House of Milk, in the Vondelpark. It ends in the suffering of men strewn across the open field. Once again the African wins. Not by chance. Afterwards, glasses of beer with Christophe in a club on Weteringschans.

### MERCREDI

I finish the drum box. Plywood and pressed wood. 34.5 cms high, the sides of the box measuring 22 x 25.5. It has a pyramidal shape. Buddha's eyes are drawn on the front, with a pentacle on top of the box. At 7:30 p.m. with Lamine, I debut "Little One," as the aforementioned drum is named. It sounds like *diable* next to the *djembes* and the *dundún*, which creates the base layer: Hey you! I'm talking to you. Lamine plans a time for next Monday.

Off to rest at Dimos's place. *Semper* good there with Dimos, *anthropologos*, cook and barman for friends. He starts to watch a symposium.

### SABATH 20

*Zazen*. To Maastricht. We arrive at 7 after four hours of traveling. My sister Amor sings tonight in the Sacred Music Festival. At 8 she sings about a pilgrim's tale in the Basilica. Afterwards, beer and french fries in a club. To bed at 2 a.m. in the hotel. The three of us are together in a room, Algerian style, Vietnamese style. As it should be.

Lilita leaves early. I wake up among portraits of the artists who have stayed the night here: Marilyn Monroe, Charles Chaplin, etc. Our admiration doesn't prevent us from eating with a hearty appetite. Then we take a walk through Maastrich, the city where they defeated D'Artagnan. A French air, modern and ancient sculptures in interior plazas, a rivulet next to the fortress.

**MONDAY 22**

Up early. I begin reading *Opus Nigrum*, which María loaned to me. Spanish trans. of the *Oeuvre au noir* by Marguerite Yourcenar, which was translated into English as *The Abyss*. The French edition was from Gallimard, 1968. *Note de l'Auteur* from the French edition, which Cesar Mora found for me in Paris: "L'Oeuvre au noir *aura eté, tout comme* Mémoires d'Hadrien, *un de ces ouvrages entrepris dans la jeunesse, abandonnés et repris au gré des circonstances, mais avec lesquels l'auteur aura vecú toute sa vie.*"

She's referring to the fact that the work was written over more than 40 years, and also to the fact that Zeno, her protagonist, would have been nine years old when Leonardo died in Ambois. Why do I read it in Spanish and not the French original? Because María offered it. I suspect that I'll need to reread it in the original.

At 3 p.m. in a café, Alverna. Interview with Lamine and two other drummers—one from Senegal like Lamine, and the other from the Ivory Coast. We agree to meet tomorrow.

**TUESDAY**

At 5 p.m. I meet up with Lamine in the gymnasium at the former silversmithing academy, which is the VOOR BEELD cultural center today. We begin with *dundún* and *djembe*, then drum box and *balafon*, with the drum from the Ivory Coast: the combination works. There are two dancers from Surinam. One of them wants to learn to dance *palo*. I teach her the little I know about it.

*Zazen*. After coffee I go home to organize papers for the interview at the office of the Immigration Police. Papers are papers.

Zeno says,

> *Je ne commetrai plus l'indecence qui consiste*
> *a essayer de montrer les choses comme elles sont.*

Up at 6:30 a.m. Meeting with the *Verfreemdeling Politie*. 4 weeks from now to wait for the Residence Card.

Cappucino in Coffee Company *avec mon amour*. Then shopping: 1 kg of bananas from the Albert Heijn, 1 Euro; with the Moroccan at the market, 90 cents; in the Natuur Winkel, 2.50. One reason that organic products are not very popular yet.

A shower and off to the *dojo*. After *zazen*, the Taoists who sublet our space arrive: "Hallo! Hallo!" *Que si jaló*. An old joke from our countryside, playing on how sounds travel between English and Spanish.

> *El gando quiere*
> *marímbula*
> *el gando quiere*
> *marímbula*

*Gando, ngando*, maybe that's Swahili: a magic box. It wants the music.

Such are the songs that can be rendered on the *balafon*. Before bed I read Joseph Bové: the globalization of hope, Gurdjieff might have said!

Gandhi may say that writing is a spiritual occupation, not work. Whatever you say, Mahatma. Just before midnight Cristina and I play chess.

To Lamine's place at 3. A certain kind of disorganization: the professorial Rastas, the New Age culture-mixing black. A boring explanation of pleasure. Enjoyment needs no explanation.

Finally we play in the classroom, but not for the public. The Grandfather, *El Tata*, was right when he told me, "It's not a drum, it's a book."

### MONDAY 29

Up at 8:30 a.m. I go out to the De Jaren café to meet Nanne Timmer, thanks to Atilio Caballero. Long conversation that ends with an agreement: A talk about poetry at Leyden University on October 24. It coincides with a performance by the Cuban company Danza Abierta, in Den Haague.

Back at home I rummage through anthologies for poems that will bring urgency to our dialogue.Continue reading of *Paysan du Monde* by Joseph Bové.

At nightfall I go to the *dojo* to lend a hand, or two, to Johann with the *guenmai* and *gomasio*.

### WEDNESDAY OCTOBER FIRST

*Zazen.* Workday at Alga's house. The chore: remove a layer of paint from various doorways using a blowtorch and a scraper, in this case a sharpened triangle with a handle. The method is primitive and highly chemical, as they say these days. After we finish, wine with Alga, who sings tangos in her particular style.

### FRIDAY

To Marije and Leonard's house on Singerstraat, in the new western quarter. With its mosques and *Islamitische* butcher shops. A neighborhood of allocthonous peoples.

In the garden, where we eat lunch, Marije proposes two hours of cleaning each week, which could turn into three, at 9 euros per hour. She talks about another possible client, Jeroen, a friend.

I go back home and make a pasta dish: *fusili, courgette, pomodoro fresco*, broccoli, onion and a curry with *pindakaas* or peanut cream. *Lekker*, as they say here. This might be the word most used in the Dutch language. At any rate it's the first one I learned. You could translate it as "tasty." But that's not the only meaning. Tomorrow, at Paul's request, I'll do the 10:30 a.m. *Introductie* demonstrating posture for the beginners. In English.

### SUNDAY 5

*Dojo*, I give an introduction for an Iranian woman. The *dojo* is full.

Then in *Kriterion, avec* Christophe who perseveres with his dream of doing something in *Italie*: a traditional Breton *creperie* and a zen-yoga center, *un monastére*. This dream, which gets modified over time and in its words, is nonetheless unchanged: to build a temple in Umbria, land of San Francesco.

### FRIDAY OCTOBER 10. *Demajagua*

Cuban independence wars started on October 10, 1868

Register in Amsterdam: *afhalen Verblijfsdocument*. I pick up my residence card and the first forms of aid in support of adaptation. Allocthonous.

October 30 will be our departure date for the fall camp led by the monk Pierre Leroux, "*sans la presence du Maitre Kosen.*" I've never been so excited about a trip before. Maybe that's why I leave home earlier than necessary and wait here in Schiphol, where I feel at home too.

I'll travel for 17 days before the *sesshin* in order to participate in its organization, experience the current state of the *dojo* in Havana, and be with my friends, my son: my Cuban family, as they're called.

What does a Zen monk do that other people don't? And what is it that the monk doesn't do, even if everyone else does? While finishing a coffee and cigarette I realize I've forgotten the precepts. They must include you will not kill, you will not steal, you will not sow discord within the community of practitioners, the last of which alone helps with adding no more violence to this war-torn world.

Not getting intoxicated or getting the others intoxicated constitutes another one of the fundamental precepts. But I pause and ask: What does "intoxicated" mean here, and what is the burden to which the precepts refer? What would it mean to "not get intoxicated"? It would be wise not to turn into fanatics, since a fanatic tends to be more dangerous than a drunk. Actually, the fanatic is a sort of drunk. Even a drunk driver tends to be less lethal than a car bomb; therefore, there are many motivations for intoxication and different statistical outcomes. A collision, an explosion, one dead, a thousand … an assault, an injury. How do you define the radius of action involved in intoxication?

I arrive in Havana at 20:30 local time. Travel intoxicates too.

### SATURDAY NOVEMBER 1

Last night I went to a birthday party for Sigfredo Ariel, where I definitely became intoxicated.

On the way I ran into Portuguese Victor who is here for the Painting Biennial, so today I'm going over early to pick him up and and drive him to the *dojo*. There's a day of meditation: around 20 people, including a few new faces, at the first *zazen*. At its conclusion comes a ceremony for Frank *el Mulatón*, who passed away recently. The space for the *dojo*, dirty and not well maintained, doesn't give any outward signs of being a place for Zen. It just looks like another abandoned building. However, everything seems to be moving forward anyway: Cuban qualities, lotus qualities.

On the other hand, there are problems paying the rent to the state. It's high, 1000 Cuban pesos, for a not-for-profit organization. Some people pay nothing, others pay what they can and sometimes it happens that Manolo the monk pays the rest out of his pocket. With friends like these …

**WEDNESDAY 5TH.**

*Zazen* 7 a.m. *Samu* at the end, repair the *zafu* cushion. What would the correct plural be for *zafu? Zafus, zafuses,* or an identical plural? This tends to happen with terms brought over from the Japanese, and grammar is just one expression of the experience of translating Zen to other lands. Anyhow, a little organizing and cleaning lifts the spirits. We still need to improve the lighting in the *dojo*, clean the other under-utilized rooms, put in a toilet, etc.

There's a faux guaguancó by Vicentico Valdés: "*Santos Suárez le tocó.*" Come on singer, let's sing.

**FRIDAY 7TH.**

7 a.m. *Zazen*, 5 people. Enrique arrives. He's a Zen practictioner-plumber nicknamed "The Destroyer," who does pretty much destroy the old toilet bowl in the bathroom. We test the drain with four containers of water, and it works!

On the way out, a young custodian in a shit-colored or khaki uniform asks us if we have permission to do what we did. We answer yes. He inquires whether the permission was written or verbal. Verbal, I answer. I'm lying. Lie and truth give way, in this case, to common sense. I remember what I learned already: A lie benefits an honest man. We've cleaned a bathroom, removed a shit-encrusted toilet in small pieces, thrown a few containers of water into the drain that shows more life and determination than many others. And for that you're supposed to ask permission.

A pathetic carnival in L'abana.

At 4 p.m. I drop in to say hello to Cintio and Fina. They offer a car and driver for picking up Pierre. But he doesn't arrive. I'll go again tomorrow at the same time.

I spend the day with Mariano. Then after picking up Laura and Manolo, all four of us go to the airport. And here comes Pierre, punctual this time. We get to my place, and there's a long conversation in the kitchen. When Laura and Manolo leave, we stay on the balcony, contemplating the carnival. We pour our first libation with rum. Then out to the street for beer. Sitting at a table at a crowded corner, an intoxicated intruder appears suddenly, reciting Hegel in German. Pierre understands him, since he has lived in Germany. The intruder has too, a romantic electrician. We go out with him for a walk through the streets of San Leopoldo.

Here I write that we find an unexpected dance, happening in a sort of hangar used as an impromptu film studio. Alex Fleites is there, apparently some kind of assistant. Actually, he offers us rum. We dance. No lack of partners. Mine rejects me after I tell her I'm Cuban: "You don't know how to dance": Relativity! I was dancing really well when she thought I was a foreigner. We walk to the Prado and down the boulevard in a circle to get home. It's 6 a.m. I shower and head to the *dojo*.

7 people at *zazen*. The preparations accelerate. Returning home, I introduce Pierre to my mother. She invites us to lunch. White rice, black beans, okra, spinach salad, tomato and cilantro. A *Pierre Leroux* salad, we call it.

In the afternoon while Pierre is resting, Mariano and I go out to ride bicycles on the Malecón. Mariano can already ride alone. Without any training wheels, he rides a circle around our course.

Then, dinner with Pierre: tamales and salad. We talk about music and French cinema, about *sangha* and *sesshin*. Tonight, more police than ever at the carnival and the *Abakuá* drummers show themselves for the first time.

### SATURDAY 15TH

8 a.m. *zazen*. 16 people. Manolo runs it. Pierre, as just one more disciple, sits by the wall. Then off to the gardens at the Hotel Nacional to sample the morning and a mojito. And to the market. There's a carnival tonight too.

### SUNDAY 16TH

We leave the zen *dojo* at D and 15, in the Vedado district, at 10:40 a.m. We arrive at the Taburete campground in Pinar del Río around one. We have to organize the *dojo*, the kitchen, get the cabins. At five there's an initiation into practice, with several newbies and a girl from the area. *Zazen* at 6 p.m. Dinner. The bar opens under Kimbo's purview: songs and guitars. There's good rapport between Pierre and the Cubans.

### MONDAY 17TH

Up at 6 and I show one of the new people the ceremony of awakening, with its rotation: the four directions, the bell. *Zazen* at 7:30. I'm acting as *shuso*, head monk, and soon I make mistakes. After *zazen* Pierre talks to me about it. It's like organizing an orchestra to create harmony as well as directing the soloist, *zazen*, to the best of oneself.

*Bon*, *zazen* at 4:30 and, after *kin hin*, an explanation from Pierre about "putting things in their places." Food at 7 and *zazen* at 8:45 p.m. Then a bonfire and a toast: "To your health, friend." Sleep at midnight.

*Zazen* 7:30, 28 people. Three people leave, female beginners. At 11:40 Pierre does the initiation into practice, and at 4 there's another meeting with the *kyosaku*, awakening stick.

*Zazen* at 4:45 p.m. with 27 people, since another one left. *Dans cette moment la, Pierre raconte l'histoire de Maitre Nyojo et son disciple Dogen: shin jin datsu raku, datsu raku shin jin.* How do you translate that? Abandoning the body-spirit, abandon of abandonment. Abandoning. Pierre also talks about self-understanding, self-acceptance.

No *zazen* at night. I rest before *sesshin*. Nor is there a bar after we eat. The sound of *claquettes*, wooden clappers for marking the hour, at 10:30 p.m. A practitioner from Lyon has arrived: Gerald.

Wakeup at 6:30 a.m., *zazen* at 7. Twenty-seven creatures, *guenmai* and breakfast. *Samu* meditation while working in the kitchen, firewood, etc.

11 a.m. *zazen*. Pierre reads a *kusen* by Master Kosen and talks about the importance of silence.

4:30 p.m. 3 *zazen* with 2 *kin hin*. Then, "*ça gasse?*": "*Au fond.*" Pierre replies.

In an aside, Pierre talks with us about the Argentine camp. The Cubans listen silently.

Dinner at 7:30. *Zazen* 8:45. Pow!

Up at 6, morning ritual.

*Zazen* at 7 a.m. Frankly the number of people is hard for me to make out. It looks like 26. It's always 26. A walk crossing the stream. *Guenmai* ceremony. At 10, gathering and tea: Pierre lays out his point of view about the organization of the *dojo* very clearly. "Find your support from those who are here, the strongest forces around. With no need to exclude anyone." It can be a team responsibility: "You are the ones capable of revolution. Stephane didn't come here for nothing." *Zazen* at 11:45. A newcomer, the lifevest of the place. After the afternoon *zazen*, a *mondo*. A newcomer asks about the importance of the physical part of practice. Response: "That's just it. Practice is practice. Without practice it would be intellectual, New Age." And to an experienced practictioner who returns to the opening theme, he responds delicately and conclusively: "There's no need to be different than the others." Dinner at 7:30; cool air descends on the mountain. People sing, and there's a guitar: "What a lovely group," Pierre says. And I think about you.

*Zazen* at 9:30. Afterwards Pierre authorizes a few beers. The *claquettes* man presses his hands together to show thanks.

### FRIDAY 21ST

After the *Hannya Shingyo*, the Heart Sutra, a long walk through the trees. Pierre: "You were asking me about the *samu* or work practice of the head student. Well, you have to keep things threaded together until the end. If you do it any other way, if you make a mistake, the energy will escape."

Departure. The bus or collective taxi arrives at one thirty, more or less. During the march money is collected for the party that's already starting, and it begins with a *Hannya Shingyo* to a rumba step. Plenty of guitars, and Gerald's tambourine. Party at Laura's house. We return to Central Havana. Carnival march by Pierre, Roberto, and me.

### SATURDAY 22ND

We go out shopping while the Frenchman cooks. Chicken with vegetables, plus a salad. There's beer, and after dark people begin to arrive. It's not late. We go out for a walk and next to the massive shape of the Hotel

Nacional we sit down to talk. It's the end of the carnival and the ocean is calling. Felix and I go for a dip.

We've invited Pierre to the alley, Trickster's Way / La Trampa in my mind. There's rumba. Back at home, a Paraguayan *torta*. Tortas have different meanings around the Spanish-speaking world—in this case, it's a soufflé: *chipa guazú* with corn, cheese, onion, egg and milk. We bake it, we eat it.

Pierre leaves at 20:30 on Air France.

I take Mariano to the Museum of the Revolution. Then we take a walk together outside the walls, the ruins left from the city's colonial period.

Up with the sun. I clean the house and get my luggage ready. When Nica arrives in the afternoon, we prepare tobacco together, a gift from the Zen group for Kosen. I take a taxi, stopping in Las Cañas to visit Grandfather. See you later.

Arrival in Madrid. Schiphol, Amsterdam. "Remember me telling you a story about the Greek police," Dimos announces.

The counterpart to the sky, according to the *I Ching*. The sky's counterpart is the motor moving the water. Tomorrow I should run the daytime *zazen*. The rule, according to the Geneva *sesshin*, is: *zazen* for 40 to 45 minutes—*kin hin*—*zazen* until 8:45 to 8:50. Those who have to leave for *werk*: they can go either before *kin hin* or after the ceremony. I continue with the *I Ching*: weak, measured, correct. The motor has to let itself run. If you were to leave it on, leave it to its own judgment, it would burn out.

Four people in the *dojo*. "Well, one quiet *zazen* morning," says glamorous Mo.

I go to clean the apartment belonging to Mr. Jeroen van der Sluis, the friend of Maria and Leonardo, the other clients: three and a half hours of well-paid work. 35 Euros.

Plus Manon has asked for my help. I'll see her tomorrow at her house. I take an herb called cascarilla, a small bowl, and tobacco butter. She prepares one solution with flowers and another with herbs for cleaning the house. In Amsterdam, believe it or not, there's a lot of witchcraft. Ever since the city was founded.

**TUESDAY 9TH**

| | |
|---|---|
| *Ik ben* | *We zijn* |
| *Jij bent* | *Jullie zijn* |
| *U bent* | *Ze zijn* |
| *Hij is* | |
| *Zij is* | |

*Ik ben student.* 1st Social Orientation class. In the neighborhood school on Elizabeth Wolfstraat. With our teacher, Omayda Villarreal, a native of Curaçao.

The majority of the students are Latinos. There are Colombians, but also Mexicans, Venezuelans, Ecuadorians, Dominicans, a pair of Moroccans, a Sudanese, and two picaresque girls from eastern Europe. Also three Cubans.

> *Mevrouw Baba, bent U getrouwd?*
> *Señora Baba, está usted casada?*
> Ms. Baba, are you married?

The classes take place in the evening, scheduled for workers. *Volwasse-nonderwijs*, adult education. The topic of matrimony, so expensive for immigrants, occupies a good part of the first lesson. For many come here thanks to the conjugal proceeding. Given the celebrated Dutch tolerance, this does not exclude gay couples. It's possible, and symbolic, to get married at City Hall, the *Stadhuis*, which has shared a building with the opera since the 1980s. A governmental operation that tries to get citizens closer to local government in an old Hebrew neighborhood, Waterlooplein. *O Waterlooplein!* Subject and object of so many songs.

### THURSDAY 11TH

In the school on Elizabeth Wolfstraat, not very far from Dimos or the over-used job placement bureau, we proceed with the topic of matrimony. We go from ordinary citizens to the prince consorts: *Het Koninklijk huis van Oranje Nassau.* It was once a small republic where queens married Germans: Wilhelmina paired with Hendrik, Juliana with Bernard, Beatrix with Claus. And here's my note that this last queen had three daughters who got married. One to a Spaniard, one to a Dutchman, and the last to a Cuban named Jorge. What has become of you, Jorge, Royal Consort?

Also I wrote that this monarchical and colonial republic, willingly or not, freed its territories: Indonesia in 1948 after a bloody war; the *Nederlaandse Antillen* in '54 and Surinam in '75, while Aruba got a separate status in 1986. Right: all the friends and future immigrants to the *Socialdemocratic Papiamento* of the Low Countries, *de Lage Landen.*

### FRIDAY 12TH

Housing: *huisvesting*; the homeless: *daklozen*; houseboats: *woonboot*. *Huur*, rentals, are not to be confused—in a very common phonetic error—with *hoer*, whore. The students laugh.

Racist outburst in class. When we're talking about the *gastarbeiders*, or "guest workers," a Dominican student calls the Moroccans "rats." Notable how these verbal habits, little by little, expand. Attacking the *marokkanen* does not exactly yield good results. They also attend these schools, and we too are "guest workers" in the progression of inguistics and citizenship. A constant otherness through which we outsiders are opposed, through subtle rules, to the natives: all those who are autochthonous.

### TUESDAY 16TH

I work at Marije's. Three hours, three floors. And I can listen to music when the vacuum cleaner allows: *Get Up (I Feel Like Being a Sex Machine)* by James Brown, and other gems. Not that one feels, exactly, like a sex machine with a vacuum cleaner. But a rhythm takes hold and for scrubbing bathrooms, sinks, and kitchen sinks, this is better than the somber and gothic Portishead, or Bjork for that matter.

In school we chip away at some verbs: *komen, wonen, heten.*

> *Ik kom uit Marokko*
> *Ik woon in Amsterdam*
> *Ik heet Rosa*

I'm from Morocco, I live in Amsterdam, my name is Rosa. *Rosa, you, melancholic.*

### WEDNESDAY

Test: at the GG & D. HIV and syphilis tests are required for the citizenship process, or *Inburgering*. We'll look for a better translation in the future.

In the Mellow Yellow, "The First Coffee Shop in Amsterdam." You climb toward the Pijp neighborhood where Jeroen and his cat Pixel live. Is it really the oldest coffee shop in the universe? Maybe not, but I liked the guy behind the counter, with his Frankenstein look.

I do two and a half hours following instructions from Alga, cleaning queen … prolix.

I do disasters, presages, decorations. *Samu*: what is it? Guevara's spirit: To whom did I give that lighter, with the effigy of Che smoking a joint?

F♠♠k the Revolution

And what are the 7 Steps of Life?

The first: for us to be alive, and without pre-history.

### FRIDAY 26

9:26 a.m. 7 degrees. Departure for Winter Camp with Paul Loomans, Cristina y *el gangling* Ernst. Passing

> Orval
> Wanlin
> Hayange, Florange, Pétange,
> Aire de Rosières, Contrexéville,
> Épinal, Mirecourt, *prochaine sortie*
> *Gendarmerie*
> Dieulefit.

*Donc*, we arrive in Lyon after dark and stay the night at the *dojo* there, founded by *Maitre* Deshimaru. The next day, after a short fast, *on' y va.* By sunset we arrive at Mas Gircos. *Automatiquement* I'm in the kitchen. *Salut* Christian. *Salut* Pierre, *et voilà, on continue.*

### 28TH

Up at 9, *a la cuisine. Zazen* 11 a. m. Normal. *Cuisine*, I've already given the Cuban gifts to Stephane. Variation: the master does *sampai* in the afternoon *zazen* and then, without *kin hin, c'est fini.* Lunch and snack without setbacks, signs that the *courgette* puree was a success. We have our dinner without wine. *Zazen* at 8:30, where the master begins to talk about Gensha. It will *continuer.*

Up at 6, prepare *guenmai*, tea and *tisane*. Today I'll receive the *kesa*. After the ceremony, the master puts it over my head and the monk María Teresa helps me to complete the process. *Bon, cuisine*, lunch, *samu, zazen*.

I prepare the fire in the room before the Turk arrives from Madrid. He comes at 7:50 p.m., the call with beaten metal, time to eat. We call our room "The Airport" because of the many entrances and exits by staff.

*Zazen* at 7:30 a.m. *Promenade. Il fait froid.* Lunch. Stephane comes to the cooks' table and offers peach aguardiente. We talk with Pierre about the last *sesshin* at the Taburete. *Zazen* at 4:30; *cuisine. Zazen* at 8:30, *cuisine. Zazen* at 11 p.m. *Apres minuit* a short fast *dans le refectoire*: soup, *pain, fromage, tisane. Zazen* until the end: *Fukanzazengi*.

2:30 a.m. The master sits down by the fire. Then we go to "The Airport." Tomorrow's wakeup time is 10:30 a.m.

I get up at 9. Lucette invites me to visit the Besalú synagogue. Four of us go in the car: Master Stephane, Lucette, Turk *et moi* and after the medieval synagogue, we get coffee in the plaza. Lucette offers a local sweet, *turrón*. Other disciples appear—among them you, Cristina, and you look happy.

We return. When we arrive, the master gives me his pipe.

For *cuisine*, couscous under the direction of Joelle Cristina. Enlivened by Lucette, dinner drifts into an amazing party. Confetti, bugles, blowout horns, total delight. Later comes the end-of-year ceremony. I put my *kesa* on under the stars, *un petit petard* in my room with friends. After the final ceremony of the year, in the bar, Stephane shows me his other pipe, with a head carved from bone as its bowl: "It's the sister of Hermes—Athena!" We close the bar and the dancing.

*Bonne année et bonne santé.*

# 2004

Tonight I sat in front of the fire with Stephane, without saying a word. "The *zazen* you all are doing is not for you but for the others. So there's nothing to worry about." He said this in the latest *kusen*.

On the way to Paul Loomans' house, Cristina and I improvise a highway haiku mostly in English.

> *The eau de vie sur l'autel*
> cold hands in the pockets
> O, Dominique.
>
> Open mouth
> yawning or devouring:
> Peak of the Dragon.
>
> Moonlight on stone
> showing the way,
> something like that.
>
> New Year, shining star.
> There has to be
> something more.
>
> Snow on the sides,
> passing thoughts:
> another year's gone.
>
> Winter Camp, New Year's party.
> Gabrielle,
> Pacha Mama is dancing too.

Await the light
knowing very well
I'm there. I'm here.

Mountain of Greece,
the sandals on the altar:
finally home.

Sounds of life,
if you get till there:
another season.

Poems on the move,
my friends discuss:
are they really haiku?


**AMSTERDAM, 2004.**

It's January 9 for us and winter in Amsterdam. Cristina sleeps, I listen.

The ginger inside the gourd, silent, listens too. Sometimes you hear a whistle. It might be the wind, or the child-God, or both. *Allebei*: the new word I learned today in school.

All things pass, including an in-house restaurant accident. "Accident!" Dimos would say to Eliah, the Berber cook, when I unexpectedly took the house bread and butter to a table that wasn't theirs. "First you have to give them time to ask for the menu," Dimos explains. The menu, *la carta*: all language is Greek, and promethean. Once I heard someone tell a German in Crete that in ancient Greek, an arrow that comes to us by chance—*incontro*—after turning down a forest path signifies a problem.

There it is: the repugnant chore of writing. Chinese New Year, new life: horse, monkey, rooster or bee, it's all the same.

Breathing through the quiet orifice, the flute. And a pipe that Stephane gave to me, the black and white horseman. When winter camp ends, the pipe is busy at the altar for breathing. The clock is going to strike eleven. I write it down. So as not to ask anything of the gods.

Sometimes you hear a sound like sirens on the canal at night. Ululation, and needless to say: seagulls. I think about Pessoa too: it is in order not to ask anything of the gods that I write. Or something like that. Stephane is a poet too. Let's go, man, the pipe is waiting.

*The comma, a rest. The period accentuates. And the semicolon analyzes: it signals continuation to the end.* It is a breath and a snort. The patriarchs will sleep. In the barrio.

### MONDAY 12

Living without decorations. And here I draw a rose.

School lesson about money: *Geld*.

*Munten en bilijetten: monedas y billetes*, coins and bills

*Betalen: pagar*, to pay

*Ik wil een rekening openen: quiero abrir una cuenta*, I want to open an account. And property: *eigendom*. Key point: property and proprietor. No one's home on earth is permanent, say the Nahuatl.

### SATURDAY 17

Swerve into straightness. *Zazen* in the *dojo*, *zazen* in the tunnel at the Rijksmuseum. At 2 pm. Long and extended. With Caroline, Loic y Barbara. Background music: Bach toccatta and fugue on the accordion.

Early evening: with Lamine and his boys, playing the African rumba.

I get up early for the 11 a.m. *zazen*. After the café, Uli, Christophe and I visit a gym, violent and well kept. Maybe we were looking for some place where we could sweat. It doesn't turn out well. Better to smoke. Christophe and I go on to the *Rokkerij* for a good Moroccan café; we plan to run tomorrow in the Oosterpark. We say goodbye. I get lost for a while as always in A'dam. I find my way home by following the Jordaan. I clean the house, take out the little Christmas tree and go for a run next to the canal. Beautiful, to run again. I go back and cook: pasta. Cristina surprises me there. Talking and talking.

*Nederlands Schrijfboek*: important! *belangrijk*; high percentage of older people, *ouders*. The Dutch, according to the teacher, sometimes prefer to have a dog or cat. They don't have young, well-trained people to help them. From which this situation arises—these lessons for immigrants who keep on arriving, "rats" or not, *ongeletterden*, illiterate, or *andersgeletterden*, followers of some other alphabet. This is a *brugperiode*, bridge-period, with its hyphen and ellipses.

*Zwartwerken*: working off the books; *watermerk & valse geld*: watermark and fake money. Holland's ancient florin dissipated into the Benelux macroeconomy: *legitemeren*! *Identificeren*! *Geldschieters*: moneylenders and *witteboordcriminelen*, white collar criminals. Launderers; nations make and unmake themselves through usury, Ezra Pound. *Kontant*!

It's my third week of classes in the new school: new pine trees. The patio is right next to the balcony at Jeroen's house. Coinciding, *dunque*, within the de Pijp neighborhood.

Adult or not, you must attend five days a week, five hours per day.

Today there's an exam. Tom is *niet tevreden*. Tom is dissatisfied, *ontevreden*; *duizelig*, dizzy, Gillespie, boos, bravo. *Hij heeft te weinig klanten.* Tom has very few clients, so he's angry. I understand Tom. I too have very few clients.

The teacher presents the first poem, maybe the first modern poem, ultra-modern, in the Dutch language.

*De Deur*
*Duwen        trekken*


*La Puerta*
*Empujar        halar*


The Door
Push        pull

And that's how the doors of the school are: pushing and pulling doors, I go at 1pm to clean Jeroen's place. In other words, I walk across the patio. *Crossing the street to escape the house*, Pavese said: but here you don't need to escape, just go in circles in order to return: fair ball! go go along the border of the garden on the left, take First, and by 3:30 the ball arrives in Café *De Balie* with his friends Cristina y Paul: safe on second. From there to third base, the movie theater. Final part of *Lord of the Rings*, New Zealand version; and though the Maoris dressed as orcs don't get noticed, the English camouflauged as elves do. The landscape is impressive and the trick photography infinite. But Tolkien's words are missing, the poems, the ancient air, the Celtic air. It's not enough for the horsemen to be blond and their columns to carry arabesques.

Gollum is still my favorite character, definitively—the only one who expresses emotion rather than making faces. Watch out, it's just a puppet! The creation of the new computing wizards. Poor Saruman, with his antiquated glass ball. This box full of quartz has a greater resonance. We go out to a Belgian beerhouse; they say Belgians take nothing seriously except their beer.

**THURSDAY 19 FEBRUARY**

*Zazen. Hannya Shingyo*

School; *soort films,* film classes.

Martial arts, *komedie, politiek drama, tragikomedie, familiedrama,* drama, *liefdesverhal* or love story: *liefde is altijd nodig,* says the docent … Love is always necessary. OK, if she says so.

With Paola from Brasil, we dream up a story in Dutch about Harold, an elderly man who talks to pigeons and thinks his bicycle is *speciaal.*

*Space Mountain* is a coffeeshop two hundred meters from the school. Juan the Spaniard invites me to go with Carlos from Punto Fijo, Venezuela. I tell him that in Havana, my mother has some maracas from Punto Fijo that were given to her by the singer Pan con Queso. It's a small world after all: *punto fijo,* a point that does not move. Companions studying in the coffeeshop: learning how to forget. *Groña polá!,* so many years, as they say in Greek.

**ZATERDAG 21**

Why don't I come up with some Dutch studies?

Summary of the pages that Paul Kennedy dedicates to the emergence of Dutch dominion, split between the sixteenth and seventeenth centuries, in *The Rise and Fall of the Great Powers: A nation born in the confusion of a revolution*—like Cuba, one could say—and those 150 vessels to the Caribbean sea! From there to the engraving by Peter Schenck, with its panorama of the port of Havana: lighthouse, schooners, the chain at the entrance, the city that grows to the right. Squemeling and other pirates wander through these waters.

97

Then maybe the story or novella by Alejo Carpentier, "The Road to Santiago," and its description of the war and the Duke of Alba.

For now, I study Dutch. Level one, exam next week. Now I have to return to Pronouns, grammatical exercises.

But surely you could talk about sugar, coffee, tobacco, and wood in Holland: a portrait of an era, of all eras, through coffee, tobacco, and sweetness. *Natuurlijk.*

And on the other hand, the Dutch USA: Rip van Winkle, Martí in his "North American Scenes," New York or Nieuwe Amsterdam, Haarlem ... When all is said and done, the child-hero has his tiny finger jammed into all of our books.

**ZONDAG 22**

Grammatical Exercises

> *Kubaanolandia*
> *Balkenende katoliek*
> *Kubaanolandia*
> *Coffeeshop De Republiek*
> *Kubaanolandia*

Jan Peter Balkenende, known as the Harry Potter of Holland, is Minister-President. De Republiek, or rather the entire republic, is a coffeeshop located on a corner of the Staatsliedenburg, one of the "bad" neighborhoods in A'dam. Actually, it looks like one of those cafeterias where they sell fruit smoothies.

And so with that rhythm I begin my reading of the essay, *From Seville to Amsterdam: The Failure of an Empire*, by Immanuel Wallerstein. Citation— *The Modern World System*, an anthology of essays from Academic Press, Inc., 1974.

From Seville's House of Trade, the *Casa de Contratación* at the center of transantlantic trade, to the decline of Spain and its allied cities "in favor of the successful rebels of Amsterdam," change moves across the economic and political face of Europe. It becomes the favorite topic of historians and poets. "I gazed on the walls of my homeland … "

The following items will play important roles in this affair: the expulsions of Jews in 1492, the year of the Hispanic-Genoan production of the discovery of America, along with expulsions of Moors, the *anusim* and Erasmians; *voilà*, even the last of the Crypto-Moors persecuted in Valencia and Andalusia in 1609. After conversion to Christianity by force, the Muslim laborers of Castile and Aragon were treated like a fifth column of the Ottoman Empire and obligated to emigrate. No few of these persecuted people ended up in the Low Countries, a tradition that continues today, in a most civilized manner. And with the same cult of fear.

In another comparison, the Duke of Alba and Valeriano Weyler offer two examples of the same scorched-earth approach that, after disasters both military and human, was destined to fail as badly in Cuba as in Holland. The Spanish policy in both territories, though in different eras, was cut from the same cloth and yielded the same results.

*Estudios Flamencos.* Miles Davis, second take. Let's pause to listen now:

> *Así que si no hay oro ni plata en España,*
> *es porque los hay, la causa de su pobreza es su riqueza.*

> [So if there's no gold or silver in Spain,
> it's because there is. The source of Spain's poverty is her prosperity.]

> Martín González de Cellerigo. 1600
> Lawyer and theologian, ¡*olé*!

Karl Marx:

> *Su realización es su pérdida (suspiro)*
> *Todo lo sólido se desvanece en el aire.*

[Its realization is its loss (sigh)
All that is solid vanishes into air.]

And in Andalusia's mountains, Huguenots and Gascon bandits,
Piedmont and Lombardy, southern Germany, Antwerp, Krakow, and
       Portugal
agitated by one and the same crisis:

Between the Reformation and the Counter-Reformation, Amsterdam constructs itself around the grain market in the Baltic Sea. With their silent boats, the Dutch overcome Antwerp, and Wallerstein announces: We depart Seville for Amsterdam. A smooth operation.

Lucien Febvre protests: These Dutchmen, prudently dragging their fat stomachs around under foggy skies. But there's nothing to be done: specialization, the new world-economy skills make it so that these Dutchmen, with their *train train quotidienne*, take over the spice trade, leaving the Portuguese behind with their regatta and bargaining.

In these successes, the global domino game is played with marine arts: boat construction, ropemaking, the production of sails, pitch and tar, ironwork for ships; plus a little Middleburg wine and the aforementioned patience for which they were already training since the 11th century in the commercial Baltic. Hurray for the mercantile marine! Flax, tar, timbers and furs.

But, was it revolution? Was this the face that launched a thousand ships, to borrow Marlowe's line?

Maybe a more enterprising, efficient and better organized revolution …

"And if it was a revolution … ", continues Wallenstein, was it bourgeois or nationalist? Consider the slogans: Tolerance, Down with Images, Freedom for Protestants, etc.

As Tarkovsky would say, we haven't learned a thing in the past 4000 years. Well, maybe something about navigation. The Water Beggars, highly organized, plowed mercilessly through the waters of Revolution. They continued trade with the Spanish, but the revolt of the Netherlands (1566-1609), non-ideological yet economic, cut the ties: "Amsterdam flies low in the Baltic"—a popular expression equivalent to "Amsterdam thrives in the Baltic"—Amsterdam lowers the prices of naval constuction, mercantile center, shipping and shipyard, waterfront carpentry, protectionist or liberal *timmerman*, as needed.

"It was, in short, ideal guerrilla country." And over the course of time, writes Wallerstein, the North became Protestant and the South Catholic, and everyone lived happy, content lives …

But no, the rise of Amsterdam marks the decline of the Mediterranean people. First Spain, then Portugal and Italy. With Greece in limbo and France & Co. repressing Provence, we arrive here. The mixed capitalism of A'dam. In 1606 the Dutch succeeded in selling the English their own cloth back, reworked in the Low Countries. And what else do they do today with coffee, tobacco, and marijuana? So much for revolution.

### DINSDAG 24 FEBRUARI. REBELLION DAY

> Here was a nation created
> in the confused circumstances of revolution.

On a day like today, that's worth remembering.

At school, *Toets Spreken*, the oral exam. With a machine: beep. *Niet zo goed*, at least two mistakes, *maar*, but *ik ben niet bang, ik ben niet bezorgd*. We also learned this today, February 24: I'm not afraid, I'm not worried. Sentence of the day: *op hetzelfde aambeeld hameren*. Literally, hammering on the same old anvil; playing on the same harp string, raining on wet ground. Rain on the anvil, rain on the harp. Rain—no lack of that.

As for the faculties concerned in this learning, listening is *receptief*: the anvil; speaking is *productief*: the hammer. I need a hammer, a hammer, says Bob Marley, to hammer 'em down.

One day in a busy year I get up early, *ma non troppo*. Breakfast and off to *zazen*. Today I give a nice free *introductie* to the practice of *zazen*: one couple. *Zazen* is crowded: "Hallo, Loic, what a surprise!" He laughs next to the shelf holding the *kesas*. Then we return by way of the Vondelpark. I clean the house and rediscover the art books in the *kelder*, or storage room. Van Gogh, Degas, Michelangelo, the insane Jan Steen, the psychedelic Brueghel.

At night we go out to the Paradiso. *Surprenant*, I didn't imagine it would be like that, renaissance-Shakespeare style, the audience standing as if in a plaza surrounded by balconies. You smoke, you drink, you dance during the concert that opens with the *djembe* drum's call: "*J'écoute le pra pra prá*," says Mousse, drummer from Senegal. Omou Sangare, the diva of Mali, and her orchestra: drum set, bass and electric guitar, chorus and a kind of lyre, also electric; the *djembe*, of course, which barely lets up, three singer/dancers with rattles. And the queen herself. When the spirit of the *djembe* blows across the face of the earth.

## WOMAN'S DAY, AH

First lesson after spring vacation, *voorjaarsvakantie*. Bodily organs: *lungen*, lungs; *hart*, heart; *nieren*, kidneys; *lever*, liver; *baarmoeder*, uterus, etc.

At the coffeeshop Rokkerij, I drink a coffee as I wait for my job interview with BOOKINGS at one o'clock, tick tock, my daily slog. *C'est quoi?* A job ad I found on the wall at school: an agency, online reservations, call-center. Any old kind of work. Another season, other means. The important part: how many hours per week, *uuren per week*, how much protection I can get through this job in the *sociale ziekefonds*, social health insurance program. If I'm not sick! In sum, *wat te doen? Geen onderwijs? Ja.*

The interview is short, by the clock. We shake hands; they'll call me.

The search, solitary impatience in the soul.

1st day of work at BOOKINGS.

*O25 2004* account view
overview—*relación de reservas*
*nombre del cliente*
*número de reservación, : factura*
*payment habitación*: check in check out!
*Ordinateur:* login password: guest-start-account view,
no password necessary, file open- *025 2004* o.k
Printing. Or Microsoft access, org
overviews      organization
design: File, access over de mountains
*Vuela, vuela alto, sobrevuela*
*Y mírate a tí mismo. Es el aire*

[O25 2004 account view
overview—describes reservations
client number
reservation number, *factura*: invoice
room payment: check in check out!
*ordinateur*: login password: guest-start-account view,
no password necessary, file open- 025 2004 o.k
Printing. Or Microsoft access, org
overviews           organization
design: File, access over de mountains
Fly, fly higher, flyover
And gaze at yourself. It's the air]

*13 uur*: meet colleagues; the secretary, Arnie, who introduces the practical
stuff with computers. Farid, Antonio, and Mariska who closes contracts.
One trial month, 16 hours per week. I leave at 5.

*Zazen.*

School: *dubbelganger*, doppelganger, someone who resembles someone else to an extreme … dubbelgangster.

Bookings. 1 p. m. I send out overviews by fax, *liste des réservations*; I call hotels all around Europe, communicate in four languages: French, English, Italian, and Spanish. I control the receipts, *i nominativi, l'argent, l'argent,* the office of *contabilitá*: *"Il faudrá bien régler les factures, Madame." "Mais, oui, bien sûr!"*

Linguistically speaking: figures, formulas for politeness and more. Musically speaking, as you wait on the hotel connections: Barry White, Mozart, Scott Joplin, R. E. M, plastic Bach; *voor de rest, quotidienne* Amsterdam: *train train.* Another stitch on the *kesa*, as Pierre would say. Day after day, water follows water:

> *Gentes chatarra, así las llama Antonio,*
> *El Belga asalariado*
> *afinad la carcassa!*
> un po' inaffarato questi giorni:
> *cuentas sobre cuentas*
> *y cuentos sobre cuentos.*

> [Throwaway people, according to Antonio,
> the Belgian on full salary who
> slaps a shine on that carcass!
> *Un po' inaffarato questi giorni:*
> process account after account.
> Listen to account after account.]

Calling South Africa: "This is too late!" Time difference. Faxing Ireland: "This is too Erie!"

*Zazen.* School. Why go on, Caeiro used to say, but to keep on going on?!

A little before one, I'm in Bookings. I eat lunch with my colleagues in the lively room whose window overlooks the Rijksmuseum. There's sun, you eat in the Dutch way: salads, bread and cheese, juice, and coffee, and back to the office. You have to exit the building in order to smoke. Arnie and Antonio the Belgian instruct me: call the hotels that didn't pay the commission to our online reservation service. The clients book via Internet. The hotels pay Bookings 10 to 15% of the price for the reservation. Or they don't. Then one must remind them, sweetly threaten them. There are many responses and justifications, dramatic ones in the Latin countries.

Antonio speaks Italian well but prefers Spanish. Arnie and I understand each other in English; my Dutch isn't so great. Farid helps me with the computerized activity: Excel, Powerpoint, Bla Bla Bla, etc. Fortunately, you don't have to wear a tie. Antonio plays music from the radio and closes the door.

### VRIJDAG

To the Rabobank to open an account. With no bank account, you don't get work. With no medical insurance, you don't get work. Vice versa, contradictions that can be resolved in practice.

I go by the Albert Heijn looking for something to defeat my hunger. *Matahambre*, the hungerkiller: the name for a European almond cookie. At one o'clock on the dot, back to Rabobank. Springtime, everything seems to speed up: it's spring, I feel like I should wake up now, maybe I'm already awake. I'm hungry.

### MAANDAG 29

School. *Toelichting*: illustration. Not to be confused *avec l'Illustration*, the Enlightenment. This is just about abundance with respect to.

To detail, to explain, to extend oneself into something.

We study the phonetic difference between "oo" and "o" in Dutch, as in:

*roos (rous)* and *los, kook* and *lot, geloof* and *gezond,* etc.

> *soms kapot*
> *zorg*
> *klok, klopt?*
> *soms.*

*Intuitie volgen,* says the teacher: follow your intuition. I agree with that. Looking out the window I think about refreshing my gaze on a brick.

> *onzin*: nonsense
> *geen onzin*: no nonsense

### WOENSDAG

School. Computer Les: *eeuwig,* eternal, *meteen,* right now, *eerlijk,* honest.

*Genoeg hebben van*: to be tired of something, to have had it up to here. Example: *ik heb genoeg van de winter.* Wintertime. *Goed!: probleem opgelost,* problem resolved, etc.

Bookings, noon. Lunch with colleagues: people from all over. Argentina, Spain, Italy, France. The sky is cloudy. Antonio and I go out with women from Italy and Brazil to smoke a cigarrette. What the hell.

Calling Italy …

> *ram raam*
> *el chivo*
>    *brinca*
>       *por*
>         *la*
>           *ventana*

*bonifici*       *contabilitá*
*vi risultano?*
       *queste fatture*
[ring riiing
  the billy goat
      hops
          through
            the
               window
*bonifici*     *contabilitá*
*vi risultano?*
       *queste fatture]*

Since you can't smoke inside the building, the employees go out now and then. Or often. Like Belgian Antonio. Marnix, department head, *diventato arrogante padrone breaks le palle ad Antonio, e anche un pó a me …* He orders the music turned down so far it's inaudible, and he says the office doors must be kept open. Medieval.

## APRIL. THURSDAY

Up at 6:30 a.m. To the *dojo, zazen.*

School. Irregular declinations.

*Beginnen- begon- begonnen.* Not so irregular after all: this music repeats. *Drinken- dronk-gedronken, vertrekken-vertrokken-vertrokken.*

*Streng:* strict: *te sterk met de regels te zijn.* Literally, to be too demanding with the rules.

I leave.

12:30 = expanse of sea.

I make my way to Bookings along the canal.

Calling France, Italy, Spain. Farid teaches, gives advice to create one's own agenda. Happiness is a thing shared. Why does man work? Happiness is not a job.

Happiness is not work (it's a warm gun, we know).

## Vrijdag 2

School, *met* Ids de Vries. *Openbare en bijzondere scholen*, schools both public and specialized: Protestant, *Islamitisch*, like butcher shops, Montessori, *Antroposophisch* … the results of the *secularisatie* process initiated in 1965.

*Meneer De Vries* abounds in suffixes. Germanic ones, like: *-heid, gezelligheid; -ing, mondeling; -schap, vriendschap.* And *romaans*, as in: *-ade, limonade; -ude, prelude; -uur, kultuur; -ie, positie,* etc.

## Maandag 5

School. *Kringsgesprek*: lit. conversation in a circle.

*muzikale vormen- onderwijs*, musical forms- teaching

difference: *grijpen*: *pakken met jouw handen*: to grasp with your hands.

*begrijpen*: *pakken met jouw hersens*: to grasp with your mind.

Bookings. Back here again. 12.30 p.m. Dutch lunch. Bread, cheese, juice, coffee, and a cigarette. *Inaffarato* amongst discarded people, *afine la carcasse*. I quit: I say goodbye to some of my comrades. Including "the Boss." I shake his hand and see that he's happy. Me too.

## Tuesday, April

After so many days in Bookings, I quit yesterday. The impatience of a spring day, disgusted with empty work and the difference between simple employees and managers, or whatever. Peaceful.

Today's *zazen* in the morning. I stay in the *dojo* to finish a bench, made from untreated wood, for the entranceway. I set up the bench and stabilize it with reed and line. Figure 1.

Then Loic arrives. We drink some coffees and talk. I go back to Marije's house and return the keys. I won't be cleaning Marije's farm anymore. I shave my hair to the scalp; it's springtime. I'll have to find steady work, something without pointless tensions, permitting more freedom to do *zazen*. As far as medical insurance, there's no need for exaggeration. Why pay men for something that belongs to God and all people and creatures? Does an eagle pay for insurance? A lizard? An ant? How is it possible that man has to pay for something all creatures get for free? *Olofi Onire Oniche Eko*: God heals us and asks for nothing in return. I go out for a run.

Expanse of sea = sign of water

## WOENSDAG 7

*Huiswerk*. Homework. Write a short story about your grade school. There in Havana. *Hoe was de school*? Good question: school was filled with fruit trees. There were mangoes, avocadoes, pomegranates, tamarind, a graft on a poplar with Royal Poinciana, plantains, and bamboo reeds. A huge patio for patriotic morning activities and physical education. Also for routine medical checkups: sometimes the patio filled with dentists and nurses who checked our teeth and made us rinse our mouths with fluoride. When you got to sixth grade, doctors came to measure the children and lined us up in order of height. I was so small they sent me to stand with the second graders.

I don't say in my story that there were hunting scenes painted on the ceiling. Or how you got up to the tower, the cathedral of Physical Education! Nor do I talk about how a lot of those trees have been chopped down, or about how little those constant studies benefited me. How I've forgotten the material, but not the adventure tales we told each other by the bamboo: I do say this, and also that I learned to write and think in Spanish there.

I go to the store run by Moudu the Baifal, a Sufist Muslim from Senegal. There I retrieve the drum that Joel found next to a trash bin, which I had taken to the store to have a skin put on it. It's still moist but sounds good. I take it to the *dojo* and leave it next to its brother, Stephane's *djembe*, which has been there ever since the master lived in Amsterdam.

> *Conseils, le hasch, l'herbe:*
> *1-Consomme le cannabis pour ton plaisir. Tu ne résoudras pas le problemes avec un joint.*
> *2-Si tu fumes un joint tous les jours, essaie de rester quelques jours par semaine sans joint.*
> *3-Le cannabis affecte le pouvoir de concentration. Evite de le prendre a l'ecole, au travail ou dans la circulation.*
> *4-N'amméne jamais de cannabis quand tu vas a l'etranger.*

> Information posted at Bluebird Coffeeshop

My first translation from the Dutch into Spanish dates to this period: "Description of the Beloved," by Gabriel Smit.

> *Los niños duermen, la casa entera*
> *está llena de su alegre descanso, alrededor*
> *el murmullo inaudible de la sangre*
> *y el respirar sacude.*
>
> *Estamos juntos en el cuarto, lees,*
> *escribo, vivimos como si este vivir*
> *en diálogo no sucediera nunca:*
> *en ambos, silencioso, el existir*
>
> *A qué, además, palabras? Un poeta*
> *ha luchado tanto su escasez.*
> *Mi palabra no hace tu vida más ligera.*

*Respirar es bastante, respirar, y a veces*
*mirar aquello en que nos convertimos.*
*Cada cual respirando, cada cual viviendo.*

[The children sleep, the entire house
is filled with their happy rest, the inaudible
rumbling of blood is around us,
and breathing brings it out.

We're together in the room, you read,
I write, we live as though this living
in dialogue would never happen:
in both of us, silent, existence

Words, for what, furthermore? A poet
has battled their scarcity so hard.
My word doesn't make your life easier.

Breathing is enough, breathing, and sometimes
looking at what we become.
Each one breathing, each one living.]

**LUNEDI APRIL 12**

We go to Zandvoort aan Zee, a beach, the ocean, to make an offering to Yemayá: flowers we buy at Central Train Station. Blue flowers with thorns, a kind of cocklebur. They remind me of that line from Shakespeare in *As You Like It*: "If we walk not in the trodden paths, our very petticoats will catch them."

The beach is wide. Long kilometers of flat coast and low sea, a cold wind, and many people out walking. There are also kites, dogs, and babies. After the offering we fall asleep on the sand and wake up when the sun goes away, around 4. We go back to Amsterdam on the kindly train. We say goodbye in the station: Cristina goes off to her horses; I walk to the *dojo* to make *guenmai*, stopping at the Ballonetjie for a simple coffee, and I get started on the vegetables. By 9 in the evening, it's ready. I close the *dojo* and go home.

WOENSDAG 14

After the break for Good Friday, classes restart. We discuss the poem "*Het kind dat wij waren*," by E. du Perron.

> *El niño que fuimos*
>
> *Vivimos lo maravilloso en nuestro pasado más lejano:*
> *en el confín del reino de nuestra memoria,*
> *la mentira de la infancia, la mentira*
> *de lo que íbamos a hacer y nunca hicimos.*
>
> *Tiempo de soldaditos de peltre y devociones ...*
>
> [The child we once were
>
> We live the wonder of our most distant past:
> at the outer limit of our memory's kingdom,
> childhood's lie, the lie
> about what we were going to do and never did.
>
> A time for pewter soldiers and devotions ...]

Someday it will continue ... In homework.

THURSDAY

*bij voorbat dank*: thank you in advance.
*een strofe*
*van 4 versregels: een kwartet.*
*Het metrum: het ritme*

*het ritme*

Kenmerken: *rasgos.*
Uiterlijke en innerlijke
*externos e internos: la postura,*
de houding, el karakter
Hier ik ben, hier ik blijf, *dice el comediante Rayman*
*aquí estoy y aquí me quedo,* legaliseer *los refugiados*
*eso es otro asunto.*
Werk-geld-werk-geld-werk-geld-werk-geld
*la conexión trabajo-dinero*
*como concordancia sujeto-verbo*
*tanto tienes-tanto haces-tanto eres-tanto ganas-tanto tienes*

[*Kenmerken*: features.
*Uiterlijke en innerlijke*
external and internal: posture,
*de houding, el karakter*
*Hier ik ben, hier ik blijf,* says Rayman the comedian
here I am and here I stay, *legaliseer* refugees
that's a different issue.
*Werk-geld-werk-geld-werk-geld-werk-geld*
the work-money connection
like the concordance of subject-verb
this much you have / this much you earn / this much you are /
this much you earn / this much you have]

To the *dojo, guenmai* with María Escala, Catalan, and "Little Barbara," a dancing *debutante.* Now there are three regular Barbaras at the *dojo.*

About the cooking of the *guenmai* I tell them, "We are not professionals, we're lovers."

*Zazen* 7:30 a.m. Coffee in the *dojo*, though the *dojo* is not a coffeeshop. You donate 50 cents to help maintain supplies for the house. Rent is expensive, so the *dojo* sublets its space to other groups, like for yoga or healing Tao, which is so very mysterious. We only know that they get together, sitting on the seats, and talk about the *Ch'I*, the *Sheng* and the *Chan*, the *Yin* and the *Yang*. They do exercises too.

At home I draw a portrait of Socrates/Bodhidharma. Serene, blue: *mu*. Pause with the coffee, confirm the future:

> *un melancólico atrevimiento*
> > *zazen no sirve para nada.*

> [a melancholic audacity
> > *zazen* does nothing at all.]

*Zazen*, school.

> *Ruziemaker en ruziezoeker*: troubleseeker.
> *kinderachtig*: related to children
> *pienter kind*: a child who is awake
> Romans: arrogant. *Germaans: verwaand.*
> Sometimes I have feelings of superiority: *Ik heb soms superioriteitsgevoelens.*
> And I feel I'm better than other people: *ik voel me better dan de anderen.*

My work is you. How do you translate that to Dutch? *U bent mijn werk. Werk*-work; *werkelijkheid*-reality. What a pair! *Meisje Mei*: my girl; or as Dimos called his black cat the other night, my *putanitsa*.

Another ultramodern poem:

> *morgen/ zon*
> *boven*
> horizon

With Professor Ids de Vries, the flamboyant, historical Frisian gentleman.

The *pronomen reflexief zich* is from the German, propagated in Protestant renditions of the Bible. In 1673, "The Book" was translated into Dutch for the first time. *God zij met ons.*

He also talks about the Calvinist writers, *calvinistich schrijvers*: Jan Wolkers, Maarten 't Hart, Maarten Biesheuvel. And he leaves his email with us so we can send him our literary projects: i.devries@rocva.nl

I get up early to work in Haarlem: Acaciastraat. As a house painter, and a painter who uses rollers, to be exact. The winning streak continues, the one that started with Ken on Friday in Van Beuningenstraat, A'dam. There we finished an apartment with Nadaf, an Israeli worker, and we celebrated at the end with beer in the infamous corner bar. The one out front is called *C'est la vie*.

Even in school you sometimes breathe the air of dictatorship by profit, the omnipresence of this civilization's god, money, which is not a god but a center, an "underlying form." But is it only a matter of money? For my part, I hope that when I finish this class, I can make the return trip: the rowboat is ready, the bonds are cut.

## 2. IF THE MOUNTAIN DOESN'T COME TO YOU

Haarlem: 7 hours. Job description: from Ken I receive basic lessons in plasterwork, but my role is to finish what he plasters, to sand off the slender lines left by the trowel, the little holes, anything not level. The rest of the job involves pulling old linoleum off wooden floors, removing thousands of staples "at all costs," vacuuming over and over again, clearing the site of all the many kinds of debris, painting with a roller, listening to the B.B.C. "God is in the details," Ken warns.

Do you all remember the child-hero of Haarlem, who blocks water leaking through a dike with his tiny finger? After eight hours of work in Haarlem, twelve beers at Don Julio.

**DOMINGO 9TH**

*Zazen.* A lot of people.

I dreamed about my son. He was alone, bored, at a family home—the place belonging to my grandparents in the Vedado district, a matter of karma. Until I arrive to take him out of there. Then he's happy, and I am too. In reality I'm sad now, and I gnaw on carrots. I listen to Cuban music. I am predictable.

**LUNES 10 DE MAYO**

Today the school is closed. I go to a coffeeshop near Centraal Station.

"Gobble up the mountain," an old Dutchman tells me from the neighboring table. "Answers are for stupid people. Only questions are for the wise." I salute him and put my thought and skeleton in order. Writing is a melancholic waste of time, today is today, now is now. How can this be grasped? I go to Haarlem on the 10:10 a.m. train. Thinkronicity.

*Zazen*; I go to school. Composition entitled "*Onze wijk*," our neighborhood.

> *Nuestro barrio* is heel rustig,
> *muy tranquilo.*
> *Entre* de Kinker en de Clerqstraat,
> *hay también* grote markt, *Gran Mercado, en las cercanías.*
> *En el vecindario encuentras otros dos*
> *lugares concurridos: la mezquita y el* coffeshop Millenium:
> *a veces, en el aire se mezclan el perfume del incienso*
> *y el de la mariguana. Frente a frente,* openbare voorzieningen,
> *instalaciones públicas. Construcciones:*
> woonboot paleis
> *casa-bote, palacio, villa,* landhuis, penthouse, park,
> *y en el parque, establo al uso de los niños,*
> etage, kasteel, bungalow, *iglesia,* maisonette
> klein maar fijn, *pequeña pero con excelente*
> *vista sobre el canal. Paisaje holandés, plano como arepa,*
> *o como sopa.*

> [Our neighborhood is *heel rustig*,
> very quiet.
> Between *de Kinker en de Clerqstraat*,
> nearby there's also *grote markt*, a large market.
> In the vicinity you find another two
> crowded places: the mosque and the Millennium coffeeshop:
> sometimes perfumes from incense and marijuana
> blend in the air. Facing each other, *openbare voorzieningen*,
> public installations. Constructions:
> *woonboot paleis*
> houseboat, palace, villa, *landhuis*, penthouse, park,
> and in the park a stable for use by children,

*etage, kasteel,* bungalow, church, *maisonette*
*klein maar fijn,* small but with an excellent
view over the canal. Dutch landscape, flat as an *arepa*
or a soup.]

As for the final result from Level 2 exams: Approved in S*chrijven en Lezen,* Writing and Reading. Flunked *Spreken en Luisteren,* Speaking and Listening. This means I'm on my way to Level 2. I go home, eat bread and smoked fish for lunch with Cristina. We send out the form for requesting Dutch residence, or *verblijfsvergunning.*

After a nap I go to the *dojo* to direct *zazen* for Caroline. Various beginners. I follow the routine I learned in Havana: incense, stick, bell. *Ji Ho San.*

Bicycle run east-to-west to meet with Lamine: "It's so powerful. You have to find a bag for your drum." Referring to the drum box.

**14TH**

I rush out after the first *zazen.* By 8:20, I'm in school. Ids the Frisian until 11:

> *spreken is zilver*
> *zwijgen is goud*

So says Ids de Vries: speech is silver, silence is gold. Speaking in silver? *Rommelig: chaotisch. Nieuwe Zakelijkheid,* the New Objectivity, is discussed. Short sentences, *geen decoratie.* Without decorations: staccato. *Als goed als oud,* as gold as new. Architecture.

The teacher gives a commentary on the poet Remco Campert: *In Haarlem.* A short tale in which Chet Baker appears, playing music and signing a record jacket for the author:

> "Thank you for everything."
> "My pleasure," said Chet.

Another proverb:

> *Wat de boer niet kent dat eet hij niet.*
> The peasant doesn't eat what he doesn't recognize.

He also mentions two debatable Dutch customs or traits. "Going Dutch," the economical or *gierig* (stingy) invitation where each person pays their own way. And "Dutch courage," the courage enhanced by the amount of drink. Collective value, as it's said in Cuba: relative value. And then, *de Nederlandse* chagrin, Dutch melancholy. Mortification. And is it with these moods that revolution was made in Holland? Was this the face …? *Chagrinig, humeurig*: a "dramatic 'g'."

At 11 I cross the school patio and go up to the house where Jeroen and his cat Pixel live. For three hours and more I clean their house. At 5 p.m. I'm cleaning mine.

> *E fece de sua vida un bricolage.*

**18TH**

Last day before the spring *sesshin*. *Zazen* at 7:30. Amsterdam School, 10 a.m.

In the schoolyard I meet up with Jacinta, the teacher, as I drink coffee and edit my homework: *omschrijving van een foto van jouw land*, a description of a photograph of your land. *Het Kameel*, The Camel, an extended passenger bus. Photograph by a Dutch artist, Henk van der Leeden, purchased in the Plaza de Armas in Havana. The Camel, *Cubaanse creatuur, langzaam en goedkoop*. Slow and cheap. It's not easy to say how many people fit in a camel. "First a camel will pass through the eye of a needle."

A Peruvian student talks about the city of Cuzco: a thousand years before *Christus*, 3360 meters above the *zeeniveau*. Judith the Hungarian shows photographs of *puzsta* and hands out a recipe for goulash:

> Potato and vegetable soup, pieces of meat, and paprika. *Pittig, pikant*. When it's made the traditional way, the pot is suspended

on a tripod over the fire. The Hungarian is from the *Fins-ongrische taal familie: Püspokladány.*

We leave on a sunny morning. 15 degrees C, from the A'dam *dojo* to the "*Bon courage*" *sesshin*, as it's called by some of the assistants thanks to the confusions of getting there, in the volcanic Auvergne valley. In the Moleskine notebook I make notes. Arnaud at the wheel, taking turns with Olivier Provilly, the young playwright; Veronique and I are in the back like tourists. By 8:48 a.m. we are passing through Van Gogh's land: Brabant. Medium speed, 120 km per hour. Maybe Van Gogh was faster. *Vlanderen*: 9:17 a.m., 18 degrees.

You have to weigh every word; the ones that seem self-explanatory are, in truth, light. The ones that get heavy and multiply in the space-time tend toward the void, toward silence. One phrase too many … They are already so many.

10:23 a.m., France! I'm traveling without a passport. Forgetting it has been a great innovation. 12:40 p.m., Paris. *Banlieu*, the city's outskirts; we brush past the Parisian damsel. I take a lovely nap. At 18:37, after a beer in the commune of Brioude, development and fashion have reached this far out: Kanabeach boutiques, we are approaching among mountains … No, we're approaching our destiny among rolling hills. We arrive after a trip of 1005 kms. I greet Pierre.

Now we're in the kitchen: potato puree, lentils, sausage and apples cooked in butter, brown sugar and cinnamon. *Claquettes*—the wooden clappers that mark the hour—end act I. Our *claque* goes to bed at about 23:30.

What day is that? Today I've forgotten. Up at 7:30, shower and off to the kitchen. I put on the *rakusu*. It's not a full robe like the *kesa*, but a partial version that I can wear while working. I drink a cold rosemary *tisane*.

Rosemary! *Rosmarino, rosmarin*, thanks the Lord that I'm here and even found myself a pencil. And a pen.

After breakfast, prepare lunch and the first *zazen* at 11 a.m. Master Stephane talks about the feminine element, intuition, which our civilization oppresses just as it oppresses women through reason, domination, sometimes aggressively: *yang*. *Zazen*, he says, is the mountain of *yin* and *yang*, it is the erection but also the opening through basic intuition, something fundamental. "The feminine revolution is only possible if man becomes aware of his *yin* side, intuitive and receptive. And if he stops imposing himself on other men, women, creatures, nature."

*Samu* at 3:30, the next *zazen* around 5. Then we'll see …. What?

Five of us leave *zazen* before the *kin hin*. Lunch: quinoa indigenous to South America, carrots indigenous to the Auvergne Region *al forno*, salted tofu with cheese. Dinner: vegetable soup, *tagliatelle ai vegetali e broccoli*, and creamed plums. Bread, water, and *tisane* are always served.

9 p.m. *zazen*. Silent *zazen*; then to bed after giving leftovers to the cats and taking out the kitchen garbage. 11:16pm.

### FRIDAY 21ST

Up at six. *Zaso* (*zazen*) at 7:30. *petite promenade, guenmai*, café, pipe, pay 70 Euros. *C'est a dire*, a discount from the cook. To *cuisine*! *Deuxieme zazen* of the morning at 11 a.m., and we're already at lunch: poison, no, *poisson*, beet salad, *tres simple* says Pierre, *mais excellente*, plus salted vegetable: carrot, *finocchio* (fennel). A short nap and a 3:30 *samu*: peel 12 kilos of potatoes.

Long 5 p.m. *zazen*. Pierre and I leave before *kin hin*, the walking meditation, in order to work in the kitchen. I prepare dessert and other things. Dinner at 7:30, *ongeveer*: chive soup, buckwheat with vegetables, baked potatoes, and fruit in a creamed cheese with almond. *C'est Byzance!* All we could want and more.

*Zazen* at a quarter past nine. Words reflecting on Gensha, who wrote, "The Universe is a bright pearl," *"et le moine avec un trés grand ego."* Then to bed after failed attempts at socializing. I feed the cats. *Mezzanotte incirca, ongeveer.*

I've spent enough time in this neigh / bor / hood to know nothing about it. *Onzin.* Dutch for absurd. Up at 6:30. *Zazen* one hour later: Nagarjuna, the Indian Buddhist thinker. *Guenmai,* as usual. *Samu,* 90 portions of cheese, a salad prepared with *pisenlit* (dandelions). *Pisenlit: plante vivace á feuilles longues et dentées, et fleurs jaunes. Loc. Fam. Manger les pissenlits par la racine, être mort.* Dandelion is *diente de león,* lion's tooth.

*Zazen* at 11 a.m. More from Nagarjuna. Afterwards I bring Master Stephane a little tea from the Greek mountains. He asks about Cristina. *Ça va,* she's fine. Lunch, nap, *samu.* Tranquil in the kitchen with Pierre. Zero stress. There's no hierarchy except through our own work choices, and the work flows easily. Simple dishes, "but with class." The issue of the leftovers hasn't been solved yet. There are too many, even for the cats!

*Zaso* at 5 in the evening: Nagarjuna and his master, Kapimala. The magic ball and the one bright pearl:

> *Mira la bolita como sube y como baja*
> *Mira como sube, mira como baja*

> [Watch the ball as it goes up and down
> Watch how it goes up, watch how it goes down]

That's how the *guaracha* goes, that's the song's rrrrrrhythm! as Pierre likes to say. It's my turn to make *guenmai* and I take advantage of that to skip our meeting, the general assembly of the Buddhist association. Dinner: leftover soup (*voilà une solution*), barley with tofu and carrots, pear and apple compote. Everything is very good but still there are leftovers. I give the soup to the animals, now joined by the local dogs, and the same will have to happen with *le tagliatelle.* What can be done? *On verrá.*

*Zazen* at a quarter past nine. Tomorrow those of us who came from Holland leave early: no *samu*, no appetizer, no lunch: it's a long way home … *Fukanzazengi*. Sung on the last night of winter camp.

"*Tu viens?*" Christian asks me, but my words don't come out.

A smoke under the Half Moon, the wooden blocks marking the hour, and time for bed.

**DIMANCHE 23**

Up at 5:55. Shower. Kitchen, warming up the last *guenmai*. Already I can make out the flickering of the lights that far away … Tea, *tisane*. I am a pillar. *Zazen* is simple, it does nothing. Just low breathing, like a sailboat at the height of one's belly button. Sometimes the ocean gets fierce, the waves high. In this one it's a calm sea, but the traveler who runs away must go back sooner or later. The sailboat is going nowhere. Wandering in shadow, it looks for you and gives you a name. Living.

> *On a le thym*
> *on l'a coupée*
> *le thym*
> *le temp*
> *descend dans la puberté*
> *monte dans la clarté*
> *de l'ivresse*
> *l'ivresse de la clarté*
> *cela lá, lá bas, o lá lá*
> *voilà, on a le thym.*

Pierre gives me permission to get our stuff. "That way we'll have five minutes at the end."

*Zazen* at 11 a.m. *Mondo*, blah blah.

Goodbyes. Farewell dear knight.

Hey! School after *sesshin*. Equilibrium. Zen: *ik heb er genoeg van.* *Opnieuw beginnen*: beginning anew. And with a prima donna complex? Ya, s'allright.

> *Vorm en gebruik* / Form and usage
> *automaat*
> *robot choppeur*
> *masseur*
> *charmeur*
> form and usage, Mevrouw Brabantius.

After the 11 o'clock *zazen*, I visit Dimos to study Ancient Greek and listen to the Cuban music I promised him. *Continuerá.*

Lord of his time, owner of his memory

Giorgios, the cook, tells me the story of the word *nomi*: opinion. So important in Holland, the land of Hyperboreans, mythical giants from the tale of Perseus. *Koiné nomé*, public opinion, was at one time *noié* and maybe *gnosis*. Knowledge; you have to study Ancient Greek to know about these things. Etymologies are insufficient, I tell Giorgios. He smiles and goes back to the kitchen to make a *spanakopita*, a kind of spinach pie with goat cheese and egg. He invites me to see how it's prepared. *Canon-iká prágmata*: everyday things are the *logos*.

**Here began summer**
**on May 24**

*Hier begon de zomer*
*al op 24 mei.*

From a press release. …Summer?

*Pinkster*, a Dutch spring festival whose name is a variation on the Dutch word *Pinksteren*, Pentecost. *Olé*!

Good morning, flamenco. I have guarana and my morning coffee for breakfast. Translating the Buffalo poetry anthology. A poem by Roberto Tejada. It flows. I go out for a run by the canal.

## TUESDAY

… of *zazen* and school. I go back to the *dojo* to make *guenmai*. And to Don Julio to apologize to the barmaid, Jamie, for my rude conduct of the other night. She offered me an early morning water, but my thirst was for something else. Apology accepted. And a beer? I talk with Ken and make a decision: I am going to Cuba this summer. This thirst is oceanic.

## FRIDAY JUNE 4

Up and off to school: *ik hou van lekker koken*. I like to cook good food. *Waar heb jij een hekel aan?*

What don't you like, what is disgusting: *ik heb een hekel van roken en alcohol*, say the elegant students.

## 9TH

After *zazen*, school: I don't know, I can't go. I go buy my airline tickets to Cuba. 880€ vía Madrid, a city I know only as its airport.

## FRIDAY 11TH

Start of the Amsterdam *sesshin*.

*Zazen* at 7:30 a.m. There are 10 people, including Dominique, the Lyon monk. After a coffee I go to school, like every Friday, to attend the lectures of Ids the Frisian. Until 11.

At 2 p.m., back at the *dojo* where Paul picks me up to go get Master Stephane at the Schiphol airport. Around 2:50 Stephane arrives. He looks elegant and his mood is good. I offer him one pink rose and one white one. "*Merci*," without touching them.

He has a new suitcase that makes him happy. During the drive he talks with Paul about Löic's accident in Johann's car. "I sincerely believe that all three of them are responsible: the one who loaned the car, for not being careful about how he did it; the one who loaned it out once more, Joel H., and the one who received the car and crashed it." According to Stephane, all three should pay a part: the one who was driving during the accident pays half, and the other two the rest.

"Solomonic," Alga says. She's right. "I can't stand injustice," Stephane kept saying on the drive.

And when Paul argues that the car was loaned with *gentillesse*, he answers, "*La gentillesse c'est de la connerie.*"

Arriving at the *dojo* he drags the suitcase along the bumpy ground: the street is being repaired. "I want to test it out, it's like Havana here." Today it's true.

Dinner at the *dojo* around 8 p.m.: creamed spinach, served with cilantro, olives and *pinoli*, pine nuts. Red wine and water. Bread, everyone happy. Tomorrow the first *zazen* is at 8 a.m.

### SATURDAY 12TH

To *zazen*. Our Indian Father Who Thunders. Good morning! I'm in the kitchen at 7 with Catalan María to organize the service.

*Zazen* at 8, 11, 4:30 and a quarter to 9, with *Fukanzazengi*. During one of the rest periods I thank Stephane and tell him about my next trip to Cuba. He looks at me with kindness in his eyes and expresses a desire to run a *sesshin* in Cuba, in some quiet place outside the city. The mountain, if that's possible, or maybe at La Coronela. Before I go home to sleep, some beer with other practitioners in *Kriterion*, a student café. There's fish to fry in the pan.

8 a.m. *zazen*. I am a pillar. *Guenmai*, service. The *sesshin* is animated; 11 a.m. *sesshin*, *kin hin* and an interesting world. An interesting world! At the end an aperitif outside in the street, a festive lunch. The master is more serene than ever. One by one, people disappear to return to Lyon, Barcelona, Geneva. With a female monk from Geneva, to be precise, I taste absinthe.

At 9 we go with Stephane to the corner bar to see the opening match of the European Cup: France 2, England 1 thanks to the divine Zidane. Stephane is satisfied. On the way back to the *dojo*, he gives me a letter for his friend, a teacher who lives in Alamar.

Then I go with Christophe Delaporte to the Thorbeckeplein coffeeshop: Bush Dokter. Christophe is at home here, always lively in these sorts of places.

By five it's already daytime. I go to the *dojo* to do *zazen* and to the café with friends. Christophe tells me about a job: *nettoyage, demenagement, opruiming. On verrá; a l'ecole* I'm falling asleep. But my colleagues, as I call my classmates, are *simpatiques*. Especially Mohammed, from Morocco, and Hussein the Iraqui. Also Paula, who talks about the Portuguese poet Florbela Espanca during the 10:45 break.

As usual I leave at noon to clean Jeroen's house, just across the patio. Coincidences, I don't believe in them anymore: I clean in the company of Pixel the Cat and Miles Davis. I'm talking about the Flamenco studies, *Kind of Blue*. Again.

I run the vacuum one way up the black linoleum in the kitchen and down the other. Everything in the kitchen has its place. Or, everything happens in the kitchen: punctuation marks amaze me. One period, two: there's a hierarchy, but it's not essential. Nor is writing as cult and refuge. To write

I'm not afraid / not being afraid, say never / and it happens right away. Maybe dumping out the wastebasket once and for all

> *Haga usted sus propias runas*
> *Sus propias ruinas, sus propias razones.*

> Make your own runes
> Your own ruins, your own reasons.

### THURSDAY 17

"You make yourself the magus of your own emotions," Alga was saying at the deserted table at the end of *sesshin*.

### FRIDAY 19TH

School trip: at 9:30 we leave in buses for the Zuider Zee Museum. When we arrive, the teacher Martina points out the name of a boat matched to a wave: *Niets bestendigt*, nothing lasts. *Precies.*

History of the present: "The nature that has almost nothing to do with commerce"; Marx was right about that one, and also he was wrong. In the way a North Sea fisherman lays his fish out to dry, like a sort of installation artist, you see the trinity of art, commerce, and nature in circular form.

*Kanoniká prágmata.* In the nineteenth century, this Villa Enkhuizen sheltered artists, the first tourists. And in 1863 an old acquaintance, Edmondo d'Amici, noted the influence of the East on the Dutch: the untranslatable *gezelligheid* is itself a translation of the image of impregnable comfort of the seraglio and smoking room: the cushion, the pipe, and the enigmatic smile. *Gezellig, hoor!*

Like an artist-tourist idealizing, I find that this country life, hard but close to nature, has a quality superior to the life-garbage they sell us, and of which they try to make us salaried salesman, and for which we have to work until we die in front of a television, a telescope for viewing life. And on the flip side:

"The international division of labor was not structured
through the works and grace of the Holy Ghost but ..."

Galeano says in his *Open Veins of Latin America*, which I read between
grasslands and seagulls:

"through the work of people, or more specifically, as a result of
the worldwide development of capitalism."

It happened here too, the breath of spirit notwithstanding. Holy or not,
uppercase or lowercase, *the spirit blows where it wishes*, especially in man
and his works: in this ropemaker/cabinet-maker/carpenter/river-fisher-
man with his pipe and fez. It blows in the seagull, crow or raven who
lands by the sea and watches us. Also in capitalism with its provisional
works. Impermanent as the Dutch boat: *een filosofisch boot*, the teacher
says.

## MAANDAG: SCHOOL

Writing in English and Dutch.

*Kangoeroe.* Kanguroo: *Ik begrijp u niet!*
What kind of creature is that?
*Kangaroe*
What kind of animal is that?
*Kangaroe!*
Ah! It's a *kangaroe*
What did you say?

## DINSDAG

Zazern *zazen* serious zen stern *streng*. School *traditionele voorkeur* prefer-
ence pestilence predilence. *taboe ik heb een tecnisch opleiding gevolgd. Tim-
merman*: electrician, Philips or Sony *als monteur. Bron* - source. *Adviseur
bowkunde loopbaan orientatie.*

Saint Thomas with a lance.

anthropologie     cosmology

psyche-logos
electricity-eklecticity
*timmerman*

Soccer night with a pack of wild Dutchmen. Holland v. Latvia: 3—0. I start to tell the story that Latvia was not even a country a short time ago, except in Jules Verne novels. In her emotional state, my girlfriend gives me words of love and the great gift: *Je bent ingeburgerd*, like saying "You're a citizen now!" Thank you.

I design a box drum for winter. Neither very large nor very small, so it can pair with the African drums, which are many and very powerful in Lamine's class. I bust my fingers on the littler one. The international division of rhythmic labor is imposed.

**MONDAY 28**

School. *Toets Lezen. Goed.*

> *Op hetzelfde aambeeld hammeren.* Hammering at the same old anvil. *Nederlands studeren, guenmai mak.*

When I get back I meet Löic, who is clearing debris out of a building not far from the Vondelpark.

> *Ça va?*
> *Ça va.*
> *Tu tiens court?*
> *Oui.*
> *Ça c'est l'important.*

Nap. Drum box, not yet finished. *Chez* Christophe: *La Loi, l'Oracle, l'Orgueil Spirituel.*

I begin my reading of *Il libro e la sentenzia*, on older Italian poetry. Dante, Cecco, Iacopone di Todi, and the Provençal poets.

Life is a conspiracy.

### Vrijdag 2

School. Ids de Vries, always open to other things: *gedichten, literatuur, geschiedenis, Nederlandse politiek*, etc.

*Na de les*, a talk with Judith, *een Hungarische klasvriendin*. We speak in English; she has a child and a Dutch partner. Misses her land and friends. Sensitive, delicate, a graduate in History, she also misses the, as she calls them, "paradisiacal times of childhood." During the Communist era. She said it, friends. And maybe walking on the steppe, the *puzsta*.

Sometimes *Opportunity* is a trap for the hungry, Hungary spirit, like the monkey with his hand trapped in a coconut. Opportunity. Detachment isn't misery.

Greece 1—Czechs 0 in the European Cup. Today the newspapers talk about the Greek miracle: *sprookjie*! A fairy tale. At last the world remembers the Greeks.

The winter drum box is 27 × 30 centimeters on top, 41 high, and 17 × 20 at its base. Ivory in color, with the Egyptian sacred bird sign: the vulture.

### Sunday 4

Running. That always feels like the beginning of something.

In Dimos's place there's no television for watching the match with the Greeks, who are going up against the Portuguese favorites for the cup. We go home without eating or saying goodbye.

Pizzas and beer, and Barbara and Ken arrive to keep us company.

Greece 1—Portugal 0. The Greeks exist in spite of the melancholic Dimos. They've played with the rhythm of a computer: 1-0-1-0-1-0. There's no reason to imagine that they'll be able to repeat that miracle: this has been a gift from the gods, celebrating who knows what!

School. Good Boy.

On the way I meet up with Florian. *Aardig.* In Dutch *aarde* is land, and *aard,* character. *Aardig,* however, is not like our word *caractoso,* having a big personality or strong character. Instead it means *simpático,* nice. The niceness of the earth.

10:10 p. m. Everything is so quiet. For the first time I go to the Hollandsche Manege to see Cristina ride a horse. The style is dressage, not jumping. It's like a waltz.

Mabel, Christa's friend, says the horses socialize while they eat in the paddock. In the stables it's not possible, so they try to socialize during the lesson, to the surprise and outrage of the riders. Some horses succeed at making friends in the stable, and then they run together when they go outside to the pasture. Posture is the most important aspect of riding. As well as communication with the animal. A good erect posture can be bareback, not needing even a saddle.

We're going to put a saddle on a white courser named Julius. I run my hand over him, then the red-bristled brush. He looks at me, smells me, and nibbles on my sleeve. The girl calls me a "horse whisperer." Actually, according to Sean the riding instructor, we're all capable of communicating with horses, but we lose the skill when we're too self-conscious. The instructor has an accent that's clearly from southern Holland.

Christa and I go to Artis, the zoo. On the way we stop in at *De Griekse Eiland,* the Greek boutique in the Jordaan district. She gives me a *rebetika* recording. *Peri Indikis Kannabeos,* a traditional collection featuring themes from 1938 to 1946, with lyrics luckily given in bilingual presentation.

For example, the song *San eyisis apo tin Pilo:*

> When I came back, when I came back
> When I came back from Pylos
> I looked for a friend.
> I went into a garden, where I heard a *baglamas*
> Saw five young men lying on the grass
> Looked them over, looked them over,
> Looked them over to see
> If I recognised them …
> An old *manghas* asked me what do you want
> "Company," I said, "but where to find it?"
> Sit down, sit down,
> Sit down with us, he said.

*Baglamas* is a string instrument. *Manghas* would be something like a handsome, romantic, Byronic type, someone who lives according to the *carpe diem* with minimal limitation from rules.

In the zoo we can finally see the wolf and the panther, which is sleeping. Unlike humans, all animals enjoy good posture. Even the crazy polar bear who tirelessly repeats a routine of circuits around artificial rock. So sad! people would say. But the bear knows what it's doing: it's like a song for freedom, its own ceremony along the edge of the abyss.

When evening comes, I give a percussion lesson to Joel Humbler. We use Stephane's *djembe* and *El Elegante,* Elegant, a drum box I made in Amsterdam. A few hours in the *dojo* and it's a good time. "*C'est rigoleux,*" he says. Not so much.

I ride the morning train to Den Hague Hollandspoor take a tram from there to Rijswijk, the rice district, to get the Dutch permission for my trip away and back, which I put in my bag. With the money from the drumming lesson, I buy a soccer ball for Mariano.

*D'apres* reading Galeano: notes on an independent capitalism. This has never been possible in the Americas for reasons already well known. The Paraguayan experiment is a sad example. Among others. But if …

I go to visit Ken at his workshop. There against the wall he has a carved Indian door, with a frame that attracts attention. The frame doesn't have hinges; instead it uses *perno*, a very simple system with a pin. We go to Don Julio to drink some beer. The female staff are more intoxicating than the beer. As my grandfather used to say, looking and leaving alone.

From there around the corner to Tom's house. Tom is British. He has downloaded material about Mister Bush from the internet and burned copies. Among them is the documentary *Fahrenheit 9/11*. Then almost two hours of some comedian, probably from New York, whose name I forgot. Deliriously funny, great mastery of the language.

*Zazen.*
*sintáxis persuasiva l'universo*
*como una puerta*
*cuya casa sos vos*

[*Zazen.*
persuasive syntax the universe
like a door
whose house you are]

I clean the house with basil, cacao and scented spray.

Greek air, I greet the Moroccan from the block. Facing the crowded mosque, the no less crowded coffeeshop.

Cost of new residence permit, the *verblijfsvergunning* = 285 Euros. Talk about independent capitalism. Emigrate, then when in Rome, do as the Romans do.

**SATURDAY 10TH.**

*Zazen* 11 a.m. Some goodbyes.

It's a reason for feeling like a rastaman.

Back at the *dojo* again at 5 p.m. A dinner organized by Julia: *Byzance*.

From there back home, and to see Dimos. Dimos always cooks well, with fresh and natural appetizers (*pikilia*) and very nice spinach pies. And *retsina* to drink. "What do you want from Cuba?" Last time I brought him tobacco. "Something I can taste," he says.

**SUN. 11TH**

Up at 8 a.m. Final preparations. Cristina to Greece, me to Havana. Schiphol to Barajas. In the usual café, where you can smoke, I run into César Alvarez, the drummer, who is returning from Argentina.

When I arrive in Havana, I have Pierre's luck: it's like a small carnival. I drag my heavy suitcase through the overwhelming crowd. My mother is waiting on her balcony, Mariano meets me in the stairwell.

*Pérez apartment diptych*

Up and jetlagged. I start cleaning the house, little by little. The bathroom and the kitchen. It works. Keeping in mind the Feng Shui directions from Stephane, who has stayed here for years and knows the house.

At mid-morning, I go with Mariano to the park. *Parque de la Maestranza,* next to the port and the seminary. It's closed on Mondays. I say hallo to the statue of José de la Luz y Caballero. And take Mariano to ride ponies. 3 rounds, 9 pesos. Then to the Museum of Natural Science in the Plaza de Armas, and to the Captain General's Palace. Adults, 3 pesos. Children don't pay, Cuban or foreign. Never pay. From there I walk to Soleida's place. She's ill but has visitors. A young couple, just married, French public school teachers. At once Soleida offers Daarjeling tea, a carpentry job in her house and a poetry reading on Thursday. Not bad. Back home, Stephane's friend comes to visit with her daughter, to pick up his letter. A beautiful woman, touched by Stephane. She gives me a letter for him.

Keep on cleaning, still jet-lagged! That helps. Two small rooms in the back and the Changó altar room, where I lay my *kesa*, and the dining room. With Mariano I go back see to Soleida, always walking. It's hot, as usual.

*Nota bene*: Mariano asks me to buy flowers for Christa, Reina, and my mother Lilia Rosa. Lilies for Christa, sunflowers for the others. I put the white, perfumed little flowers in front of my love's photograph. "She's beautiful," says my mother.

Still a little jet lag. A cup of *mate* and I start this Cuban diary. In English, so that you, Cristina, can read it.

I clean and do *zazen* by Deshimaru.

> *cadenas de pensamientos*
> *cadenas de producción*
> *diez mil palabras!*

> thought chains
> production chains
> ten thousand words!

Clean the patio, bathe La Negra, my black dog who once again has an infection. Now it's on her left ear. I go with Mariano to the park to play soccer and ride a bike.

Lunch, shower and siesta, and back to the park. Play with children. Write a poem: "*Dos naranjas y un cuchillo*," or "Two Oranges and a Knife."

I call Sandra. We'll arrange dinner. The house is clean, the sky is blue, the music is loud. As loud as usual. I go on reading *Il libro e la sentenzia*. Boring and academic, but full of the right information.

Middle Ages: *il poeta é spesso chiamato sophista o sophus*
IX Century: new poets: *moderni philosophi. Voilà.*

Up around 7. No more jet lag. *Zazen* with a cat.

*Poiein—costruire*

The doctor made a cut in Negra's ear to let the dirty blood out. Tomorrow one opens it, then cleans inside for seven days with antibiotic.

Around 8 we go to Quinta de los Molinos for a poetry reading. The music is blues. The reading starts a little late. I read four poems from "*Lingua Franca,*" my unpublished work in progress. Then there are live blues; Migue, an old friend, is the bandleader of Sociedad Habana Blues. Nice atmosphere, beautiful girls, free rum. Mariano is totally at ease. After a while Soleida leaves; she talks about a new reading with music in Old Havana, for a more "cultivated" audience.

In the end the organizer, who's been very gentle, asks us to read one more poem. I read two short ones. The other poet is also called Omar. Going back home through a silent Cayo Hueso, we eat pizza. And then to bed. Mariano is happy.

Up at 5 a.m. To the Housing Office. I'm number 1. Yet I have to wait long enough to forget what I'm doing there.

"No," says the guy, or the lawyer. "According to Disposition 17, you cannot obtain property if you live on the Malecón."

In the most everyday situations of everyday life—the post office, housing office, etcetera—there's a potential dictator. Anybody can be anybody's dictator for a day. In a dictatorship like this one, it's very easy to put the blame on the government or the supreme leader for each and every ailment or evil, when in reality it's easy to see that people create all sort of petty dictatorships everywhere. They sort of enjoy doing so in order not to change anything, in order not to feel really responsible.

Because in the end, the condemnation goes always to an abstract, distant dictatorship that does not necessarily exists here & now. Whereas to fight the petty/immense dictator inside us is harder. But also simpler, in fact: inner revolution. In our families, in relationships between couples, or parent and son, even with other animals, we can put a stop to dictatorship, we can stop waging war against each other.

In this transformation, intellectuals can play a crucial role. But here, as elsewhere, intellectuals behave more like *literati*. They are charlatans always complaining and criticizing with second-hand concepts and ideas rather than organizing their lives and actions in a different, austere, and generous manner. I / me / mine is the energy that moves this world.

Back to the house, and to ordinary decisions.

As we already know, austerity is a common combination of economy and joy.

First healing of Negra. She's absolutely passive. She surrenders to my hands in absolute love. No person I know, indeed, trusts me so much. It must be painful, yet she makes no sound, no movement.

I lose my temper with Mariano. I kind of recognize in him the fundamental selfishness that appears in childhood: not seeing, not thanking. It's part of me too. He's just a child, but karma is karma. Once again I acknowledge, with pain, the necessity of letting go. We go to the park again.

### SATURDAY 17TH

First *zazen* in the *dojo*; 15 people. A couple of beginners, one young fellow with a good spirit, it seems. Stephane has answered with his typical brevity: he's coming on December 10th.

I come back home and Mariano doesn't say hallo. Neither do I.

I wake up from my siesta, as if by premonition, just before the summer rain. Mirabilia. A shower with thunder and lightning, which helps to clean the house a little more.

Mariano and I go to see Cintio and Fina: a refreshing breeze. We have wine and sweets. I read a few poems, which they enjoy. Laura is also there.

Leaving their home, on the elevator, I think for an instant: "Back to reality." But, no. This is reality! Reality is what we create with friendship, poetry. The rest, just a noisy dream.

> *Cavalcando l'altr'ier per un cammino,*
> *pensoso de l'andar che mi sgradía,*
> *trovai Amore in mezzo de la via*
> *in abito leggier di peregrino.*
> *Ne la sembianza mi parea meschino,*
> *come avesse perduto segnoría,*
> *e sospirando pensoso venía,*
> *per non veder la gente, a capo chino.*
> *Quando mi vide, mi chiamó per nome,*
> *e disse: "Io vegno di lontana parte,*
> *ov'era lo tuo cuor per mio volere,*
> *e recolo a servir novo piacere".*
> *Allora presi di lui sí gran parte,*
> *ch'elli disparve, e non m'accorsi come.*
>
> DANTE. Vita Nuova

> *Farai un vers, pos mi somelh*
> *e. m vauc e m'estavc al solelh*
> *Companho, farai un vers covinen:*
> *et aura. i mas le foudatz no. y a de sen,*
> *et er totz mesclatz d'amor e de joy e de joven*
>
> WILLIAM IX OF AQUITAINE

*Zazen*. Just four people.

I go to the UNEAC for my travel permit. It takes the whole morning, but I complete the elements: walking in the sun, waiting in line to buy a stamp, sitting in an office with a smile on my face.

The idea of writing a novel pops up again. I don't have the most common motivations: first, to become a novelist; second, to make money. Writing for money is not an issue here. Yet the idea is attractive for its own merits. A good model is *Zen and the Art of Motorcycle Maintenance*: an appealing structure, simple and right to the point, yet comprehensive. Autobiographical, mushotoku. "*Mushotoku?*" the main *karakter* would say!

Feelings are like a placebo. No real essence, no root. Yet they work, they help. Then there's a feeling that rises from below, up from the belly like mushrooming laughter, and it puts this smile on your face that makes people talk to you if they're children: they play with you, or they sniff at you if they're cats or dogs. Call it love for lack of better word, call it solar energy, call it "my real self." Call it "My way," like the song.

I go on with *Il libro e la sentenzia*: "*dato che la perfidia é una caratteristica ereditaria di tutte le donne.*" This is about Cecco, of course, and not about Dante or Cavalcanti: both sides are right. Anyway, this novel could be a diary plus action, plus dialogues. *Etica di navigazione*, a logbook. *Left Foot: A solar diary*, we'll see.

Siesta is a powerful thing here. 3 hours, fruitful dreaming.

As agreed, I go with Lizabeth, Mariano and his friend Cinthia to a park. In less than an hour out walkin' we meet three poets: Rito, Victor Fowler and Alex Fleites. At the coastline Mariano takes a sudden bath on the rocks in the quiet, afternoon sea. As we walk back, he climbs on a statue.

"Watch out," says Cinthia, "He's gonna bite you!"

"No." Mariano takes a good look at the patriot. "He's already dead."

The workers who repair the building's facade ask for help.

They've seen the Buddhas: "Is your family Chinese?"

*Soy budista*, "I'm a Buddhist," I say.

"Big belly guy who brings money?"

"Exactly."

I show the mason a photo of Stephane in *zazen*.

"What's that? Something to do with the parabola?" I assume he means "pyramid."

"That's the *pirámide*."

"It gives you energy and all that stuff," and he looks attentively. "It's true!, *es como un entrenamiento*," it's a sort of training.

*Voilà*, training. As María Callas would say, *on devrait considérer tout ce que l'on fait comme une répétition*. I proceed with *Il libro*, the Provençal poets. Comedy, paradise. A matter of tuning: music, tools, time.

*Zazen*, four people

Take Negra to the Doctor, but the Doctor is not there.

Go on a walk to Nuevo Vedado to look for photography book on Che Guevara. A real *ganga*: 30 pesos each.

Drop by Sandra's place. We pick up her boy on the way to a birthday party for Igor and Xenia's daughter. Everybody seems to be there with their kids. Mariano comes after a while with his mother. We talk. Nice party.

Run. Ominous feeling this morning. *San Pai. Pater Noster.* It's gone.

Here I am, listening to the Goldberg variations like Hopkins in *The Silence of the Lambs*, while I give Negra another bath with alcohol in the water, to doze the fleas away.

I start reading *L'amore in Grecia* and go on studying my *Nederlands*.

At midday I go to Old Havana; it's hot. Soleida wants to cut a new window in her living room and has a Dalí painting as a model.

We go to pick up some old beams from a neighboring carpentry studio to work out a frame. It's pinotea, very old wood.

Coming back with a load of wood, I see Sandra with three other dancers on the corner of Mercaderes & Obrapía. They're working out a clip for a piece of choreography: *Drinking & Smoking: Made in Havana*. Seeing in order to create.

Back in Soleida's living room, I take some measurements and mark the wall, like a work in progress. With the Dali painting, ingenious.

In the magazine *Revolución y Cultura*, I pick up copies of my contributions published there: poetry translations, an essay called "Martí y Buda." Then I buy a bottle of rum for Pierre and slowly wander to the *dojo* like a sailor with plenty of time. It's too early: I wait for the *zazen*.

Mariano is more mature now and starting to understand issues with words. I asked him if he wanted to go to Lazaro's, and he said yes. Then he said he'd go with his grandparents to the Ermita de los Catalanes. He changed his mind, which can happen, and I understand that here, in the quietness of a room.

## SATURDAY

*Zazen.* I go to see Lázaro. *El Tata.* Two days that don't fit into two lines. The creek, the soccer game, the family. The conversation with The Tata:

> *Bla bla bla bla bla bla bla*
> *Bla bla bla bla bla*
> *Bla bla bla*

## MONDAY

I wake up in Lázaro's house and ride with him and his grandson back to Havana. It feels like I have a virus, so I rest and drink tea.

In the afternoon Ruben S. comes, and we have a friendly conversation in the balcony. He talks about people who are cutting their ties with this country as a new wave of "outscape," a new stampede. I tell him, I haven't cut my links to Cuba. Only the links to what some people call "reality," which is not at all reality.

It's a thin mental apparatus, which is of their own invention and for which they blame the usual suspects: the government, "the situation."

I don't want to have anything to do with that kind of reality, here or anywhere.

## TUESDAY

Take Negra to the Doctor; give up after two hours: a couple of young Dobermans undergo the canonical ear & tail operation.

Later Roberto comes over, and we drink some *mate* and talk about the *sangha.*

I finally make it to the dentist. She fills the hole again, very fast, and asks for no money.

I take Negra to the vet. He sees her and starts dancing: "I'm very happy when the wounds go like this." It's clean, in fact; 10 to 12 days, it must close on its own. He doesn't ask for money either: "Money isn't everything," he says.

It's very hot here, around 35 degrees Celsius, and the sun is as ruthless as Mamita's tape player one floor down.

The Tata wasn't very enthusiastic about showing me the sign of Mama Chola. I saw it written on a piece of rough paper: "Give me that." But I managed to remember and reproduce it. What a beauty. *Chola'ndengue, ndengue Chola.*

I translate Emily Dickinson, study Dutch: *de oudste tekst*, the oldest literary text by a known author, XII century: a colorful fictionalized version of the *Aeneid* by Hendrik van Veldeke. The oldest prayer ever to be preserved:

> *Hebban olla vogala nestas hagunnan*
> *hinasse hic anda thu*

> *Hebben alle vogels nesten begonnen*
> *behalve ik en jij*

> All the birds began making their nests
> except for you and me.

From the epoch of the wandering troubadour, *rondtrekkende zanger. Luze* and sword, just one name remains: Bernlef, the blind cantor of Friesland.

Up at six. Running. *Zazen*. I ask Roberto why he's not leading it. "Inertia," he answers. I run home and try to fix the table saw: Help! Help will come tomorrow. Instead Roberto comes now with two guitars and two bottles of homemade wine. We go through old songs:

> *No hay exceso d'equipaje*
> *no hay equipaje ligero.*
> *Paraíso sin imagen*
> *gaviota, canción, velero.*
>
> [No luggage in excess,
> no luggage is light.
> Paradise with no image,
> seagull, song, or sunlight.]

Study Dutch.

So I fix the table saw myself, the old tank. Swedish motor: 1 & half horsepower. I clean up the room.

Late in the afternoon, with Andrés, we visit a couple of squalid bars.

"Why don't you become a monk," I ask him, "and give your life some good flavor?" He laughs. The barman rustles up two glasses for us. Later, I dream of Master Deshimaru: he's small and strong and sweet. Very friendly.

To the *dojo*. It's drizzling. We have a brief meeting after *zazen*. The Habana *dojo* and *sangha* should not emphasize their difference from other *dojos*. Difference springs up spontaneously; the way to designate a responsible *zazen* should be regular and not totally *ad libitum*. The direction, collective and not based on an individual trip.

It could be good to form a group of 3 to 4 persons to look for a place suitable for practice with Master. A small temple.

If we don't try, we'll never know if such a thing is possible in Cuba.

With Michel I agree to go and see the place for the next *sesshin*. I'll wait for his call on Monday.

On TV I watch *Memoria del saqueo*, a documentary about the Argentine catastrophe. An outstanding page in the book of evil. Comparable to the Nazi period—if not in the amount of human losses, though human lives were lost by the thousands, then in the depth of its betrayal of the ideals of solidarity and trustworthiness.

### ZONDAG AUGUST 1

I go on with the translation of the "American Anthology."

At midday, Old Havana, where Mara lives with her boyfriend, her mother, and a Pekinese dog. A bottle of red wine. Talk. Lunch. Talk. About an exhibition in Amsterdam featuring artists from our Habana *dojo*.

Back home, I go on translating William Carlos Williams.

Ezra Pound. Canto XLV

At home, I can be part of the city too. The collective soul.

It's not a European city. It's Babylon.

### MONDAY

Warm, 32 degrees C. Damp. I cut wooden beams to measure, and there's the window. Nothing but dreams, these beams. But they're real. The window is there.

Later I put your photograph in the kitchen, while I warmed up *guenmai*, my lunch. Words are too old, my love.

Up at 4, I cannot sleep. I've been drinking a *Yin Seng* tea, and it's interesting. You wake up with this warring, joyful spirit. Mariano too, at 5.

One *Kameel*—a camel or extra-long Cuban bus—to get to Cuatro Caminos, then we walk to the Esquina de Tejas, and then one more bus with Michel to get to the Botanical Gardens. See the place, discuss the price and the matter of painting. They understand and are very kind to Mariano; we walk through the park and move on. This is the road to Las Cañas, I say to Mariano. "Why don't we go see Lázaro?" O.k.

When we arrive, Regla is on her own with four kids. I bring one more kid, or two. It's really hot. We play soccer in the yard. Then I realize I have nothing left to take off, except my shorts. *Vamo'p'al río*, Let's go to the river. Mateo takes his horse. But first, more soccer in another field close to the river. Then to the river, then back to the field, then back home with the littler ones. The others stay there, playing soccer.

After a while, Lázaro arrives. He asks me to check the roof for work over the weekend. Then we eat and watch a couple of videos.

Back to Havana in the *Tata*'s car. Mariano is tired, so am I. I get some sleep before resuming the day's activities. I wake up around three to finish my letter to the *Historiador de la Ciudad*, the City Historian of Havana, to give more of the story about the house. The Historian's office makes a lot of decisions about building restoration and maintenance. Abruptly, The *Tata* comes to pick up the roof material and wood he needs to build something for his chicken. We'll meet on Saturday.

To UNEAC to pick up the letter permitting me to pay the Havana airport's exit tax in Cuban pesos; otherwise…. The cost in other currencies is too high.

I try again, in vain, to get on the internet. Internet access is only available in limited places. I go to a government office and get as far as having the form in my hands. "But you have to fill it out here," says the lady in the Actors Association office. *Dat kan niet*: I can't, I'm a writer. I belong to the writers' association. But our association is closed again. Anyway, there's a blackout, a neighborhood electrical shutdown due to energy rationing.

The form is really something: stamp & signature from the head of the department. Or association. Sometimes it's the same as it ever was. At the market, the same pace, the same rhythm. I can get everything I want except for sweet potatoes. The line is slow. I leave, take the camel bus home, slowly, slowly by the sea.

Am I any less intolerant than before?

I go on translating: the neighbors' noise is appalling. Close the doors, play my own music: Gary Snyder.

*Mal rayo parta talanquera congo* / Screw this! Guardian at magic's door

    Fu

    *como servir una taza de té*
        *la vida.*
    somehow unexpected, *por allí va*
        *vereda congo*
    midnight, naked monk
        eats *guenmai*

    [like serving a cup of tea
        life.
    unexpected somehow, the Congo road
        runs that way
    midnight, naked monk
        eats *guenmai*]

To botanize: set the alarm clock.

> None of that
> *el monje se durmió*
> *es ya viernes*
> *sigue echando flores.*

> [None of that
> the monk fell asleep
> it's already Friday
> keep tossing flowers.]

### VRIJDAG

In Maggie's house, at Maggie's farm, around thirty people or so. Old friends, acquaintances. Nice drumming. I notice that some of my friends are more into the rumba spirit. Sometimes I forget the *palo* traditions. They're very good though. Sandra dances *palo* as beautifully as ever: she's completely enthralled. And electric. There are some guitars also and Manolo with his flute. Thank you, Maggie. Alejandro, her son, brings us back 'ome in the car.

Midnight. I bring my bongos.

### ZATURDAY 7TH

Up around seven, six people in the *dojo*. We talk a little afterwards. You might as well close the *dojo*, I tell them.

Drop by to see Jesus, and Jesus hears me!—I can get online for my email. Jesus is very nice.

Dream: Sandals in the middle of the road, me leaning against the wall, throwing pebbles, looking at faraway children. Valencia. I've never been there.

Finishing Marianne Moore (and listening to Descemer Bueno's music), I realize that very often in Spanish, and in poetry mainly, articles can be as useless as they are absent in English.

Hart Crane: two poems. As a continuation to these sea poems, Mariano and I cross the street and go diving.

Mariano's siesta. A freehand drawing of this island. Later we go to the park.

At 8, translation again. Zukofsky: They listen to hip hop, I listen to flamenco. If one strain is not too loud, they can combine. I get as far as Larry Eigner.

There's a chance to rent a place on the beach next week. Mariano insists on judo. We practice the basics on a straw mat: falling and so forth. Funny how he goes intellectual as soon as it gets rough. It happens to all of us.

He asks what a *dojo* is. Back to translation: Jack Spicer & Robert Duncan.

### Dinsdag

Up at 8:30 with the violent sound of building-destruction: a pneumatic toy. Powerful sexual dreams, universities, travels through the *laggelanden* from Waterloo to a place where Amsterdam and Habana mingle: lost until I found you. A concert; I cry to the sound of Venezuelan *llanero* music.

I must admit I go to sleep with the same kind of excitement others have, or seek, at the movies: such landscapes, such situations.

 Go on with translation: Oppen. H. D.

                              "What the skull can endure!"

Soap-opera music mixes well with Jamiroquai. Dorn's *Gunslinger*. I finish.

10 p.m.: Mariano's crocodile tail. Or tale.

Here I am, tempted to continue my translation: Gertrude Stein. But first, a list of things to say in the *dojo* meeting:

> Key in its place.
> Responsibilities, including *guenmai*, sewing, and flowers.
> Black kimonos.
> Wear *kesa* to lead *zazen*.
> Carry out the ceremony with precision.
> Improve publicity and information.

Learn to translate by the clock. Or by the hour. Gertrude Stein: the writing is *Cantinflesque*, reminiscent of the Mexican comic Cantiflas. He speaks rapidly and in fragments, which has its charm. But enough, I go with Mariano to Soleida's place, bringing the window beams. We have lunch together, which she arranges. I check my mail at SGAE with Darcy, & Darcy says she needs a translation of Yusa's lyrics for the new record: there could be some collaboration.

I go on reading *L'Amore in Grecia* & Martí's *Apuntes*, notebooks from his travels.

There's danger of a storm. My left eye is not right: lack of vitamin B. I see to it, salt water. I go up to the roof to prevent leaks, then go shopping. Signs of a storm, crowded shops, no bread or sausages left: priorities. Fight the storm with bread and sausage. I buy fruit, oil, beer, rum, yogurt and some kind of dubious jam. Signs of a storm at 5 p. m, rain & thunder. No wind.

Gigi calls from the Lunigiana. I talk to my sister also. She's in Italy with them.

Back in translation: good old T. S. Eliot, the marine quartet. Ready for the storm. Mariano & I organize a flute, drum & voice concert. Neighbors in absolute silence.

Storm comes finally at midnight, scattered rains at 3 a. m, storm is gone at 6. A cleaner city, now. Although we have to face a storm of inefficiency and noise, the everyday storm. I go on translating: Eliot.

### FRIDAY 13ᵀᴴ

Minor damages. Translation by the clock.

Etymology of *repugnantia*: opposition or contradiction between two things; logics: repugnant terms> for an essay on the writer's condition: *La repugnante tarea d'escribir*! The repugnant labor of writing.

At 5 I finish "The Dry Salvages."

### SATURDAY

Finish translation of Robert Creeley. *Voilà*: "Papi, let's invent a fishing game."

Like a logbook or campaign diary, we talk: Roberto, María Cristina his wife, and I. She mentions the possibility of me writing a novel. It's an idea. Writing a novel as the common commerce using words, no. Instead, to tell the path of a teaching. That's what my Tata refers to when he asks me about "The Book." A memory of a flight, a journey, jour.

Félix's invitation: Focsa building, floor 24. Dinner with Paraguayan students. Good food: cassava, rice, salad and *natuurlijk*, meat. Also a medical student from Argentina, and one from Britain, with the mother who came to visit her. She wants to know how her girl is doing in the brave new world. She's doing well: she speaks Spanish with a Cuban accent, she has first-hand contact with the ill and illness. Cheaper than the first world, much less complex. Think of what Italy meant for the English Romantics, or what Greece meant for the German youth or Lord Byron: the Greek town of Vyronas. What Cuba means still, but it's ever-changing. Paradise to crisis, crisis to Paradise: a roundtrip. Chauvinist?—give me a break: keeping mystery, between one system and another.

After finishing Creeley, Whitman will travel to A'dam to undergo treatment there.

Up at 6. I prepare Mariano's things and leave … I feel the future.

We arrive around 10 a.m. at Boca Ciega beach. The landlady, América, takes us to the apartment: it's small but has a great view, good energy. Félix and his Californian bride Hadley made it there with us. At 11 we go to the beach, which is full. We meet Soleida, Darsi, and son Martin. "Why do you have red eyes?" he asks me. And Yusa, the musician, comes too!

After lunch, Félix gets his own little house: a Cuban/American honeymoon. Hopefully, this is how at last we will ensure an end to war. Yusa brought a laptop. We work on musicalia. Lyrics with translations sounding good to the ear. We do half, then we go for dinner to a pizzeria with *forno a legna*. Pizza is good enough and cheap. There are Italian tourists by the pound and Italian pop music. At night I dream about my *kesa*.

A Saturday for the *orisha* who is queen of the sea. I go out 'n vain to search for a market: they're all closed, so now I know. Back home, *L'Amore in Grecia*. Greeks, they knew something about it.

At dusk we go for a walk. It's drizzling, and two boys are racing horses on a slope. More children play around them. Mariano wants to be part of the group, but children are not so diplomatic.

Early in the evening, we go to a *paladar*, a small, privately owned restaurant. Very slow. Cuban food, a drunken European sailor with his missie. Nice palm-tree shirt he has. I talk about the future with Félix and Hadley: when mankind finally loses its control of the world, Félix dreams, nature shall take over. Then the animals convince man, worst of all animals, to get rid of the garbage that poisons Pacha Mama, startin' with weapons.

Today I told Mariano that wizards don't follow the same way back when they make a return. "I'm not a wizard," he says.

"But I am."

Then he wants me to make a single pebble disappear. I tell him to throw it, which he does. So the stone in fact disappears. Then he tries again: the stone falls into a little pond on the street and, slowly, it begins to vanish in front of our very eyes.

Life is cheaper by the sea. Or you have fewer needs. Or both. Have the sun, the salty pond, the fresh fish, the fruit. A telephone to make a call once in a while. A boat. Maybe with sails. No, not maybe.

*Cerveza, naturaleza*
*en estado civil*


A beer, nature's sphere
in civil union

Mariano makes some progress in swimming. He takes things easy. It's very very quiet. Waves. Windy, no mosquitoes.

I improvise a *zazencito*, a mini-*zazen* with my backpack. Tea, reading *L'Amore* ... Along come Roberto & Family, including guitar.

*Rastaman*

*Hay un león en la tierra*
*y un jardín quemado en Afganistán*
*todos conocen el circo de la guerra*
*pero no todos conocen el pan.*
*Mira la luna que brilla cuando llena*
*tiene el rostro de la eternidad*
*el colibrí conversa con l'abeja*
*y la paloma les dice 'qué más da!'*

This is a reason for feelin'a rastaman
This is a reason for feelin'a rastaman.

*Hay un águila en el centro de la nube*
*una serpiente al fondo de un palmar*
*hay un tatuaje en tu vientre*
*y todos te quieren contar*
*historias  historias.*

*Mira Mamita lávate los dientes*
*compra tu pasta, no seas indigente*
*la chuchería que le gusta a la gente*
*televisada como pan caliente.*

This is a reason
for feelin'a rastaman.

*Mira esta vida sensible*
*mira esta vida sensible que llama al bienestar*
*yo cambio el agua por oro*
*yo cambio el sol por petróleo*
*unos pagan por lo que ya tienen*
*otros compran lo que nunca tendrán.*

*Mira Aristóteles, déjame tranquilo*
*de tanto hablar, ya se me perdió el hilo*
*la lagartija camina por el filo*
*cuando me callo, suspiro, suspiro.*

This is a reason for feelin'a rastaman.

*Yo no soy más cubano que tú*
*Tú no eres más cubano que yo*
*Yo no soy más cubano que tú*
*Tú no eres más cubano que yo.*

[Rastaman

A lion moves across the earth
a garden burns in Afghanistan
everyone gets it, war is a circus
but they don't all get bread in their hands.

Look at the moon that shines when it's full
it has eternity's manner
the hummingbird talks with the bumblebee
but the pigeon says, "it doesn't matter."

This is a reason for feelin' a rastaman
This is a reason for feelin' a rastaman.

There's an eagle in the heart of the cloud
a snake at the foot of the trees
there's a tattoo on your belly
and everyone wants to tell their stories
to you, tell all their stories to you.

Look Mamita brush your teeth
buy toothpaste, don't be a bum
trinkets are for people on tv
so is bread that arrives warm.

This is a reason
for feelin'a rastaman.

Look at this sensible life
look at this sensible life to feel content
I trade water for gold
I trade sun for oil
some buy what they already have
others buy what they'll never acquire.

Aristotle, leave me in peace
without so much talk. I lost the thread

a lizard walks down the sheath
when I stay quiet, I breathe, I breathe.

This is a reason for feelin' a rastaman.

I'm no more Cuban than you
You're no more Cuban than me
I'm no more Cuban than you
You're no more Cuban than me.]

As usual, when we meet in favorable conditions, Roberto Garrido and I work out a couple of ballads. Next one.

*La cerveza.*

*Va, va, sientes que va*
*sientes que pesa*
*pereza*
*en estado civil*
*naturaleza*
*cerveza*
*en estado sutil*
*yerba que besa, que besa.*

*Siento el resplandor de los motores*
*de la naturaleza*
*vida que da vueltas al azar*
*barajas en la mesa*
*quedo extasiado ante un camión*
*o el cante del sinsonte*
*y me siento en casa en la estación*
*o en lo hondo del monte.*

*Dejo mi simiente en la ocasión*
*Cada día nuevo una razón*
*levadura, pacto, corazón*
*melodía de mi sinrazón.*

*Llevo el aliento del lugar*
*montado en la cabeza*
*y me cuesta mucho caminar*
*te juro que me pesa*
*yerba en estado civil*
*me da pereza*
*vida en estado sutil*
*pónme una cerveza.*

*Dejo mi simiente en la ocasión*
*cada día nuevo una razón*
*levadura, pacto, corazón*
*melodía de mi sinrazón.*

[Beer

It moves, it moves, you feel it move
you feel it pull down
it drags
into civil union
nature's sphere
in subtle union
with beer
kissing the ground, the ground.

I feel the glory of motors
the motors in nature
life that circles around its fate
packs of cards on the table
spellbound by a truck for some reason
or a mockingbird song, it's strange,
I feel right at home in season
or under a mountain range.

I leave my seed when the time is right
Each new day brings new cause

Leaven, a pact, a heart, the song
melody of my newest wrong.

I take the breath out of the place
it rides along in my head
which makes it hard for me to walk
it weighs me down I said
smoking grass in civil union
makes me draggy here
life in subtle union
pass me another beer.

I leave my seed when the time is right
Each new day brings a new plight
Leaven, a pact, a heart, the song
melody of my newest wrong.]

He wanted to write a song about the hurricane. This is what came out:
beer, breeze, breathe, and put some melody in there.

At Yusa's place, and the house is big. Fabian is in Havana, says Yusa. Jam
& translation session: the record gets finished by candlelight. Blackout.
The laptop-guitar combination is promising.

I get up at 7 to pack and clean. Wake Mariano for a swift swim. He
doesn't want to, preferring to stay and play on his own: bushes, discov-
eries, lizards. I go out to say goodbye to the sea, whom I'll meet again at
home.

Great party tonight. Around 7 p.m. it gets started with electric bass &
acoustic guitars, *bongó* and *cajón*. It sounds good, with feeling, though
you can observe in some of my friends the same qualities that you can
observe in the Habana *dojo*: Indolence & Co. Many of the friends who
come here to sing and play practice Zen there. Same family, same trou-
bles. The party is *magnifique*, anyhow. And with Yusa, some pleasure in
playing music together.

I worked out my first drafts by hand, with no computer. And now, all day, a transcription on a rusty typewriter while listening to songs in my head. Then I try to get some sleep. I can't. I try to sing and find this:

*Que se duerme la tormenta*
*se callan los ruiseñores*


[So the storm may sleep
nightingales fall silent]

Typing until 3. Lunch, etc. Ania & her brother come to invite me to Telmary's concert in La Casona. It starts a bit late. She recites one of my poems: *Sip at your thirst, sip at your thirst, add to it ...* We go back to Central Havana and have our own party with Roberto & neighbors till 6 a.m.

I hunt for the water tank in the morning. Bingo. It's plastic. I buy it later. Sleep, sleep, and to the *dojo. Zazen.* Walk back, eat-sleep. Tonight, this dream: By the Malecón, a tiger is chasing a deer in the seawater. I just want to show it to you, but we get too close, and we fall into the tiger's water. There are two of them. I try to kill them with a broken beer bottle to defend you. Not to kill, but to make them disappear; we're saved. Another scene: magic mountain, fountain, waterfall or spring. The tiger and the deer live together.

The noise is remarkable: they're demolishing the neighboring buildings with pneumatic hammers. I go on typing. It can't get any noisier with the old typewriter. Around 3, I pick up Mariano from his grandparents' house and bring him back home.

I dream about a very special horse. At 11, I finish typing the majority of the poems. I walk with Mariano to Old Havana. We drop by the museum at San Salvador de la Punta Fortress: the sea, the sailors, and the sailing. We drop by Soleida's place too. Lots of walking and even running. She offers tea.

Yusa comes later and we finish the last song in English:

Today I'll tell you no
there'll be no promises
love me like this, like this
this case is closed.

"Let's look at Shangó and think of him as someone whose spirit is here and is good." So says Mariano to start his pre-bedtime ceremony. Then he makes a few very precise movements, as in a dance, and it's time to go to sleep.

**FRIDAY 27**

Ginger tea. *Sampai* and work. All day, the new site for the water tank. In the afternoon, Roberto comes with news: Cristina has given birth to a new patriot. Another male. Then comes Yusa, who gives me some money for the translation and 'scapes as if ashamed. Sometimes money love energy.

Shall I translate Whitman? Never boring, and well paid: the whole universe with a hand in its pocket. So, I finish bearded Whitman with my beer. The only way, translation on the clock: at 10:43 the anthology is finished. With the water sweated by a glass of beer, I clean our house.

All around the house is demolition.

Soleida asks for some drumming in her café. At the Palacio del Segundo Cabo, ...some friends already there with drums. We play a little on the square until the policewoman arrives to sweetly say it's not allowed: sweet forbiddenness. So in we go. The party begins with poetry, drum and flute, song & verse. Sigfredo swings and reads along. To close it up, Soleida asks for one more poem: we do it with drums *alla maniera del guaguancó*. Out again on the square, we play our fill.

Two hours: too many people to close down the party. Police don't show up.

I go to see Lázaro. I bring a drink of *chamba* for the *nganga*; the Tata is ready to make a request. He does, and Saint Lazarus says yes. He prepares

163

the herbal concoction for Sonja. Ready to go, 'til next year. I leave at midday.

At home, a few friends come by to celebrate. In anticipation of his birthday, Mariano's emotions run really high. He sings and improvises with the small guitar his aunt bought for him in Milan. Then he plays percussion as we sing.

SEPT. 5

7. 30 and the demolition crew is already on. Mariano goes on sleeping, undisturbed. I wake him up around 9. Happy birthday. Cake in hand, and guitar, flute, plastic saxophone, and maraca all in the backpack, we go to Almendares park.

Today's wonders: so many friends and children. Roberto and his two little men; Sandra and hers, Pablito; Manolo and his Rafaela. So much of this joy.

Both of us kidnapped, they say, by new friends. We go to a restaurant by the river. Good food, not such good service. Mariano and a girl called Isla start a revolution here, make waiters nervous. Children are not supposed to eat under the table, sir.

Back home, Mariano still wants to party. After a warm bath and a Chinese story, he goes to sleep.

Wake Mariano up. Breakfast and a cab to Santos Suárez: he starts school today. 1st Grade and he's happy. Say good bye to him and come back home to finish packing: I take 15 canvases of congenial Cuban painting with me for the Amsterdam exhibition. Félix drops by before lunch for a quick visit with gifts. *Nsallah malek, malek nsallah.*

VRIJDAG 10

Up 7. Amsterdam: School. *Eerste les na de vakantie.* Summarizing my flight from Habana to Madrid: long layover, jumpy landing. Boom!

Ecuadorian classmate in Schiphol: he didn't want to come back, but his love awaits. So does mine.

Next day, Vondel Park, and then sea and dunes: for the first time I take a swim in the Dutch sea. Cold tonic, so cold that I go back to my everyday tasks with fresh body & soul. Life continues.

**ZATERDAG 11**

In *de dojo*. Some eleven people. Loic directs and asks to dedicate the day's ceremony to the 9/11 victims—not only in the United States, but around the whole planet.

I propose the Exhibition of Cuban Painters, practitioners from the Havana *dojo*, to Paul. The proposal is accepted.

Visit to Haarlem. Ken always has a good story to tell. He says he'd like to write a play using his conversations in the Tax Department. For example:

Ken: So, what can I do if the Tax Department wants to take the money directly from my clients? (It's the income tax.)

Tax Man: You put that money in your wife's account, but don't forget to pay the VTV tax through your own account.

Ken: Ain't that fraud?

Tax Man: No, as long as you pay your taxes, that's good.

Ken: So, over time I can pay off my debt using my client's payments. Is that good?

Tax Man: No, that's bad. It's profit. Then you have to pay tax with the money you owe.

Ken: Then, I have to declare myself bankrupt and claim I'm in debt. Isn't that bad?

Tax Man: That's good. You pay your debt with the loan's money.

Ken: That's good.

Tax Man: Yeah, but if you declare a debt, that makes it harder to get a loan. That's bad.

*Waiting for Godot* in an office.

We talk about *Le Droit à la Paresse* by the Parisian born in Santiago, Cuba, Paul Lafargue. Then Ken gives us a lift to the train station. Good knight.

## SUNDAY

The category 5 hurricane is getting closer to Cuba. It's important not to complain, *niet zeuren*, get angry or lose your sense of humor. Also physical exercise and *studieren* come in handy. Concentrate on just a few things.

I interrupt this note abruptly in order to clean my pipe.

*Va bene.* On my way back home, I throw the paper away, try in vain to withdraw money using my card, buy bread, and all of this is Cubanology.

—That I listen to Cuban music and work happily on my translation of the North American anthology. I prepare the artworks for the painting exhibition. I clean the house, make a phone call to one Mr. Thomas, a Spanish Caribbeanized Dutchman, who contracts helpers for cleaning, *schoonmaken*: "I don't have much, everything's tight," he says in a serious voice. Well, okay. I puree potatoes with onions, mushrooms, chives and celery. A little bit of TV and off to sleep. I miss the reading of *Women Who Run with the Wolves*.

## WOENSDAG

*Sampai*, do de dishes. Congo prayer, Dutch breakfast work. Off to school at 8:30. Something is changing in me, around me. It's presence. Prescience, the science of foresight. I know, but it's something more: ahselleraytion.

*Niente traduzione oggi.* I try to fix the plumbing on the kitchen sink. Well, after cleaning out pipes, it's clear I have to call in the experts. I quit, listen to Irakere and discover new things.

Sometimes school is indecent.

At noon, I go home. My afternoon nap helps to pause the flow of events.

I wake up, finish reading *The Open Veins of Latin America*: thirty years later, things haven't changed much. Watching some Moroccan flamenco singers closely on television in Amsterdam, I discover structural contaminations between overlapping poems in Dutch and Spanish, at the same time, with a beat.

*Bij voorbeeld*, for example,

*Het Poem, the Pum, el Poema*

| | |
|---|---|
| *Probeert niet, Nederlander* | *No intentes ser, holandés* |
| *te origineel te zijn* | *demasiado original* |

Don't go trying, Dutchman,

to get too original

Cristina invites me to Artis, the Royal Zoo, to visit the new giraffe born five days ago. It's bigger than a Doberman. Mother giraffe greets us. Giraffes give greetings with their eyes and ears. Their eyes move as if winking, and their ears flick in all directions. We also visit the African turkey buzzards, or vultures, and they give us four feathers. The gorillas eat while maintaining thoroughly abandoned postures. A girl sitting by a giant window that separates her from the male exclaims, "What a beautiful stance!"

We go home on the streetcar, and I think about the book. A novel of three 100-page sections, *ongeveer*. "For the wise, few words are enough." The first volume tells of the encounter with Gaspar Guevara, an *andante* poet with *allegro*. And a character we will call Homer, poet and storyteller, also itinerant. Slang: Gaspar, a flamenco singer, without hurrying his rhymes, goes rhyming down his path through Spain, France, and other lands, where he learns an urban English: the English of advertising. Homer operates in Donne's elusive compositions: mystical gibberish: they converse in Tuscany, *terra antica* for poets, and in Provence. In Marseille, they eat at an African restaurant at the edge of the Old Port, and in Paris they attend a jazz concert directed by a Brazilian woman whose last name is Teresa. Their rhyme, *Teresa Teresa. No interesa.*

I discovered Gaspar Guevara on the day that I launched a new novel: Into the Wind. It was the first volume of the trilogy, "To Someone Understanding," a hundred pages stewing with religious, social, domestic, and virile passions. *L'Andría*, as the Greeks would say, about a nomadic Havana gentleman in the twenty-first century.

He reserved some passions for the feverish joy of activities leading down roads of the saints. To others he dedicated great surges of yang energy, as experts would say. He would lose himself, or escape stealthily, to varied celebrations: carnivals, parties folkloric or otherwise, a *bembé*; or a wedding, in a Catholic church in Miramar, of an Austrian and a Colombian. There he plays bongo and sings a rumbita. Open-air concerts. Nor did he reject the crooning called *el feeling*, or what he himself described as "flamenco with no relationship whatsoever to that tradition." A concept difficult to explain, which manifested in *romerías* with a guitar and mint tea. You could say that this gentleman is Gaspar himself, who finds his recollections in the flavors of mint and mendacity, but there is no other meaning for "expertise" in the first section of the story.

Homer will compose a short essay, two pages, about the aforementioned novel. What will happen to Gaspar inside my novel is not what happens to him within his own novel: the first is implicit, a vision of what is to come: science fiction. Meanwhile, the other novel conveys what happens inside the legendary reality. Neither this nor that. Polyfiction. For example:

> Similar to the player of soccer or chess, warm by the time he reaches the middle of the game and field, someone testing an unexpected solution from a distance of various meters or moves, I write these notes. They're as uneven as I am. But suddenly, they're warming up. My name is Gaspar and for the moment I'm waiting. I'm aware that I'm inside a bunkered office by the Bijlmer prison, in a not-so-tidy Amsterdam neighborhood. How I got here, what I'm waiting for—like any other player, that's what I'm moving to tell you.

I arrived in Europe one steel-gray morning from Havana, then in flower. I had no reasons to abandon my walled city, only an impulse to set sail and stretch my frame toward other regions, like a buffalo crossing the steppe or a salmon swimming upstream.

Like so many others, I crossed the open sea with a doctored resume, a fake letter of invitation, and twenty nasty dollars in my jacket. I don't feel like describing procedures. It's the wrong time to lay out details, and I won't offer an emigrant's political explanations, much less economic explanations, or any of the other chatter that humans invent in order to do what other species—supposedly inferior species—manage to do without any thought.

But some nights, looking out through the open square window in my kitchen's back wall, between two large buildings, toward infinity, I had observed a star's sigh. Then, blinking slowly as I exhaled, as though my eyelids and bronchial tubes were working in unison, I felt a great nostalgia for the unknown. At the start of late spring, stretching myself, I set foot, a shaky foot, in the city adjacent to the Marne.

I'll call my friend, my smartass sometime girlfriend, by the appropriate name of Mademoiselle Savante. She was waiting for me on firm footing in her apartment. I won't say that here we managed a walk toward some famous cemetery or residence of illustrious rubble, or that at sunset the mist from a seminal river clogged my throat. These trivialities were quickly forgotten in the little bars nearby, in cheap food troughs that don't even provide a place for sitting down. Well: sitting down will cost you. And as I heard *ça va ça va* and said *ça va ça va*, the whole thing became real: I became *savant*, nothing mattered to me at all, and I learned how to shell and eat this nut.

*Pérez apartment rear window*

Mademoiselle had a cat. Not a fine cat, not fine like a grand piano, not fine like a dress with a train, just a plain old cat … *Moche! pour quoi?* Demoiselle would get angry, too often. *Pas du tout!* She meant he was stubby, because he had no tail: his name, Tzigane, gypsy. Sounding a lot like Zidane, the soccer player. She and I no longer felt attracted as lovers. No pure drama. Instead we enjoyed walking arm in arm, yes, sleeping together because the spring was still too cold; there was no more to it.

And still, at times, a reminiscence, and we would curl up together: Out, *Zidane!* Out of the bed, stubby cat … And she, now more softly, *C'est pas moche, pas non plus Zidane …*

Journals, pieces of letters, notes from newspapers interweave. Homer is a monk. At a retreat in the city of Amsterdam he meets another monk: "An expert in vacillation and in the theories, the most current versions, for accelerating the spirit." Meanwhile Gaspar has a good time in Rotterdam. He is invited to a poetry festival, garlanded in new euros and the smiling discipline that emanates from his well-earned social status. What gets written down is crucial; what happened is indispensible.

Dimos isn't here anymore. Yesterday we went to see his restaurant, and it has been replaced with a *Neederlands eet kamer*, literally a "house of Dutch food," with smoked ribs and endless beer. There goes quality. I give a roar. I feel happy, and that's the end of it. Will Dimos end his Dimosian agony? We won't ever know, but the restaurant no longer exists on this corner. Things transform. Enjoy yourself and take good care.

## ZATERDAG 18

To the crowded *dojo*. Alga leads, Löic cries, Paul invites. In fact, after lunch, oh and a siesta, we leave for the North for a delightful night out, in which our neighbor Nedine will take part. After a few drinks I let loose in Dutch. Sonja's plants are so lovely, the children so sweet. Especially the littlest one, Ebony, Pierre's little goddaughter.

Paul also thinks that culture, or the current way of life in Holland of *samenleving, gaat over geld*, is a money thing. *Consumptie maatschappij.* Was Van Veblen not Dutch? A society that is sumptuary, superfluous, impermanent. *Ukiyo.* He also talks about Stéphane in the last Zen summer camp: patient, compassionate. Talking about our hidden motivations: discover them. Also about the "impossible" chip in our minds. Nothing is impossible, says Nike.

Take the chip out, make your own reality, try to be a *buddha. Voilà.* Blast off. Before we fall asleep, Cristina says to me, "You have to find the job that you like." She suggests that I write a list of possible jobs. Carpenter? Editor? Baby sitter? Astronomer? Marvelously imaginative.

After school, I call one Larry O'Tool about a job in Amsterdam Forest. He's not there. In one corner of the forest you can collect nice autumn leaves. Search and capture. I prepare frames for the Cheleny artworks, with help from Caroline, who is very *handig*. Manual: the combination of intellectual and manual work is *geweldig*. Barbarous, violent, as the Dutch say literally. The encounter between barbarism and *tekne*: hand-made intellect.

⚭

Rock around the clock. Half *zazen* at the *dojo*, 'scape to school. (As I leave the *dojo* in a hurry, Florian helps me to untie the cord of my *kesa*, with a smile.) *Goed op school. Geen probleem.*

Except my concentration inside the study isn't good enough for learning: relaxation is not happening in the study. I go back to the *dojo* with Cheleny's red oil painting. "Through the streets." Caroline is already there with tools, making frames for Mara's canvases: the *ndoki* (someone who casts spells) amongst sunflowers, spirit of the glade. *El Lucero*, with signatures. Jute. Johann arrives, *parliamo italiano*. I do introductions for a young Dutch woman. *Zazen* again. I do *kyosaku* and in the end, I sit facing the large bell. I forgot to stop. It was good there, calm.

Put into order around its things: the person or the ego. I pay the *dojo* 30E. We go home on the route past the organic corner store. In the doorway a rasta plays the flute for money. Cristina goes in for food, and I stay outside with the bicycles, listening to the flute. At home we make squash and chive soup. And put some Indonesian *sambal* on the pasta. When it's all ready, I feed the queen. The queen falls asleep in front of the television. Today she did not ride horses.

Now it's a question of Dutch. *Huiswerk: Informatie over werk.* Ethnic minorities, revalidation of diplomas, seats. *Test u zelf,* test yourself, are you flexible enough?! Dutch Curriculum Vitae: send it, print it, turn it in. *Flexibel, economische.* Internet, mainly commercially oriented. Boring. *Werk.* Netherlands: *translator (Spaans) niet gevonden.* Listing not found.

One is busy. Later. On a different note, Barbara's new child is born. I talk to Ken; he calls for a quickie at Don Julio. Mo calls to get details for printing. *Expositie Kubaanse Kunstenaars*. A4 CD ROM.

## HANDMADE/ HECHO A MANO
*Exhibition of Cuban Paintings at the European Zen Center*

*15 piezas en venta y una que no:*
Zen Monk playing *cajón.*

[15 pieces for sale, and one that is not:
Zen Monk playing *cajón.*]

*en un bar de Amsterdam Noord*
*hija auténtica de O Chung*
*vientre calabaza china*
*tras la barra del "Don Julio"*
*ojos rasgados al infinito ámbar*
*papaya hervida en aguamiel y otra cerveza?*

[in a North Amsterdam bar
O Chung's real daughter
Chinese pumpkin belly
behind the bar at "Don Julio"
eyes scratched to amber infinity
papaya boiled in agave syrup and another beer?]

Not today. For every thing there is a day,
says my friend. Hallelujah.

*No siento envidia de la mente. sola*
*característico* karakter, *a la mierda*
*ni superior al perro o al gorrión.*

[I'm not jealous of the mind. Solitary
*karakter* characteristic, fuck it.
Superior neither to dogs or sparrows.]

The friend is Ken.

Caroline works well with her hands and creates solutions for framing and
hanging. Who said that women … ? Not me, man! *Ik ga*, i go, *naar de
copyshop*, not the coffeeshop! 40 *kleur* posters: 60 E. *Werken met de posters.
Hoe?* Take them to Cuba, distribute them, sell them. More things to take
to Cuba: tools, paintings, material, charcoal, incense, needles, sewing
items. Merchant sailor, A'dam. I write in English:

C.V.

I was on that corner one afternoon
it was raining.
Yesterday at night i was looking
at the fool moon in the garden
i have a son and it was
one afternoon and it was raining
i was looking
at the full moon in the garden.

Pollen: the greatest trip. *Je suis chez* Christophe de la Porte, Eliah is there.
Arriving back home, the key doesn't work. *Natuurlijk*, one thinks…is it
my fault? But the key is the key, not the lock on consciousness. I wait for
my girl, watching the white wolf moon, the fool's moon; I analyse the
trees on the corner, in a Λ formation, delta-tree formation coming from
our chamber in the direction of the drawbridge. I do four laps on the
bicycle and return to find her at the door: What good timing!, she says.
Tell me about it.

The lock is broken.

We get up with the sun and *lawaai*, the racket made by roadwork, at Vero's place. Vero is our neighbor and *dojo* companion after last night's drunken evening. Her husband, an Israeli, plays the guitar. Their daughter, another man's daughter, an Australian: seven. We wait for the locksmith, *il miglior fabbro*, who finds a quick solution: his drill. I take a shower and go out to get the copies of the poster.

### FRIDAY

I go to the *dojo* and then to the copyshop. Not only are the copies not ready, but they lost the CD ROM. *Hoe kan dat nou!* Sorry, sorry. Always sorry. Sorry, I'm going to school to learn sorry. Luckily, Cristina calls Han and he can make the copies: 50 in total, big and small, for just 20 euros! And the text is free! Bad becomes good. *Allah akhbar*. I am happy.

Caroline, the monk from Alicate, is already in the *dojo*.

The weather is magnificent at the start of fall: soft, relaxing rain. From cool trees the green, yellow and red leaves are falling. The temperature is right for taking a walk in shirtsleeves, if you like. Back at home I listen to Camarón: Old World! Florian calls to ask me to take care of his cat Nefertiti, just for three days. Living. Taking it literally is no good for anything: all is dream. Lights, rain, Danae, the Greek woman singing with the piano. Singing a Greek bolero to it.

> *Por qué t'engañas soñador hermano*
> *por qué sus alas tan cruel quemó*
> *Icaro, Van Gogh…si de cada cual*
> *según su trabajo a cada cual*
> *según su necedad*
> *también la luna*
> *tomarla en sentido literal: peligro*
> *como una broma fuera de lugar*

[Why do you fool yourself, brother, dreamer
why do you burn your wings so cruelly
Icarus, Van Gogh … If from each
according to his work, to each
according to his lunacy
the moon, too,
take the moon literally: danger
like a joke made in the wrong place]

There's a way to have a fine touch. As in baseball, where a good hit doesn't have to go in a particular direction.

*como la uva*
*por ser alta*
*no tiene que ser agria*
*las elevadas metas*
*no tienen zona.*

[like the grape:
growing tall
it doesn't have to get bitter
the heights of aspiration
have no exact zone.]

Going out for bread, doing *zazen*, these things have no exact zone. And in the end, Hunger makes brothers out of all men.

### ZATERDAG

I go out for bread. Immigrants don't look at anyone. They go along with their head down, looking at the future, the one they already found: ah, a coin! Ten cents. To the *dojo*, *zazen*. I do what Paul requests. Then Cristina and I go to the public protest against the Balkenende government. *Museum Plein*, 300,000 people. Blessing: when the demonstration ends, the rain begins. Back at home, potato puree, the Dutch *stampot*. The afternoon is more peaceful than any other. Life, a succession of accidents comprehending all actions of the body in reality and dream. Accidental culture. Magical biological. Hey man!

To the *dojo* on bicycles, Cristina insists. I prefer the trolley and at the end of the day we'll see. The bike tire gets punctured. We return home on foot, arguing about it. Is listening to intuition now valuable on its own terms? Following intuitions makes it possible to study them in relation to life. Believing momentary intuitions nourishes the more fundamental intuition, which supplies all of these voices or sources.

Today is a *zazen* day: 4th. I help to make guacamole in the kitchen. The Hungarian, a disciple of Ivon Beck, also makes the trip for the day. At the end, I have a conversation with Alga, with whom I've been in contact throughout the day. She directed the session and did her *kusen* in Dutch. We talk about the meal for the opening of the art exhibition: fried bananas, plantain chips, black beans and rice in coconut milk, a broth with sweet potato, yam, malanga, squash, yucca and onion. We discuss the prices for the paintings. With the earnings, we can contribute money for the master to travel to Havana. Alga also tells me that when entering the *dojo*, one should first go to the master's spot, make the *gassho* gesture of placing the palms together, and then prepare the meditation cushion, the *zafu*. Then the place will be fresh, alive. Alga says that when leading *zazen*, one must also speak, in order to transmit the source of the *dharma* so that it will stay in motion, according to each person's experience. And she tells me about her life, how she became acquainted with *zazen*. How she started back then, angry and arrogant. Full of internal fury. She shares her story about being a foreign woman.

# 3. THE OCTOBER CRISIS

MAANDAG 4 OKTOBER, SAN FRANCESCO

Up to the Office of *Immigratie*, to pick up the new *Verblijfsvergunning*, residence permit, and up to the school for immigrants: summarize a position, *positie van de Parteid van de Aarbeid*, the position the party holds regarding public health, proper health, funded by a base of social taxation. And the insurance, where does money from medical policies go— health for money? And up: from Löic I receive 40 € for a small painting job. With it I pay for daily *zazen*, and I buy bread and bananas. And up: home. Eat, sleep. Sometimes that's enough.

> You don't speak Dutch? That's fine! If you want to work with us in Randstad Call Centers, no Dutch is necessary...

Tomorrow, after *zazen*, school, I shop for Cuban food that will be served at the opening for the Havana painters:

> Arroz congrí, rice and beans: 500 gr black beans, 600 gr white rice, a coconut, 2 peppers, 1 red 1 green, 1 onion, rosemary and a little sambal, an Indonesian chile paste.

> Caldosa, stew: 5 malangas, 5 potatoes, 2 sweet potatoes, a piece of squash, a large yucca, plantain, lemon, garlic, onion and corn.

> Tachinos, smashed plantains: 6 green semi-ripe plantains. Oil and salt.

> Chicharritas, plantain chips: 6 green plantains. Oil and salt.

> Picadillo de soya a la habanera, Havana-style soy mash: 1 kilo of soybeans, onion, olives, raisins, tomatoes, pepper, chives. Sambal.

No one puts a bridle on a crow.

*Reel* is both real & reasonable!

Four Cuban artists show their work in the European Zen Center. They represent no trend or group, yet they have a few things in common: they're young, they work and play with their hands, practice *zazen*, believe in gods and in godly life: reality.

Mara, actress and singer, paints not only to earn rice & beans, but also to find a path for Nature's sullen creatures. Lucero is one of them. He opens doors as a child opens a book of tales. So is the Ndoki Yaya, colorful and silent like a daughter of the Two Waters.

Cheleni is a street artist who plays with drums and stilts. A giant in red, like a brush stroke in an urban collage. Abstractions, you'd say, though you can dance on them.

Ania is a sandpaper weaver, a sawdust contralto: her spirits, like African Rouaults, bring thunder inside linen.

José Francisco is the youngest, the proverbial student. Coming back from a party, he paints this untraceable icon: a zen monk playing *cajón*. The gaze is stony, the naïve hands are shells on the dark wooden drum. Handmade.

They're my companions tonight, plus María la Catalana. And the ones who are always here.

With these people I drink and keep quiet / with those people I talk and bide my time. Like a naïve drummer with a stick face, an island buster-keaton, a scarecrow who distrusts winter during the fall. *Dáme mais vinho que a vida é nada.*

This week Ramadan begins. Not that I fast, except timidly and for one day. For a thousand days more, I don't. *Ayunar*, to fast: it's not so hard to recognize hunger or feast. *Solidariteit*. The Muslim students talk about flour, soup with meat and vegetables.

*Ja, spreek toets*, oral exam, like always. A mute parrot, *stom, sprakeloos papegaai*, speak after the beep: *spreken na de biets. Biep*!

After *zazen*, a reading test. Here I write Paul's words from *kin hin*: "Do you know the difference between a monk and an ordinary person? At a party? The following day, the monk will come to *zazen*. This is not about morality. It's just that *zazen* is the most important thing that he can do." He's referring to the party with our art opening, and to those of us, like me, who didn't show up at the *dojo* on Sunday.

Proverb of the day: *Gods water over akker laten lopen*. God's water upon God's acre: let it flow. Today there's a transportation strike. The Wait.

*Aanhalen*: to show, but also to quote. *Aanhankelijkheid*: devotion, but also attachment.

*Aanhouden*: perseverance. *Aan aan*, like the children's game of tag, like the *I Ching*: Instinct.

The silent person grants consent—silence is consent—*wie zwijgt, stemt toe*. A supporting vote. What a meager understanding of silence. To fall silent in every language, *zwijgen in alle talen*. Silent as a stone. A rude person, I slide along the avenue:

> The Devil is human
> *brood met pindakaas*
> and beers, uncountable

—a human devil of bread with peanut butter and beer tugs me to that place. The secret of active listening, says Prof. Martina: *actief luisteren*:

> *meedenken*
> *voorspellen*
> *categoriseren* means
> to think about,
> to foresee, and to categorize.

Categories, *trefwoorden, sleutelwoorden, symbolen*. Words as blows, words as keys. *Wat bewegt je?* What moves you, what gets you to listen? Symbols. A coin split in two, *accuratesse*: when sometimes in Dutch, with an Anglofrench swing, Latin breathes. *Accuratesse*. At the city gates, this coin, this metaphor: *in kaart brengen*. To bring into a map. But the map is not reality! Nor is the metaphor, thus the Muslim distrust: spirit, where are you going? To take care of Florian's cat. To feed her, to clean her litterbox: her name is Nefertiti, and she sleeps like a sphinx. Next to Nefertiti, I study this linguistic variant:

> *gaastarbeiders-buitenlanders-medelanders-allochtonen*

It reveals the progression, in terms of what is linguistically/politically correct, when referring to the immigrant: from the "invited workers" of the 1960s, mostly Turkish and Moroccan, to the non-natives of the XXI century, mostly Turkish and Moroccan, without forgetting the Surinamese, who were not invited to work but responded to the call from the financially solvent mother country: Goethe would say they were Germanized strangers. They became Dutchified. According to the tiny *Nederlands-Engels* dictionary by Dr. G.J. Visser, that verb exists: *verhollandsen* = dutchify. Many Dutch people don't know the word, and they even dislike it. Dutchify yourself. In reality I Provenzalize myself. The cat is still napping.

*Illustrated Dymaxion world map*

Via Milan Linate Airport, which while an airport is inside the city. Night in Milan, the eternal light rain, the empty streets, the mela- mela- melancholy. My sister, who has pasta ready for me when I arrive. Da Vinci, today you can have your appetizer in Amsterdam and your dinner in Milan, and even this time "they will call ancient."

> *Notturno*
> *pioggia*
>> *lavanda*
> *croce*
>> *via*
> *perdido entre dos mundos*
> *cuáles.*

> [*Notturno*
> *pioggia*
>> lavender
> *croce*
>> *via*
> lost between two worlds
> which ones?]

*La famiglia*: I've come in order to see my sister Amor, *Love*. Strong among the stars and filled with a silent thrill: love for the goddess. Perched upon a silent song, among lavender flowers and *culmine*, the final rose. Force: it's not about who holds her by force, but about who can get her to pause in joy. Invented, not inventoried. But by means of books there's no way to calculate force: the secret of force, secret of the rose.

> *Milano secreto*
> *arde mal, arde mejor*
> *Arde*
> *lo erónimo.*

[secret Milan
burns worse, burns better
Burns
eronymity.]

Chased by a rose, I achieve *l'iluminazione*. *Ma!* In spite of occasional insomnia, you sleep well in Milan.

### DINSDAG 26 OKTOBER

Back in A'dam after fall vacation, *herfst vakantie*, I ask for help with *taal werk*. Language and work, work with the tongue: *contact met Nederlanders, geschiedenis*, history, crossing the Low Countries in search of norms and values: *normen en waarden, tradities en gewoontes*. Traditions and customs. Smoking a pipe, for example, and riding a bicycle. Respecting the traffic lights. And the schoolday dream: *als ik minister-president was*. If I were minister-president. A composition of *150 woorden*. If I were *Balkenende*, I would retire from public life. Ah, putting these words into a wheelbarrow and pushing them toward understanding: *s' io fossi fuoco*. If I were my own self. *Als ik mezelf was*. Gentle force.

### VRIJDAG 29

After *zazen*, studying poetry: Mr Mc Mental, from school to school, examines the possibility of giving no opinion. Dear athletes, maybe you've noticed the problems caused by smoking, so you find weed in all the bars. Tea, then? Taking letters on the subject and sending opinions in every instance. Opinions. For example: The city will close the nursery school, *questione di soldi*. Write a letter, get classmates to participate. It's not about money but about solidarity! Use the structures and keywords that you learned in school. Still another example, in a *gesprek over de Politiek*, with the referendum as its theme. Pan-European themes: the European's daily bread, to belong or not to belong. That is the question. Objective: discussion itself. Tools: opinions, intonation, arguments. Definition of Sector Chief: *wijkagent*, neighborhood agent, or *buurtregisseur*: director of the district. We learn certain bad words. *Plasser, piemel, pieps* & *tolie. Tolie* in Surinamese: *tolete. Ongewenste intimiteit.* An unusual degree of intimacy. A *tolete*, a short stick, is attributed to the district director. *Eerlijk is eerlijk*: let truth be told.

### Maandag

*Ik vertel je dit sub rosa.* Conduct or direction: *handel en wandel,* they say. Negotiating and moving forward, putting something into play, setting out. As for *karakter, identiteit?* Land: *aard.* How can this be, in an amphibious country, land without land, land without *karakter?* That's not right: amphibious, ambiguous, but not without character, even if it seems hypocritical to Latinos. Homework: search the internet for Holland's *politieke barometer.* On the internet?

### Martes

The learned Ids De Vries brings us a present. A poem that comes like water, from the rain, for chocolate. I translate it into Spanish.

*Noviembre*

*Es lluvia y es noviembre:*
*Regresa el fin del año y nos acecha*
*El corazón, esa tristeza, pero también costumbre,*
*Que se arrastra en secreto.*

*Y aquí en el cuarto, donde olvidada*
*La vida diaria se pone en juego,*
*Brilla de la avenida inconsolable*
*Una incolora luz de mediodía.*

*Los años se van como solían,*
*Poco a poco no hay cómo distinguir*
*Entre el recuerdo sordo*
*Y el devoto esperar.*

*Perdido estás camino tierno*
*Para evadir al tiempo;*
*Siempre noviembre, siempre lluvia,*
*Y siempre este vacío corazón.*

J. C. BLOEM (1887–1966)

[November

It's rain and November:
The year's end returns and stalks
our hearts, that sadness, but also the custom
dragging itself in secret.

And here in the room, where forgotten
everyday life puts itself on the line,
a colorless midday light
shines off the inconsolable avenue.

The years go off as they always did,
little by little there's no way to tell
the difference between deaf recollection
and devoted hope.

You are lost my dear path
for evading time,
always November, always rain,
always this empty heart.]

## WOENSDAG 10

*Een voet tussen de deur krijgen.* Holding the door open with your foot:
a foothold. Or, following Archimedes … *Genuanceerde denken*, giving
exhaustive thought. For example, *het doen*, to do it: *tener seks*, sex. To do,
not to make. Poiesis.

In *De Twee Zwaantjies* I drink a few beers with Gaspar Guevara. The two cygnets, *typisch hollandsch*! Music from the movie *Shane*, the beers are not tiny, and Gaspar puts the article on the table: Was Huizinga right? Is Nederland *proper, nuchter en tolerant*: clean, sober and tolerant? Would it be enough to take a quick look around The Two Cygnets? A bar in the Jordaan neighborhood should be a good laboratory for testing Huizinga's myth …

> Truly, should we recognize, as a national characteristic, an urgent desire for simple, unadorned truth, for honesty and trustworthiness, for order and harmony—in a word, for spiritual purity?

A bar is a bar, Huizinga, a clean well-lit place, says Gaspar. He finishes his autumn beer, brown and tough as a billygoat. *Bok bier*. There's something sickly sweet, however, like the surroundings that always tend toward *gezelligheid*.

"But is *gezelligheid reel*?" He looks around. This comfort out of a period photo, this efficient patina, those smiles? Are we really tolerated?"

"*Bon*, you don't have to try to squeeze milk from a stone. The surface is the part that's real."

"Okay, of course, it has already been seventy years since Huizinga talked about *la qualité d'un defaut*: what isn't there is what is there. But the bar's all right."

"Within reason."

"*Voor illusie en rhetoriek*. Cheers!" And he retakes the texticle:

> It's understood to be an expensive luxury, one that we can allow ourselves, this recognition of the foreigner. The interpenetration of communities continues, in spite of the delusions that rattle the world, its course. We should let it work freely upon our territory and …

Here he interrupts himself, sips at his billygoat,

> ... *en houdt uw Nederlandsche hoofd koel.*—How would you translate that?

"Keep a cool Dutch head."

"Got it."

After *zazen*, school. A participatory story: *By the Crocodile River*. Anna and Dorus are a couple. They live on opposing banks of a river infested with crocodiles. The bridge is closed for urgent repairs (here they usually put up supplementary bridges, but that doesn't happen in the story). The lovers become desperate. Anna decides to ask for help from Simon, captain of the boats on the river. She can get help if she consents to *het doen*. Sex. Anna consents and crosses the river. When Dorus finds out what happened, he repudiates her. After a beating, Anna complains to their friend Ivan and asks for his help. He refuses to get involved. A political story, if those exist: what do the students think? Their opinions, *jouw mening*, the cornerstone of Dutch society. Rank people in the most humane manner possible, which is to say, from bad to worse. Anna impatient, Ivan unsupportive, Dorus uncomprehending, and Simon a fucker. Students are learning. Let there be discussion.

For the Muslim Maghrebis, in general, Anna is the worst of them all. For the Europeans, in general, it's Simon. The North American blames Ivan. The Brazilian women, Dorus. The river carries the opinions away, or the crocodiles swallow them.

It's my turn to do a *spreekbeurt*, a mini-presentation for the class. I choose Summerhill, the free school founded by A.S. Neill in 1921. Suffolk, England, 100 students at the primary and secondary levels. Optional lessons, free attendance, collective assembly where the voices of the student and professor carry the same weight. Freedom shock? Naturally. It happens to us adults sometimes here in Holland. *Onderwijs zonder angst,* says Erich Fromm. Education without fear: www.summerhillschool.co.uk

*zazen*

> koffie consumptie
> *pipa, y la profesora que me ve tan atildado*
> "Hoe houdt je vol!" *Como dice?*
> "Gedisciplineerde!"
>
> [*koffie consumptie*
> pipe, and the teacher who sees how elegant I am:
> "*Hoe houdt je vol.*" What is she saying?
> "*Gedisciplineerde!*"]

Learn to know your neighbor, learn to imitate him. Gradations. Degradations, and all kinds of fairy tales!

Writing, time and time again, application letters: *een solicitatie briefje schrijven.*

> Dear Sir, Madam, *geachte heer, mevrouw*
> Based on *l'informatie op u internet site,*
> it is important, *belangrijk,* that I get in touch with you.

*Wie je bent?,* who are you,

> *Ik ben,* I am bla bla bla seeking work:
> a poet/writer, *een dichter/schrijver*
> *met ruime ervaring* broad experience
> as translator/teacher *als vertaler* docent.
> *Gespecialiseerd,* specializing *een Nederlands dichter career:*
>        *Romantisch Letter*
> *dief,* lit. a thief of letters, a plagiarist

*Wat je wilt,* what do you want?

*Ik zoek,* I am looking for freelance *werk* but also
*maar ook,* Maroc, temporary or permanent employment
in the countryside, *het veld van letteren en vertalingen.*
For more *informatie,* if U interest *heeft, mijn C. V opsturen.*
*Met voorbat bedankt,*
O.P.

French windows: *De Kabinet.*

The *kabinet Balkenende* and their Boys, a Dutch proposition: six ministers and, *voor de rest,* a fistful of *staatsecretaris*: vice ministers.

The government is formed with names and high fives, clap clap. A cabinet unpopular with the voting public and maybe someday to be tossed out in the street like a useless piece of furniture. Something common in Amsterdam.

*Kabinet* is the government, but also *een mooie, kostbare houten kast.* A nice, expensive piece of wooden furniture.

A foreign embarrassment: *plaatsvervangende schaamte!* A shame that changes place, that moves from one place to another, translates from me to you, to other people. Shame.

Classes with the Frisian Doctor De Vries give rise to reflection. They stimulate speculation, looking into a mirror, *een spiegel tussen Holland* in Cuba. Like Alice through the looking glass.

The Frisian remembers some poet who whipped this one out:

> Ik voel me zo bijzonder
> De zon gaat onder
> *Me siento tan peculiar*
> *Si el sol se pone en el ma*
>
> [*Ik voel me zo bijzonder*
> *De zon gaat onder*
> I don't feel like me
> When the sun is setting into the sea]

And speaking of sarcasm in poetry, an epitaph:

*Hier ligt Gijs van Amerongen*
*In de grond een goede jongen*
*Gijs was niet een gemakkelijk iemand*
　　*Nu dat hij dood is,*
*is een beter person geworden.*

Or in Spanish,

*Aqui yace Gijs van Amerongen*
*En la tierra un buen muchacho*
*Gijs fue en vida un mamarracho*
　　*Y ahora que está muerto*
*Se ha vuelto un buen hombre.*

Or in English,

Here lies Gijs van Ameroy
On earth he was called a good boy
Alive, he was a real mess
　　But now that he's lifeless
He has become a good man.

A Dutch saying, *iemand de grond inschrijven*: literally: inscribing someone in the earth, burying them or, what amounts to the same thing, relentlessly criticizing them.

In school we talk about the rules of the immigration game. The class is enriched with four young women from Thailand and Indonesia. One of them resembles an indigenous Mexican. They're marvelous: they know how to give a look: the eyes and gazes of these Indonesian girls are intact.

Barbara Queirolo calls for a *babysitteraggio*, as she puts it. Mondays and Thursdays, *sera*, in the evenings. In his *Nuevo Catauro de Cubanismos*, Fernando Ortiz explains the two meanings of *cajón*, the instrument and its dance: "It's a dance with the drum box, poorly executed by Afro-Cubans

(…) who lack a drum." That is to say, the *cajón* exists "in an absence," as a substitute. There's a story that Paco de Lucía brought it from Peru to Andalusia. From there, the flamenco *cajón* becomes endemic. *Flamenco Sketches*, an alternate take, continues to be the favorite on these and other nights. With Cannonball Adderley's sax, which sounds like Moraima Secada.

La Negra, our dog, dies on November 18. From age alone, according to my mother.

Today in the Jordaan neighborhood I've seen *spionetjes*: spying-mirrors, according to Dr. Visser's dictionaries. A Dutch style of voyeurism, attaching mirrors to building facades in order to look into the street from the window, or through it. Open spying, yet with discretion. Or direct spying, with familiarity: *gezellig*.

With Elia, three hours. Well paid in games, plus 15 Euros. We play *la lotta*, wrestling. On the floor. Then we draw at the table, drink artificial juice, draw some more and throw colored pencils around. He likes that a lot. Singing, for example,

> *E caduto nella mano*
> *un giallo che e proprio strano*

or,

> *il rosso cade per terra*
> *il colore de la guerra*

Then I talk with his mother about her Christophe's employment situation; something about it resembles mine. As Pierre said that afternoon in Cuba, too many talents. Not in vain, talent: imaginary money of the Greeks, equivalent to 60 minas.

*Nubes que suben al cielo*
*Asi se nutre y se reposa el hombre noble,*
*Contento y de buen humor.*

[Clouds rising toward the sky
A noble man finds energy and rest like them,
Content and good-humored.]

—This is the image (Hsii ["Nourishment"], 5) given by the *I Ching* in Dutch translation. Skies, water, clouds, signs of rain. *Het wachten is geen ijdel hopen, maar bevat de innerlijke zekerheid.* Waiting. It is not in vain that we wait, encouraged. It suggests internal conviction.

Weakness, *zwakheid,* and impatience, *ongeduld,* don't resolve. When clouds ascend in the sky, it's a sign that rain is on the way. People can do nothing but wait for it to fall. *Overmachten,* a lovely word for superior forces. "Superior forces" sounds like a military phrase. And it is: you don't have to try to take the initiative directly. Strengthening your body with food and drink, strengthening the mind with happiness and good humor. What a combination for winter!

Leonardo in Milan, the relations between Cuba and Italy. Fernando Ortiz—who, in some way, was a student of Lombroso and discussant in Amsterdam in 1905—closes the triangle. Cuban religion in one place, Italy and Holland at the corners of history. Not to even refer to Paris. That long-ago night of February 28, a full moon, doing *zazen* with the master in his mother's apartment. Rue Croix Saint Simon, not far from the flea market. *Cubanology,* filled with good ideas, like the mind of a commercial traveler.

Amsterdam, noviembre 26, 2004

Este cuaderno comienza con una consulta al I King —y deja suspendida por el momento la relación del encuentro de ayer noche con Alga del Mar, en su casa de Amsterdam hoy dice así: 777876

零

Siu . La Espera
HeT WachTen

boven K'an, heT Onpeilbare, heT water
beneden, Tj'ién, heT Scheppende, de hemel

Continúo el sábado 27/11/2004, la lectura de HeT WachTen en el I King.

HeT Oordeel

HeT WachTen.
Als je waarachTig benT, heb je lichT en welslagen.
STandsvasTigheid brengT heil.
HeT is bevorderlijk, heT grote water over Te sTeken.

HeT Beeld

Wolkens sTijgen op aan de hemel: heT beeld van heT WachTen.
Zo voedT en laapT zich de edele, blijmoedig en opgeruimd.

La espera: Si eres sincero, Tendrás luz y éxito. La perseverancia Trae forTuna.
Es propicio cruzar las grandes aguas. EsTe es el juicio.

*"Amsterdam 2004" journal page*

I'm waiting for the lesson to end with Ids de Vries. He hopes for something from his students. That they will write to him.

Today he talked about television: *de verrekijker*. The telescope. From *treurenbuis*; from *treuren*, to cry, and *buis*, tube. The tube of lamentations. From there to Jeroen's, to clean for a few hours, cleaning the life residues from fifteen days of a solitary man and his cat Pixel, speaking of television. Today he's at home. It's a glorious exception, since Jeroen, like a good solitary type, is fine company. We talk, drink coffee and smoke. We talk about the history of coffee in Holland, about the 16th century *koffiehuizen*, with their libraries and coreligionists. *Hollands glorie*. Where did the idea of revolution come to Holland from—when it wasn't Holland yet? Jeroen answers that it came out of indifference toward the German emperor, who on the strength of an apparent Spanish intervention, turned up in the Low Countries as if an emissary of God. Both of them, the emperor and God, were seriously dysfunctional. They were questioned. No blind serfdom to god or man: revolution, yes, says Jeroen. You can call it that.

Today, babysitting with Elia. What does "babysitting" mean? Sit on the baby? Anyway, we play. His mother arrives, we talk. Sometimes Elia has nightmares, which he calls dreaming tigers and lions. Or it's the other way around and we call that "nightmares." In Germanic languages, as Borges noticed, the bad dream is a nocturnal mare. *Nachtmerrie*, nightmare. But lions and tigers are something else, Elia.

I resume treatment for Alga, who has trusted me with some sort of rash on her legs. For seven days, she'll apply lotion made with a Cuban medicinal plant, *caisimón de anis*, which Tata Lázaro mixed for me. She'll stop visiting the dead man, her routine. The cemetery is behind the house: she waves toward it with one arm. On the other side of the ever-present canal. There's always a canal. I help her with a power switch and we eat. There's red wine from the Cape. Once the Cape was a land adopted by intrepid Dutchmen, and it still recognizes their language of colonization: *Afrikaans*, a sunnier Dutch, and a stormier one. Like the wine.

We talk about the American guerrilla fighter, Geronimo. Algo carefully collects photographs of Apaches and Navajos, of Bolívar, Che Guevara and Rodobaldo Yagunzo, who is a literary guerrilla but no less real for that. The mythology of the guerrilla fighter in America. "According to you," I ask her respectfully, "did Che Guevara die defeated?" "Are you crazy? What have we been talking about all night long?" Alga's personal history is a book in its own right. Its episode in the sewers is noteworthy.

At that time Alga lived in a squat, or a house occupied by non-owners, in a fierce part of Amsterdam. Her companions, demanding and bossy, made her life into yogurt, as the saying goes. This yogurt contains flowers and song, *floricanto*—another word for poetry. But it's still yogurt, and in the end, it goes sour. Alga goes into the street, remembering drifters in her birthplace of Colombia. Where they slept and how. Under bridges. This is no problem in Amsterdam. There are thousands of bridges, 600 to be more precise. Cardboard boxes abound, as does rubbish in the streets. Trash from a wealthy nation. She takes her things to rest under bridges the width of sidewalks. Hidden from onlookers, she finds a sewer entry. She asks herself where she'll end up. It's cold outside, so she just enters the sewer.

The pipes are dark, and Alga is afraid of rats. She keeps going until she arrives somewhere deep inside, at a warm place: she has penetrated the Botanical Garden, its tropical zone. These plants know her. Alga talks with the plants. She stays overnight there.

The following night she returns with her precious belongings, a little gas burner and matches. She can sleep naked, she can make coffee. She spends her nights in the Botanical Garden for two and a half months.

A more simple monster.

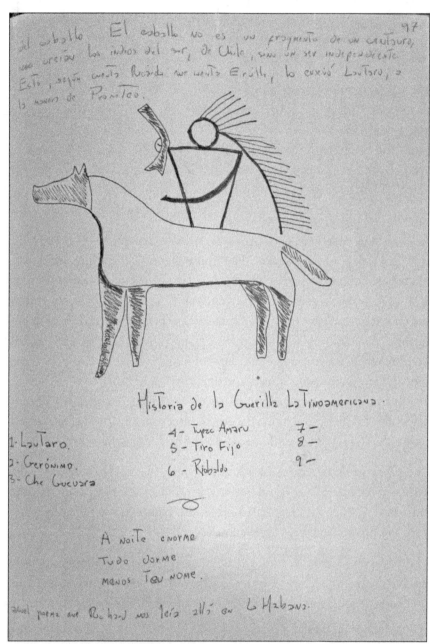

del caballo    El caballo no es un fragmento de un centauro,
con creían los indios del sur, de Chile, sino un ser independiente.
Este, según cuenta Ricardo me contó Ercilla, lo curvó Lautaro, a
la manera de Prometeo.

Historia de la Guerilla Latinoamericana.

1- Lautaro.
2- Gerónimo.
3- Che Guevara

4- Tupac Amaru        7 -
5- Tiro Fijo           8 -
6- Riobaldo            9 -

A noite enorme
Tudo dorme
menos Teu nome.

aquel poema que Richard nos leía allá en La Habana.

*"History of the Guerrilla Presence" journal page*

198

*Bijlmer Prison*

To our little *dojo*. I haven't been able to go to class. Better said, I go in, drink a coffee, and leave without saying goodbye, what the Dutch call taking a "French leave." With the drums silenced, *met stille trommelen vertrekken*, as they say it in this language … Instead, passing the notorious Bijlmer on my bicycle, I'm going to study next to the Gasperplaats lake. What am I studying? *Spijbellen*: the English translation is skipping school. Escape to the water, go out in a boat, play the truant. The enlightened truant who smokes his pipe and reflects next to the swans' lake:

The difference between *spijbellen* & *procrastinare* is relevant. When procrastinating, you don't abandon the place or activity. You just go around it or beat about the bushes. I forgot to mention that there are plenty of bushes here: slacking off in bushes. But no, *spijbellen* is already doing something. It shows a determination, for better or worse, to change things, or to change a scene, whereas *procrastinare* is a "sin" of indetermination.

Going out in a boat, slacking off: aquatic or amphibious images tailored to the landscape where I effect *spijbellen*: a lake wide as a gulf, as a *golfillo*—which is another synonym for a truant in Spanish—where birds give their bad example of passing time while doing nothing. Why, dear lake, ocean or river, does *spijbellen* tend to take us toward water? It's the purification of a mania to do things, a mania for routine. *Schoolverzuiming*, literally omission of school, takes me then as far as Diemen, lost as a wild duck. The bicycle drops a pedal. We return at a walk together to North Jerusalem. Mokum is its Hebrew name.

Elia wants me to read the stories about Asterix and Obelix to him in Italian. Tonight he won't accept that the Gauls might speak French, like his father, only his mother's Italian. I'll try for a Gallitalian, like the sort spoken in the time of Marco Polo. I have to translate the dialogues between Asterix and Cleopatra on the spot. And those two, if they ever met—in what language would they understand each other? What would be the *lingua franca* between a Celt and a Ptolomeic? Greek.

### VIERNES

Daily life escapes like usual, silently. It's not about lethargy. My mouth is closed.

### SABADO 4 DE DICIEMBRE. DÍA DE SANTA BARBARA

A blessing, Siete Rayos, that you have come to the birthday of a little boy named Noah here in Amsterdam Noord. He is turning 3.

His father Guno, native to Paramaribo, tells me: "I'm not going to give a Dutch party!" What's a Dutch party, Saint Barbara? You who know everything about parties.

We eat dishes from Surinam, somewhat resembling our food: piles of white rice, cassava or yucca, *bacabana* or *plátano macho* (plantain), *bacalao* (cod). The seasoning is different. Their emphasis is on coconut milk and a hot pepper, an Asian species. There's Dutch beer to drink, and the men gather to talk; the women are a bit isolated. A sort of family representation with the usual formulas of courtesy, but there's not a whiff of insanity. Only that gentleman with mustaches who plays with the children, whacking a balloon through the air. I drink palm beer, highly fermented. I help to wash the dishes. "*Ga weg*," I say to the lady of the house, who's rather overworked, as they say here. Burnout: it happens a lot to women who face the obligations of a working mother alongside the social stereotype that women must be beautiful, infallible, trustworthy, available (in the sense of her labor). It causes a short circuit. Once the mother gets sick, the worker is gone. The woman is burned out and not with flames of love. What do you think, Saint Barbara? They say that if the housewife's productivity were recorded, in financial terms, her annual salary would be 22,000 Euros. But in fact, even with the rules of the social state, the woman is as unprotected as any Mary elsewhere, and at times she cries like a Magdalena: *ga weg*, take it easy, I'll do the dishes.

### Zondag 5

In the *dojo*. I explain the posture of *zazen* to a gentleman who drove 70 kilometers to get here. We communicate in Dutch. That's easy when the topic is posture: *lichaams taal*, body language. After *zazen*, while we're changing clothes, he asks more abstract questions. Now we don't understand each other. "What a way of speaking!" Alga says.

### Lunes 6

For the first time, I go to school on foot. I leave the bicycle without repairs, its pedal resting at an absurd angle. Today I walk.

In class during a *Luisteren* test, listening, the radiophonic speaker reasons about housing. A familiar theme: during the 19th century, everyone lived close to their job: *labora et ora*. In the 1930s, cities became impoverished as the wealthy moved to the more rural outskirts. You have to see the photographs of a working-class home in this neighborhood, Pijp: one room, the bed inside a kind of wardrobe, the bathroom in a closet (literal, water closet: W. C.), the table by the window, back to the kitchen: 4 picturesque square meters. Today the majority of young people want to live in the city, in order to work more and dedicate more time to house-keeping. They like to live centrally, since that's how they save time and take advantage of the flexible rules of urban life. On the other hand, states the phlegmy lecturer, *cluistering* dominates: the separation of groups into different social sectors. The youth, the elderly, allochtonen, autochtonen, etc. *Is goed: gezellige apartheid!* That way, people find more things they can share. Criteria, for example. In Almere, one of the zones recently stolen from the sea, the majority of inhabitants live in family nuclei. I've ridden my bicycle through Almere—it's cold as hell. "*Sinter Klaas, denk ik!*," says the teacher when she notices a horse passing by the school. But it's the mounted police.

> *Of je Christen, Zen Boeddhist bent,*
> *Islamiet of Jood*
> *Er is leven*
> *Er is leven na de dood.*

After break, Martine Haak makes us listen to a little cabaret song. Whether you're a Christian or Zen Buddhist, Muslim or Jew, there's life after death. She also tells us a homosexual joke with the word *flikker*, which means both a flicker of light and someone gay.

> "*Ik zie geen flikkers,*" I can't see even a flicker, says a man after entering a dark movie theater.
> "Yoohoo!" replies the *flikker*.

### MARTES 7

The rain is simple. So much time in Amsterdam without understand-ing. *Wat maakt je een Amsterdamer*: nothing. How different fear is from respect: can't believe it's so simple: rain.

⚜

*Schrijven is schrappen*: to write is to redact. Rules for a school assignment, *spreekbeurt*. One's turn to speak:

> A good argument: not too broad, while also interesting for you.
> Collecting information: *verzamelen*, one of the arts of the Dutch, idiosyncratic collectors.
> *Alles op een ritjie zetten*: line everything up. Organize.
> Organize the media: overheads, photos, citations, slides, epics, triptychs, maps, symbols.
> Presentation: direct, clear, in your own words, utilizing *lichaam-staal*, body language.
> Practice *voor het spiegel*: in front of a mirror.
> Breathing: slow exhale, like in *zazen*.

### MIÉRCOLES

After *zazen* and a coffee with Alga at the corner, I go to school to listen and converse about *vrije keuze*, free will. An Odyssey in the form of a cartoon, a legend for readers and viewers: *De Vrije Keuze*. Odysseus training Telemachus.

Tomorrow I work *d'imbiancatore*. Painting in *bianco*, like *pasta asciutta*. Informal graphic work: zero etiquette, etiquette 0. *Nul et nu*: the naked zero. Straight or backwards. Now it is one.

How for example did this little white feather end up on my tobacco bag? What bird dropped it? Working as a painter in a friend's house: white on white, Malevich, malefactor. As I lay magazine pages across the floor to avoid action painting, I find this:

> *La Havane jour et nuit*

and as if glowing against so much white, a photo from 1994: classic corner at San Leopold where some building might fall down, forever enduring its ochre barrage of debris. *Le Monde Diplomatique*, not so *diplomatique* after all. *Tapijt bombardement*, they say in Dutch, a tapestry of bombardment: remember Cambodia. Here a young woman crosses the tapestry in a dressing gown: make yourself comfortable. A barefoot boy waves at the camera. I know that corner. The ocean, which you can't see, collaborates on the erosion. And the light. Central Havana. Distant palaces.

*Palais lontaines*, Abilio Estevez's latest novel in a French edition, is the theme of this page that I rescue from the ferocious dripping of my paintbrush. It deserves a reading and I'll do that after finishing work. I go to a coffeeshop providentially named *Irste Hulp*, First Aid. *Le monde des livres, le monde de la lecture, de la rupture*:

> *Trop d'exils, trop d'incompréhensions,*
> *d'abdication, de colère et d'injustice*
> *semblent s'être inteposés entre La Havane*
> *et lui. Il sait qu'il est à La Havane*
> *tout en sachant qu'il n'est pas.*

I could transcribe those words inside Amsterdam's first aid centers: I even copy them down. But I lack the rage. Calmly I drink my mint tea, and eventually I say "*Goede avond*" to the happy waitress, to the customers who are just as Arab as me. Because we're all of us Arabs and, after a day of work, I'm going to sleep, *tout en sachant…*

⚜

I dream about El Tata. The road to Santiago. To Las Vegas: next to the highway, in the fenced pasturelands, there are lions who sleep, frolic, or nap. These lions don't seem to be in very good shape. Maybe they're malnourished? Too enclosed? Long-term captivity engenders a kind of malignity. It's not healthy. I'm boring the cat, as a recluse said many years ago in Pinar del Río. Along the road, inside a room, I find El Tata: "What can I do?" I ask him. "I'm not going backwards!" "This table is set, so that's it," he answers.

Irving, a young Havana painter whom I've never met in person, asked me to be his long-distance tutor. From his thesis he sends some "topics." I draw out these ideas:

Affect and Signification as the Basis for Poetry

"Poetry is the aspect of the art," you say, "that deals in a fundamental way with the affective life of human beings, their relations with others and with themselves" *Trasumanare*, says Dante. But poetry is also about what is superhuman.

Poetry is the "maximal crystallization of the image." Only in the fashion of a quartz, let's say, which also inclines toward becoming, decants into its becoming. The solid, set becoming of poetry. Parmenides. Speaking of becoming, what is the value of meaning, of commonplace? These tend to be affirmed, ay, even we take action "without questioning our activities." Without the critical exercise of the conscience, how can a commonplace come to be quartz? Through simple decantation, simple becoming. A fact of nature. "Our inventiveness wastes them," the Nahuatl used to say, regarding the flowers and songs of poetry. Their rolling stones.

As for the archetypes … "There are foundational ethical images over which we only work the surface." And behind them, you say, is the basic landscape of the human condition. There it is defined; that landscape, that veil, is all we have.

> *Nadie tiene casa fija en la tierra*
> *sólo poesía*
> *sólo flores y cantos*

> [No one has a solid home on earth
> only poetry
> only flowers and songs]

The writer writes as though he knew what he were doing.

The imperative of archaic consciousness. It addresses man through the interstices of silence, which span mental activities: Stop looking for a place for consciousness.

Imagine these interstices like tiny rills that flow branching through cerebral mass. The mass of thought: tributaries ... "*che'l suo verbo non rimanesse in infinito eccesso.*" Dante clarifies, the eagle chatters. Canto XIX of *Paradiso*.

The eagle's second imperative: Stop looking for imperatives to human consciousness.

Archetypes, archaic types. Figures. Stereotypes, affluent types. In stereo, confluent and affluent. The stone and the mold, unity and reproduction. Stereotomy: the art of cutting stone and wood.

### 17 DE DICIEMBRE. SAINT LAZARUS

*Pobrecito Oggun guerrero*
*cuando llega a tierra extrana.*
*estereotomia: arte de cortar piedras y maderas.*

[Poor little warrior Oggun
arriving in a strange land.
Stereotomy: the art of cutting stone and wood.]

In the afternoon I walk toward The Jordaan: "*O, Amsterdam, wat ben je mooi!*" There's no reason to live in A'dam unless you walk through the Jordaan district.

Night falls quickly. The houses glow with yellow light. High on the facade from the XVII century, stone deer announce the presence of winter: about 5 degrees. People are talking, animated. Chinese shadows in the customary bars, an insistent cold drizzle. I pass close to the protected Anne Frank house, a road deep in Jordaan. On the facade of the house with green stained glass, 1648. From the XVII century forward, what were the visible ties between Cuba and Holland? Exquelemin, the illustrious buccaneer (1645–1707). Peter Schenk (1660–1718) and his apocryphal view of Havana. Fernando Ortiz visits A'dam in 1902 for a Fifth Congress of Criminal Anthropology. Capablanca playing chess against Max Euwe, Queen's Gambit, A'dam 1930: "in order to set the knight free." De Kooning paints *Suburb in Havana* in 1958, a festival of splotches. Joris Ivens creates *Cuba, Armed Pueblo* in 1961.

With an air of cultural studies, maybe, one asks the researcher about interpersonal relationships between Cubans and Hollanders through the centuries. Travels, exchanges, translations, marriages, commerce. I have at hand the story of our neighbor Aleida de San Leopoldo, servant in a Havana mansion with Dutch owners. She was invited by them to vacation in Amsterdam. Was it cold, Aleida? I never asked her.

Alexander Oliver Exquemelin: A native of Normandy, barber-surgeon, buccaneer and sailor. On the orders of Henry Morgan, he travels to the Caribbean. In 1672 he departs the port of Havana for Amsterdam, where he is based for a while and brings to light *De Americaenche Zee Roovers* (1678), a testimonial about "American buccaneers." It is eventually translated into Spanish by a Dutchman, Alonso de Bonne-Maison, and from the Spanish to the English in 1684, where his name gets anglicized: John Esquemeling.

So doctor and buccaneer John comes and goes between the Antilles and Amsterdam, following the breeze and various orders, piratical or soldierly. Did he ever meet Schenk, as mentioned by Ortiz? I don't know.

GOOGLE NEDERLAND CUBA

> Nederlanders in Cuba: *página porno*
> Amateurs free sex picture 4
> *donde aparece, a más de* lekkere kontjes,
> *la frase* "animierte potentie cuba"
> Nederland-Cuba: related history 25 seconden

another porno page
nederland cuba parts &panties
discount air travels
Nederlandse boeken over *Cuba:* geen document
*una biografía acaso*, Columbus *de* Hans Koning

[GOOGLE NEDERLAND CUBA

*Nederlanders* in Cuba: a porno page
Amateurs free sex picture 4
where *lekkere kontjes* appears along with
*"animierte potentie cuba"*
Nederland-Cuba: related history 25 *seconden*
another porn page
nederland cuba parts & panties
discount air travel
*Nederlandse boeken* over Cuba: *geen* document
sort of a biography, *Columbus* by Hans Koning]

And the diary of Anne Frank, and the letters from Vincent to his brother that debuted in print like a revolution, and the story about the heroic child of Haarlem in our textbooks … Looking for Cuba in Holland, I find a ship that sailed from Hamburg on March 18, 1897, under the name *Coblenz*. Which at some point during its passage through the Antilles was renamed Cuba. It wrecked "there in the '20s" (to borrow the rhythm of the Trío Matamoros song about the S.S. Morro Castle), thus becoming famous. Famous, the ships that wrecked.

SABADO 18

*Je n'ai pas l'etoffe de la valse viennoise.* Chopin. Creator of waltzes. I take another walk through the Jordaan. Consultation with a Tibetan doctor in an alleyway: in the window, Medicinal Buddha holds a bowl with the magic herb that the Tibetans call … in his other hand, the *mudra.*

Eat neither a lot or a little, says Buddha. More pasta than bread, and the latter, whole grain. Not coffee but tea, little to no sugar, and move around a lot: this is the secret for eliminating phlegm. Move like a waltz by Chopin. *Vivace, Tempo Giusto, il giusto tempo umano.*

Velvet: *terciopelo.* Verve: *vitalidad.* A velvet verb.

❦

Cuba's National Ballet is in Amsterdam: *Cubanen brengen top uit het balletrepertoire*: Swan Lake, Amsterdam is for swans, the Nutcracker and Don Quijote … Although Cuba brings salsa to mind more than ballet, claims the local press. Well. Is salsa not also choreography? And does *balletto* lack for sauce? Come enjoy Don Quijote in his Cuban Amsterdam gala.

❦

One Petrus Schenk appears, editor of maps in the golden age of Dutch cartography. View of the port of Havana edited by ICAP, which hangs from the wall of the cubicle that we privately call the African shop: seventeenhundredwhenagain?

❦

Exhibition featuring neighborhood artists at a space in the Oud West. Free beer, fresh *taboulheh.* And the paintings? I'm not a critic. Morgana Velterop, *alternativartist,* alternadiva dressed as a clown, recites some poems standing on case of a Heineken: green on green. "Let's go to the ocean!" she says. Kind of difficult at this hour. She shows me her serpent-shaped ring: "Are you a poet too?" Well, I'm making something: *perch'io non spero di tornar,* Cubanology. "Although Cuba brings salsa to mind more than ballet …"

❦

Understudy. According to *Collins Dictionary*: to study a role or part so as to be able to replace the usual actor or actress if necessary. Should I understudy the part of Morgana? Standing on a case of Heineken, reciting, for example: "There's a tulip light in the shadow and silence in the sea," or "A scandal is the same as an homage to me"?

### ZONDAG 19

The most beautiful day this winter. To the *dojo* on the bicycle, from there to the Jordaan to meet Cristina next to the protected Anne Frank home.

Quality is Respect for the Community, and now on the wall of *El Pez Saltarin*, an artists' bar, the word *Kwaliteit* leaps out of an ad for Van Nelle Tobacco. *Pirzig, kwaliteit*, is respect for the community. "Strange, so many different people coming from different places," says Mónica. We're celebrating her birthday here. "Maybe you're the connection," I tell her. Sure enough, I meet Nanne Timmer, her old friend. Ha, ah! We talk with Nanne about a future company: Descartes South American. A business for collecting, processing and transporting objects found in the street. The *object trouvees* would be transported to Havana in a container, which would then return to Amsterdam full of toys manufactured by Cuban children.

### LUNES

To school on my bike. The teacher hands out a text about *"Fietsen als emancipatie middel,"* the bicycle as a means of emancipation for women. Grammatical dictation.

1900: the bicycle contributes to women's emancipation. Previously only men rode bicycles. Within twenty years, women take up bicycles *en masse* in seach of their freedom of movement and self-confidence.

From dictation to market: I buy brightly colored winter gloves in De Pijp. Five euros, seven colors, and from there to sit with my Amstel and read

*Women Who Run with the Wolves* ... or with the bike. At noon, I park my bicycle and make myself physically present in the coffeeshop Het Ballonetje, in order to collect their house Rules and Norms:

> *Pas op! Hier geldt betaald parkeren.*
> Careful! Here you must pay for parking.
> *Consumptie verplicht!*
> Purchase required!
> *Helaas is het onmogelijke om op onze toilet te poepen!*
> Unfortunately one must not poop in our toilet!
> *Bejaarden zijn hier ook welkom!*
> The elderly are welcome here too!

At two on the dot, I head out eastwards to work as an electrician. A lady offers South African wine and we listen to tangos as I install outlets, switches, lamps.

**MARTES 21**

*Descartes S.A. Dromen Leveranciers.* And off to *zazen*, five people. School starts late today, and I wait at Space Mountain, a coffeeshop two blocks from the institution. I meet Martijn Blok, a sailor who says he wants to learn Spanish. Joseph, the Jewish bartender, explains his theory that communities express, through language, the development of their consciousness on all levels. And he highlights the economic level. According to his premises, the Spanish language, whose sound is definitely not pleasing to him, is not a language of strong values since its original speakers, the impulsive Iberians, gave nothing of substance to European culture. By "European culture" he refers to the technology, consumption, and waste that we can admire here.

Martijn Blok doesn't agree. He puts on his hat and says goodbye. I don't agree either and do the same. Before leaving I ask the Israelite what Spanish he has heard: the one on television. I who similarly do not know Hebrew leave without saying anything. *Shalom.*

At school the theme of immigration/emigration comes up again. In fact, in *Nederland*, there are more *emigratie* than *inmigratie*. Most go to Canada and Australia. I take advantage of the hour in the computer lab to continue my search for the missing cornerstone: *Cubanolandia*. Schenk on Google proves to be fruitless: Bacardi cocktails. Havana-style eggs, Cuba Libre, etc. As for Willem de Kooning, emigrant from Rotterdam: "*na een trip naar Cuba maakte hij in 1959* 'Suburb in Havana,' a creation giving off the heat of a slow summer night."

In postings at the bookstore I discover Huib Billiet, who recently wrote about the rumba. *Variaties op een Cubaanse bekkenbeweging*: 20 euros. *Bekkenbeweging*? Pelvic motions.

Other news: Harry Mullisch, the great Dutch novelist, dedicates his attention to 1960s Havana. XXI century: Holland defeats Cuba in baseball. Sketches for a book. Drawn in the chalk from the mountain that Van Gogh praised.

On an avenue of the *Ceinturbaan* there's a store for orthodox imagery: icons, books about the Athonites, various paraphernalia. I buy two postcards from the congested Montenegran woman, with her warm voice and velvet eyes. An icon of Edmund, king and martyr, with an arrow shooting through the rectangle. XIII century. The other icon, a Christ Pantocrator from the Vatopedi monastery in Athos, XIV century.

### JUEVES 23 DICIEMBRE

Sendoffs from school and the *dojo* for the Christmas holidays. At school we pull a breakfast together: alongside the Dutch *kerstbrood* are the Moroccan sweets rich in honey, the now classic potato chips, the *rmpeiya* from Indonesia that would be called *empellas* in Cuba—what a coincidence!—made from flour, salt and nuts. We watch a film, *Shouf, shouf habibi*. A comedy about customs in the life of a Moroccan family in Holland: we student-immigrants, allocthonous scholars, *nieuwkomers* who have recently passed level three Dutch, we laugh and sympathize.

*Cubanolandia*: Carpentier's "The Road to Santiago." Stories about nomadic soldiers in the Low Countries.

Dante: Canto XIX of *Paradiso*. To the classical forest, urges the demon. The dialogue with the Eagle begins here.

I do *zazen* at home. Kitchen: *tagliatelle alle spinacche e formaggio*.

### SÁBADO 25

Sometimes the sky is a strong cobalt blue, without the light diminishing at all within a 180-degree radius.

Van Gogh, in his letters to Theo: "Here everything has a perfect beauty, just as I like it, love it. I mean that peace has come." And then he expands on the color: "Properly understood, to see it this way you shouldn't look at the color in a local, isolated way, but consider this local color in relation to the tone of the sky." On that December day in Amsterdam, 120 years ago, the sky was gray, "but so luminous that our 'pure' white probably can't reproduce the light or splendor." Today the sky is blue.

We go out for a walk. Empty as on Sunday, the street has a faintly melancholic air, an air of family parties. Businesses are closed, people eat at home, and a faraway man crosses the street with a bottle of wine in hand.

*Dromen leveranciers*: transporter of dreams. I wash my kimono and pack my suitcase. Off to Winter Camp.

At Winter Camp. Cataluña.

### 27, LUNES.

Arrival at 6, late. I greet the kitchen and Pierre. The air clear, subtle. A full moon is starting to rise.

I wait out dinner's slow tempo reading poems about the land: an anthology of Cuban poetry, a souvenir from Guadalajara. Meanwhile the Master arrives. It's 9:20; soon we'll eat. And after the dinner of soup, quinoa and

Alsace sausages, I will shake Stephane's hand. "*Ça va, Stephane?*" "*Oui, ça va, et toi?*" And his eyes sparkle.

## 28.

I wake up at 6:35. The sun hasn't risen yet. Minus 7 degrees, announces a local. I doze by the chimney and start dreaming again. Wake up again.

My job: with Florian, to heat the *dojo*. We have to change out the recently painted pipes on the chimney for other new ones, substitute one stove for another that's even older. It works. *Zazen* at 11.

After lunch and with the saucepans, I find Stéphane. I give him some tobacco and the jute bag that Ania sewed for his wife Lucette. "It went well in Cuba, but there aren't many people. I won't go back again until there are at least eighty." He laughs and thanks me for the presents.

Next I go to the refectory and give the money from the exhibition of Cuban art to his secretary, Ingrid. It's 450 euros. Next is *zazen* at 5. We have to heat the *dojo*. It heats up! During *kusen*, the woman who is both translator and monk addresses Stephane in an authentic Spanish that initially invites mockery. I think about Joseph the Israelite. Nonetheless, what she says is no laughing matter. *Donc.* I go to the forest in search of firewood. I find a dry treetrunk, ready to burn. It's so big that I'll work on it in stages. Dinner and *zazen*, 8:30.

Mara's painting, *El viejo sueño de engendrar jimaguas* (The Old Dream of Engendering Twins), was raffled off for two euros fifty per ticket during the Geneva *sesshin*. The winner was Jossy, the Master's mother. Loic Vuillemin brought it from Amsterdam in his pickup. Jossy saw it and was terrified. She gave it to Dolly, Paul and Pauline's daughter: "*Elle l'adore.*" The painting will return to Amsterdam.

I'm a pillar for the entire day. You have to be sitting in *zazen* before the others enter, and you stay there like the trunk of a tree in a corner. First the heating job, then *zazen*, the walk. *Guenmai*, coffee and a cigarette. My girlfriend Cristina pays for my *sesshin*. Someone else with no money, the monk Laurence, has to leave. The wind took the cold away and left the sun.

Happier than a dog with two tails, says El Flaco, the one from Rosario. I talk with him for a long time. We haven't seen each other in seven years.

Christian invites me to learn the art of making seitan: 300 grams of *glutan de blé*. Cover it with water containing tamari and olive oil. Move it around so the water gets into all of it, and homogenize the flour. Touch it as little as possible. When this sticky mass—Dogen's brain, according to Christian—is ready, you cover it with cloths for a few hours. Within that time you heat water with an onion, a carrot, thyme, chives, etc. When it comes to a boil, at just the right moment, *si butta la masa a fond* for an hour. Then you cut it to taste and cook it like this: in tamari, white wine, and white sauce. *Voilà!*

For maybe an hour it has been drizzling with a little sun, but I don't see any rainbow.

After lunch it's time for a siesta, but it's too beautiful to sleep. I go out in the forest to find firewood, and I play the flute for a dry tree that has given up nearly all of its branches. Almost all afternoon there were drizzle and sun. No rainbow, no delusions. As Gandhi would say.

At five Gabriela Sobel leads a meeting about how to correct posture. We talk about mine. She highlights my hands and tilting of the pelvis, little to none at all. *Bekkenbeweging*, an imperceptible rumba, helps *zazen*. Coincidentally Master Stéphane talks about hands and how they represent man's evolutionary leap. He concludes, "None of this is complicated.

It's just about evolution from the monkey to man, and from the man to Buddha."

Dinner. The Turk arrives from Madrid. He's in our room, so now we are four: a Frenchman, a Dutchman, an Argentine, and a Cuban. Like those jokes about wrecked ships, crashed planes, or international competitions in *conneries* (stupidities). The fundamental word in the French language: *Voilà*. When you know how to say it at the right time, you really speak French. *Voilà!*

### JUEVES 30. 1ST DAY OF *sesshin*.

Up by 6:15. My wristwatch, which serves as a silent alarm, runs 5 minutes behind for every 6 hours. 20 minutes per day. *Donc*…run, heat the place, *zazen* at 7:30. Stéphane continues to talk about the master Fujo Dokai. Fujo, from the homonymous mountain; Dokai, ocean of The Way. He talks about the tradition, according to our lineage, of rejecting social honors and political sinecures. During the second *zazen* at 11, he resumes, and from a reference to the *Soto Shu*, which Sawaki hated, he calls functionaries of Zen "of the Vatican variety" traitors. He affirms that the place where the devil can act with the greatest efficiency is, precisely, within religion.

Lunch around 1pm, and I rest until 3:30. I can't fall asleep; the day on the mountain is too beautiful. I go out to greet my treetrunk friends. In the 5 o'clock *zazen*, the master remarks on the phrase "cutting off two heads." I think of the two tails on Flaco's dog. The two heads chat ceaselessly in the flow of our thought. The disciplines laugh at the explanation. You also have to cut off the third head: the one watching. Now no one laughs.

Dinner. *Zazen* at 8 thirty. Pause. *Zazen*, 10 thirty. Pause, dining hall. *Zazen*, 1 a. m: Grand *zazen*, said the *shusso* at the dining hall. Indeed. Stéphane keeps talking about the *Gyo Ji* of the patriarchs. What is the *Gyo Ji*? Continuity, a peculiar way of not stopping. Then we go to the room, talking straight through until four.

Breakfast with *croissants*. Then some *mate* tea with friends, in the sunshine. And when evening falls, I prepare the two fires, and while I'm looking for wood I find treasure, palm fiber. Treat me gently, for it's my person!, says the palm. I use the trunks as seats by the fire.

Pierre and I converse: Are you going to return to Cuba? When? It's a matter of deciding how to get organized for the future. Organization on the mental level. Sometimes there's no real poverty, just a lack of order. Pierre contributes 50 E. for Master's journey to Havana: I ask him to accept a painting from the show but don't put much emphasis on it. In return, he recommends, with great emphasis, that I use gloves when doing manual labor. He always uses gloves and has a pair for me in Barcelona.

I have to laugh: I feel about gloves something like what I feel about shoes. But I always listen to Pierre.

New Year's Eve! Just as I finish preparing the first, the master asks me to play the drum for the ceremony of *Hannya Shingyo*. "Rumba!," he says. I don't know how to play a rumba without the patterning of the *clave*, so something else comes out. Everyone is perplexed. Stéphane laughs loudly. On the other hand, as Pierre says, "It plants a seed." Later Stéphane insists: "I'm going to play the *Hannya Shingyo* like a rumba," and he explains to me that the *clave* doesn't matter. The continuity of the *mokugyo* is enough. He's right—a question of mental habits, but rhythm isn't mental. It's something else.

Fiesta: Stéphane finds himself in charge of the music. He presses the keys for sounds and observes the effects they have on the dancers. He smokes his tobacco. Alga and I are dancing a tango-bolero with Descemer's music. I sense how a rose takes shape between us. She plays shy but moves like a cat. Stéphane calls me over without saying a word. "You have to go to Cuba," and he widens his eyes like some ancient bird. "Don't worry about the money," and then, "Where do you want to go?" I think about Greece. I hesitate a second but can't put my finger on it: "To Cuba," I respond. Same thing. We say goodbye. *Gassho*, tomorrow will be another day, and another year.

# 2005

A very informal breakfast. Final *zazen*, short but sweet.

Collecting our things again. Goodbyes. Pierre set a date for Barcelona.

Cristina accompanies me, and we travel from Girona with The Turk and Ana from Madrid. She tells us that people from Madrid call people born there, to *madrileño* parents, "cats." She isn't a cat because of her father. It's like a tale about native Hollanders. They go on to Madrid, and we meet Pierre, who is waiting.

When we arrive in the city we get lost, but the ramble with suitcases helps to wake up our bodies and minds.

More about the monumental welcome from Pierre and Gabriela. Whenever there is some kind of frugal abundance, Pierre says, "*C'est Byzance.*" Indeed, this way of becoming a prince with a little bit of wine, a cigar, a few words and two or three smiles updates our idea of what is Byzantine. Excess? Lack? Neither one nor the other: "*C'est Byzance*" and that's good enough.

Today at noon César Mora arrives with his friend, Hook the Dog, and we go out to see Parc Guell, which glitters in the sun like a rhapsody of broken bottles. It has a certain zoolike air. There's no shortage of animals, of course, or varieties. But we're especially drawn to the *pulpo a la gallega*, the Galician octopus that César is offering us, so off we go. It's a bit of a walk. Sometimes we're thoughtful, sometimes euphoric. Little by little we approach the Gràcia area, its market, and at Pierre's place we'll watch a film: *Sato Ichi*. It lacks the panache of the older films but presents the same blind violence. *Appunto*.

We approach the Gothic Quarter. Cristina leaves tonight to go back to Amsterdam. César and I empty a bottle of red Spanish wine with Pierre: tsunami, Martí and Cuba. That's what we talk about. I have two homelands, and it's midnight.

**4.**

Tonight we invite Pierre to watch Kurosawa's *Seven Samurai*. You have to see Pierre sitting there, silent. He doesn't like martial arts, but when the youngest samurai goes walking down the hill, Pierre exclaims: "That man is a ballet dancer!" As we go off to sleep, he asks me to go out tomorrow after he finishes work.

**5.**

I have breakfast with Pierre, who leaves for his job as a gardener. Like Monsieur Le Notre, Louis XIV's landscaper, César remembers. The one who put a slug on his coat of arms. At noon I cook Cuban food: rice, black beans, yucca and sweet potato. A farmer's meal. César helps me with the shopping. He knows who has the soft rice, the freshest foods, and all of the vendors know his taste. Cuban. Talking with him, I realize that this is a new era. The one that officially started with the death and resurrection of Christ has ended. As César is commenting on the millenarian movements "preceding our own era," he bursts out, "That's not our era anymore."

Pierre and I go to the Blues Bar in Gràcia. The street is filled with people, as though it were summertime. He sees in me going in a direction clearly marked as "Cuba." Conversation about sailors.

These past nights Pierre has given me lessons in music appreciation. Transforming himself into a DJ and master of ceremonies, he makes me listen to a sort of extended symphony: Steve Lacy, Brigitte Bardot whispering "*Je t'argentinisairé!*," Don Cherry, King Crimson, James Brown, Guy March- and who howls "*l'Appassionata!*" Today we say goodbye in the right way: 'til next time.

The year 2005. Reigned, according to the horoscope, by Changó and his consort Oyá. Sigfredo Ariel gives me to know this, again, from Havana. And with those influences, a waltz: *My Gondolences*.

## LUNES

School, by bike. The teacher proposes to create a booklet with participation from the students. An A4 college: a souvenir. For example, a map of time, a photocopy of your residency card, European Zen Center sticker, Dutch sea cartoon, map of A'dam, drawing from school of teacher Jacinta, drawing from school of teacher de Vries, poem and *vertaling*: "Victory of the Disobedient," *De overwinning van de ongehoorzamen*. Then an oral exam until noon. *Ay Hussein, ay Hussein*!

Rijksmuseum, to visit its library. It's no longer there. It moved to Frans Mierisstraat, near the Pijp and school. Free, well guarded. I can observe prints by Petrus Schenk close up. The pleasure is mine. I should say.

Pieter Schenk. Elberfeld, 1660-A'dam, 1718. *Graveur*, according to the *Allgemeines Lexicon Der Bildenden Kunstler*, published in Leipzig, an expensive city for an actual artist. Between engravings and mezzotints his repertoire varies: saints and biblical scenes, acrobats and tumblers and kings. Landscapes, vessels, ports. I look for the port of Havana.

It doesn't appear in *Hollstein's Dutch & Flemish Etchings, Engravings & Woodcuts* (A'dam, 1981). What do appear are three mezzotints dedicated to blessed Saint Barbara. Rubenesque, at the entryway to a tower; by the balustrade, Saint Barbara Martyr Fortis; on her knees before the landscape, the tower to her right. Later on, *maris ingredientibus*, great ships in the calm. Also an Indian chief, Tee Yee Neen Ho Ga Ron, leader of the Six Nations. Schenk is tireless: even a portrait of Portocarrero! — Luis Manuel, the Spanish cardinal. The prologue warns that *most of his prints are not of his own invention*. They're adaptations from other artists.

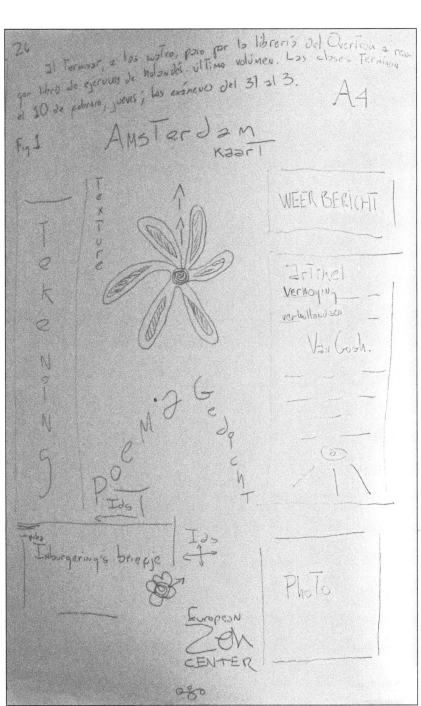

26

Al terminar, a las cuatro, paso por la librería del Overtoon a recoger libro de ejercicios de holandés, último volumen. Las clases terminan el 10 de febrero, jueves; los exámenes del 31 al 3.

A4

Fig 1

Amsterdam
Kaart

Tekening

Texture

WEER BERICHT

Artikel
Verhoging
verhollandsen

Van Gogh.

Poem Gedacht

Poem
Ids

Inburgering's briefje

Ids

Photo

European Zen CENTER

*"Rijksmuseum" journal page*

Martes 18 de enero,                                              27

      tras el zazen, spijbellen.
      sexuellement spijbellen. Tras el zazen.
      boelets al kashmir Lounge, cerca de casa.
      Ik werk aan het vertaling;
      La Victoria de los desobedientes.

Al mediodía me voy al RijksMuseum, a visitar su biblioteca. Nueva, se ha
mudado a la Frans MarisStraat, cerca del Pijp y de la escuela Gatis,
bien protegida. He observado de cerca los grabados de Schenck. Finalmente
el gato es mío. Deh, deur.

Pieter Schenck. Elberfeld 1660 - Amsterdam, 1718.
Graveur, según el Allgemeines Lexicon Der Bildenden Künstler, o enciclo-
pedia de artistas plásticos publicada en 1936 en Leipzig, ciudad cara al propio
artista. Entre grabados y medias Tintas, el repertorio es variado: santos y
escenas bíblicas, acróbatas y saltimbancuis. reyes y compaña. Paisajes, navíos,
puertos. Busco el de La Habana.

    En el Hollsteins *Dutch & Flemish Etchings, Engravings & Woodcuts* no aparece;
aparecen sí, tres medias Tintas dedicadas a Santa Bárbara bendita: a la
manera de Rubens, a la puerta de la Torre, junto a la balaustrada, Santa
Barbara... Martyr. Fortis.; de rodillas ante el paisaje, la Torre a la derecha.
Más adelante, maris ingredientibus, grandes naves en calma. Y También
un jefe indio, Tee Yee Neen Ho Ga Row, capo de las seis naciones. Ina-
gotable Schenck, probablemente hijo de Shangó.

    Hasta un retrato de Portocarrero! Luis Manuel, cardenal español.

    Se advierte en el prólogo que "most of his prints are not of his own invention"
sino adaptacoones de otros artistas. Visitante en La Habana. Tal vez, por el internet
de Los grabados. Pero Schenk es alabado, sobre todo, como impresor, en la época.

*Adam, 1981

"Rijksmuseum" journal page

A visitor to Havana, yes, but thanks to an internet of prints. Schenk is respected, above all, as a printer during Holland's golden age of cartography. The same time when Exquemelin travels to Cuba, a translator bandit. Would they have met? Did Exquemelin serve Schenk for his mapmaking, when he was tracking cows around the Caribbean? Butcher and doctor.

I notice three pipe smokers and those two women, Mozarabs, who face each other as though caressing each other: solemnly. Effigies that describe "*afectionum animi,*" actually policing them. They register mingled facial movements through coordinates that are practically millimetrical. Tranquility, stupor, rage: all reflected as if in a study of criminal anthropology. Fernando Ortiz would have enjoyed them. Titles in four languages: Latin, Dutch, German, and French. And so *la laetitia* is *la Ioye*, is *de vreugt*, is *Die Freude*, is *la joie*.

### MIERCOLES 19

School. Cleaning at Jeroen's measured in time: two and a half hours. In a moment over coffee, Jeroen warns, "You cannot fight water. In the end water will always win." Which, when said by a Dutchman, has a particular resonance. On the other hand, he says, "We'll get it all fixed up." With the certainty of someone who has always lived on the water: "We'll turn Amsterdam into a houseboat." A *woonboot*. It's not a bad idea. We were talking about global warming, which now they're calling a global dimming, the dimming of the winter and migrations. Maybe the Dutch will become a nomadic population in the future, definitively Flying Dutchmen.

### JUEVES

Half *zazen*: whole *zazen*. School: *discussie over religieuze feestdagen*. Discussion centers around the Muslim request for official recognition of its religious celebrations in Holland. There are four Christian ones: *Kerstmis*, or Christmas, *Pasen*, Easter, *Pinksteren*, the Pentecost, and *Hemelvaart*, Ascension. It seems that many people no longer know the real meaning of the festivals today, so they're pure style or social inertia. In the case of Muslims, there are two: the sugar festival at the conclusion of Ramadan, and the holiday for victims. Arguments in favor: Muslims are part of Dutch society, these festivals are part of their tradition and express their culture and spirituality. Arguments against: Holland is not a Muslim nation but a Christian one, too many holidays are bad for the economy, it's not fair to other minority religions, Muslims don't live in small provincial towns, just in the big cities. Despite being a true statistic, the last argument doesn't seem to help reason out the real issues. As for the two earlier ones, they contradict each other: if Muslims are not a mere "minority" in Holland but an important group in the social body, so much that their economic contribution is noticeable, all the more reason to give official legitimation to their religious festivals.

Emil, a Czech student who is moderating today's discussion, inquires whether in Morocco the Christian holidays are official too. He argues that there are 15 million people in Holland and "just" a million who are Muslim. Then he lays out a theory of the steps: first, the Muslims arrive in Holland. Then they want to build mosques and practice their faith. Now they demand the right to celebrate their holidays with official sanction and finally, he says, they'll want to bring Osama Bin Laden, the new Antichrist, to Holland. Here I can't restrain myself, due to the flavor of that incitement: "*Dat is een fascistisch argument!*," I tell him. Emil, by the way, does volunteer work in an old folks' home.

Irritated, I go off to Space Mountain to talk with Joseph the Israelite, who is especially fiery today: "Bush, fuck fuck fuck." Then he calms down. A young woman from Kosovo shows up to ask for money. Her paper creased with badly written Dutch, her head covered in the Muslim manner. "*Salaam*," she says at the bar of the coffeeshop. I give her a Euro. You, Joseph, you give her three.

Do you believe in the chosen people? I ask him.

"And, what is that?"

"For example, the Israelite or Israelis."

"I don't know. But if such a thing exists, it is to help other people, not to kill them in the name of a god."

In De Balie that afternoon I meet the Chilean poet Ricardo Cuadros. We exchange poems. His are outpourings in his native tongue: "The horizon of these poems lies in Holland," he says in his prologue. He's a friend of Paul Loomans, from their years in Paris.

## MIÉRCOLES

After *zazen*, not school but the *Bibliotheek* in the *Rijks Museum*. The library's curator of prints, Huigen Leiflang, is waiting for me. We get right to it: Schenk, and Havana on the table: a reproduction printed by a Cuban Institute dedicated to friendship with other mations.

Curator: "*Dit lijkt wel een detaille van iets groter*," this seems like a detail from something larger.

Me to myself: "*Zeker! Het is een detaille van iets groter*," thinking about the connection between two nations and two times.

Anyway, in this library—"and this is very strange," mutters Leiflang, there is no presence or news of Schenk's engraving. There's a chance, *un kans*, he says, of finding it in the series of 100 impressions called *Profile Views of Cities Throughout the World; Hecatompolis sive totius orbis terrarum,* with a commemorative mezzatinto for Prince Frederick Wilhelm. For this, I should keep searching in the Amsterdam Historisch Museum, as well as the library at the University of Leiden, where I've been one time thanks to Nanne Timmer. In brief, looking at Schenk's engraving,

> *Al centro el Morro y la Punta, con su cadena*
> *un galeón, 4 barcas.*
> *una montaña a lo lejos*
> *la ciudad y la intemperie*
> *oh, perspectiva marinera,*
> *oh, mano alzada sobre olas simétricas.*

*las iglesias parecen holandesas*
*el Morro molino de viento*
*y las gaviotas, gaviotas.*

[Morro Castle and the fort at La Punta in the center, with their chain
a galleon, four boats.
a mountain in the distance
the city open to the sky
oh, marine perspective,
oh, hand raised above symmetrical waves,
the churches seem to be Holland's churches
the Morro a windmill
and the seagulls, seagulls.
oh, marine perspective.]

Huigen inquires about my interest. I talk to him about De Kooning and Mies van der Roer—the one and his designs for the Bacardi family, the other and his 1959 Havana outskirts.

*"Van der Roer is een Duitse. De Kooning...Wilhelm? Hij is niet echt een Nederlander, maar ... ja!"*

De Kooning, a native of Rotterdam, isn't really Dutch? Murmuring, Huigen Leiflang offers a consolation prize: the maps by Johannes Van Keulen and a drawing by Bonaventura Peeters: "The Sail of the Spanish Fleet from Havana." The conservation of these pieces, all from the 17th century, is impressive. These maps are ready for new navigations, their drawings and engravings fresh.

On a map for Mediterranean navigation, the name of Crete stands out: Candia. On a map of ancient Mexico and the Caribbean, you can see the vast territory, today lost, of the *Terra Apachorum*. Finally, a chart of the *Zuyd Kust van Cuba* and all of Jamaica, 1687. Printed in Amsterdam and sold by the *Nieuwe brugh*, or new bridge. The rendition of the Sierra Maestra recalls one of those Taoist mountain drawings: lines calming themselves.

As for Bonaventura Peeters, *uitseyle van de galions ... havana 1662*: out-sailing. The Morro Castle and la Punta are off to the right, almost the same height. Four galleons and various boats at the entrance to the port. A blurry sea, a strong breeze, a city in the distance more compact than the one by Schenk: however, the image is an analogue. The galleons pick up supplies, they leave. The drawing is spanned by three vertical lines and one horizontal. A sign that at some point it traveled folded up in the Flying Dutchman's pocket.

### Viernes 28 d'enero. The apostle's birthday

I go to school in search of De Kooning. I can't find *Suburb in Havana*, but I do find a small series "on waves": Waves 1, Waves 2, which look like Zen inkwashes. He also has a yellow pirate and a variety of portaits depicting women. Abstract or figurative? Born in Rotterdam (1904), died in Long Island (1997). A student at the Academie van Beeldende Kunsten from age16 to 24. Emigrant to the U.S., a New Jersey house painter, a New York abstract expressionist. In '68 he returns to Amsterdam for a retro-spective. A precursor to action painting, a student of the urban landscape: that's where his Havana suburb comes from.

> *Andar el mundo como un perro*
> *tallado en un hueso de perro tallado*
> *en un hueso de perro*
> *tallado*
> *en un hueso de perro.*
>
> [Wandering the world like a dog
> carved on a dogbone carved
> on a dogbone
> carved
> on a dogbone.]

At 3 I go to the Kashmir Lounge for a break. I ask why the mint tea costs 20 cents more than the other ones. Mint's spiritual qualities? As

I'm leaving, some young men question me. It's the Oud West, a neighborhood of impulsive foreigners. The boys, maybe Turkish, Moroccan like the mint, call me *pooier* and *homo*. *Pooier* is sort of like *chulo*, which often refers to a pimp in Spanish. I don't know how, but they've mistaken me for a gigolo lost out here, far from the historic, touristic, and prostitution sector. Or maybe they're just trying to shake up their afternoon, or to exercise a democratic taste for giving offense. I move away without talking back to them, walking off toward the *Open Bibliotheek*: a reading of poets from southern Amsterdam. There are four of them, three men and one woman.

I try to follow the thread of the poetry with my foot. There's definitely rhythm. Sometimes like a waltz, sometimes like a rap. First, I clap for them. Then at the end I identify myself: Translator, Show Me Thy Documents. Two of them give me their books of poetry; the other, a biography of Dylan Thomas in 127 pages: the first one in Holland.

We live surrounded by birds and don't even notice.

> can you bridle a bird?
> can you sit on an eagle and say
> *naar Centraal Station, alsjeblieft?*

### LUNES 31

Dutch language exam. *Spreken*: talking with the machine. Like talking on the radio, no babbling. You pay attention to the language of the questions and, whenever possible, you cite that text directly. Then the beep! Until you have done twenty questions. Forty minutes.

At three thirty I work on a catalogue of translation businesses taken from the internet, eliminating and perfecting until I get down to 10, to begin my essspiriment:

The Language Lab. Elan Language, "experts in Language." Foreignaffairs. nl. A.R.T. translation services, *kunst*. Tekstwerk, which says, "Translators can't be good if they are not also good writers," *voilà*. Adept Translators, "in this era of globalization, quality, price & speed." WYO Talen Nederland. UvA Vertalers, university. La Puerta, *"literaire en culturele vertalingen."* Jomadu, *"jong en dynamisch Spaanse taal contact."*

It's about making contact, sending forms, resumés, etc. Playing the lottery in the *werk market*: light a candle for Archangel Saint Raphael.

## Martes 1ro de febrero

*Zazen. Lezen* exam, reading. 25 questions: 1 hour 45 minutes. Topics: memory, its relationship to the senses, short-term and long-term memory: on remembering. Supposedly Freud said that to forget is to remember oneself. Relation between social position, range, and maternity among gibbon monkeys, something for Malinowski. Dental ailments and age-related behavior. The caloric properties of mint!

From there to the open library in the Prinsengracht. From the large window, the water is green; on the Kostverloren Kade, it looks brown. A matter of light? Thus, *Willem de Kooning* (Harry N. Abrams Inc., New York, 1975, text: Harold Rosenberg).

Born 1904, Rotterdam. At age 22, emigrated as a stowaway. *Polizonte*; house painter, New Jersey: *I don't give a damn about the Pacific*, says De Kooning.

In 1948, teacher at Black Mountain College. Did he meet Robert Creeley? Most probably. Ten years after, visited Venezia. And *l'Abana*, Havana? Anybody is a genius. Painting was a "beard thing" there in Holland: t*he idea of being a modern person wasn't really being an artist* but a designer or commercial artist. Better a house painter in New Jersey than a thing painter in Paris. But, *l'Abana*? Specifically, a recollection of a visit back in 1958. The *new symbol of metamorphosis is the highway: Suburb in Havana,* 80 x 70 (Collection of Mr & Mrs Lee V. Eastman, NY). A recollection of a visit … on what highway did De Kooning find himself? To Fontanar, Los Pinos, Alamar? And when he saw it, what did he see? Three lines, black and far away like windmills, and that splotch might be a yellow palm.

I get a response from Mevrouw Kay at WYO Talen Nederland: my proposal to teach is very nice, but how would one combine their domicile with our facilities? I ask myself the same thing now, Mevrouw. For the moment I fill out their form, send the resumé, listen to Miles Davis, *Birth of the Cool.*

## MIÉRCOLES

*Zazen. Schrijven* exam: writing. Finally! Surprise: in the topics we are to cover, there isn't one single reference to Dutch culture. Or is that itself Dutch culture? Relationship between schedule and the number of automobiles that enter and leave the city of Rotterdam during one working day: comment on the graphics. The construction of a highway next to a southern city, and its economic and ecological effects: real estate depreciation, decimation of green space: write up a short article. Publicity for the sale of new car models, one small and one large: give your positive opinion about how you like both of them. Regarding reasons to buy a new pair of glasses; a new and attractive model? An antique, chic model? More resistent lenses? (than the ones that Spinoza polished): a description based on graphics. Young people with guns at the school entrance: what should be done? Should they be registered? Should security systems be installed? Give your opinion. Opinion, so cherished by humans and, according to Gottfried Benn, never getting to the point. Yet each one of these topics could launch a short essay in Montaigne's style. Or maybe, in combination, one in Adorno's style: "Modern Education and Writing."

A letter of inquiry, *sollicitatiebrief,* to Adept Translators. I reread *Black Sorcerers* by Ortiz: since Ortiz had a decided criminalistic orientation, he flaunted Cuba's official representation at the Fifth Congress of Criminal Anthropology celebrated in Amsterdam. From the prologue by Dr. Isaac Barreal. 1905: De Kooning was a baby. Capablanca had already defeated his father in chess, but not yet Max Euwe, with whom he would play 25 years later in the same city: Capablanca moves the white pieces against Euwe in the round that closes the volume *How Do You Play Chess?* Today I go through Max Euweplein, where the cold doesn't prevent outdoor play with pieces 20 inches tall, and I wonder what Ortiz learned at that Amsterdam congress. Maybe there were already blacks there? Black sorcerers? The first mixed marriage of a Surinamese man and a Dutch woman wouldn't happen until the 1930s, and it was a rarity. Even in the present day, when now several generations of people of color have lived in the so-called "midst of civilization," people still say that there are black thugs who demonstrate unbalanced psychological evolution, and while they are relatively "civilized" in an intellectual sense, they maintain traces of their African morals that launch them into criminality. —Says Ortiz. Today black thugs are plentiful here, like the Surinamese who control the cocaine market, and there are black sorcerers who, like psychics or for-tunetellers, offer services in the classifieds. As for "African" morality, it's the same one that we have in Cuba. It helps us to be a little less enslaved to the Judeo-Christianism that all of us, black and white alike, receive. In the end, wasn't the Indian Hatuey "an uncivilized infidel," and weren't the black revolutionaries "criminals and *manigueros*" in the eyes of the "civilized" Spanish Christians who faced off against them? Their African morality, my African morality.

From *La Perle delle Antille*, by Gallenga, I rediscover this pearl that got Ortiz's attention: "The religion of State, as it exists here, also has no influence over the masses […]" Whether it's an evil that there are few or many priests, that question doesn't interest me. But the fact is that Cubans don't lament the scarcity of religious preceptors.

*C'etait une de ces epoques ou la raison humaine se trouve prise dans un cercle de flammes.* That's how Ms. Yourcenar describes the context for Zeno in *L'Ouvre au Noir*. In Amsterdam, at the home of the blessed merchant Simon Adriansen, the new heretics hold *conciliabules de marins*. Among them is Bernard Rottman, a disciple of Luther. Meanwhile I send a form to WYO Talen Nederland. I work to earn time: time is money. Or vice versa?

Returning to the topic, Norman Cohn says, in search of the Millennium, which the prophetic cloak dropped over a Dutch Anabaptist, the baker from Haarlem named Jan Matthijs. The latter, who died fighting at the front ot thirty men and an army of angels according to Yourcenar, baptized John of Leiden, perhaps the most radical of the Dutch prophets. In this environment, according to Cohn's formulation, one so charged with supernatural hopes, Yourcenar's work *au noir* takes place.

Is the air we breathe in Amsterdam today perfumed with supernatural hopes? At this point, the two men who could aspire to the title of new Dutch prophets have already been sacrificed: Pim Fortuyn, the *politicus carismaticus*, and Theo Van Gogh, the no less daring *kunstenaar*. The first one was shot by an environmentalist. The second, shot by himself, and stabbed by a Muslim fundamentalist to boot. All -isms flourish in fear of the unknown. This is exactly what prophets talk about.

When the dog is dead, is the rabies gone? First they chained John of Leiden for public display, then they tortured and executed him. Keep everything among Christians. When a Muslim with a different opinion intervened to assassinate the revolting Dutchman in a public place, an atheist even, they invoked the "Muslim threat." The threat of reacting to difference with fear, fury, ignorance and impotence has always been among us: dead dog.

*Tabak van hebben*: literal. To have tobacco from something or someone: to be weary. The story of tobacco, putting the tobacco's flame out, in Cuba.

You can't ask the eagle to fly low to the ground, or the mockingbird to sing level with the earth.

All this time in Amsterdam just to learn two things: continuity and rhythm.

*Zazen*. As for the exam in *Luisteren*, listening: a failure. I can understand word by word, complete sentences, but relating that string of phonemes to a meaning, choosing between A, B and C, that's impossible for me, or I just don't care. Sour grapes? Maybe. The topics are still dry, as if in addition to learning the *Batave* language one must go through the weave of social, political, and economic life in Holland tied to the ship's mast, like Odysseus, so as never to disassociate from the Europeanist goal: integration into the fortress. Ithaca?

What is the *Batave* language? *Baatafs*, Batavian, pertaining to the Batavian Republic. And what republic is this?

Mailed translator application to The Language Lab

Back to *bataafs*. What's this language? *Baatafs*, Batavian, pertaining to the Batavian Republic. And what republic is this again?

I reflect on it from the upper level of the Jolly Joker coffeeshop. Across from the Café Cuba at the Nieuw Markt, with a plaza between them. I put the language aside assuming that it's about the *gewoon Nederlands*, simple Dutch. I ascertain that 1793 marks the foundation of the *Legioen Bataafs*, in partnership with the *Republique Francaise*, to fight against national nobility. In 1795 in the Dam, then by the way called Revolution Plaza, *Plein der Revolutie*, the advent of a *Bataafse Republiek* is celebrated. France recognizes it as a vassal state. In 1798, Joseph Fouché, the embassador of the *Republique Francaise*, travels to Holland for secret negotiations, according to Zweig, and he achieves "quick successes." But Bonaparte is even quicker at crushing both republics.

I still have the same questions about *bataafs*: is it a community, a culture, or just an ideological trend rescued in the hectic times of revolution?

Encyclopedias are good for some things: *Kroniek van Nederland*, from the publishing assocation AGON Elsevier—for which the deceased Pim Fortuyn once worked as a columnist:

In the time of Caesar, the Batavians lived on humid land between the Mass and the *Oude Rijn*, the Old Rhin, near what today is the city of Nijmegen. They were just one of the many tribes who occupied the Low Countries. What's the basis for the ancestral revindication? The Greeks, in the person of one Pythius, had arrived here by sea three hundred years before the Romans. The Hellene navigated 10,000 nautical miles to disembark on the coasts of the *Nord Zee* around 350 AC. He called this area *Metuonis* and the people living there the *Guionen*, probably a Teutonic clan. What brought Pythius from the sunny Marseille to the North Sea? Maybe the feats of Perseus, traveling to the Antipodes, to prepare his mission against Medusa among the people of the far north. Perseus traveled using the winged sandals stolen from the Nymphs, and under the tutelage of Hermes. Pythius put his trust into Poseiden, and Hermes too, since without this partnership no voyage is possible: Hermes / Elegguá.

**LUNES 7**

> *Piet Heijn*
> *Piet Heijn*
> *Piet Heijn, zijn naam is klein*
> *zijn daden bennen groot.*
> *Hij heeft gewonnen de zijlvervloot!*

A popular song in Holland. Piet Heijn (1577-1629): small name, great feats. He captured Spain's Fleet of La Plata. A treasure fleet from Perú by way of Panamá. Thanks to this feat, the Dutch West Indian Company acquires cargo valued at 12 million florins, and Matanzas Bay erupts into Dutch engravings.

School: *gespreek over de Cursus*. Now that it's about to end, our recommendations: *Meer Cultuur!* Not just formulas for social survival, which are also *cultuur*, a point not to be doubted. The teacher advises, if you want to perfect your Dutch, look for someone who wants to learn it. A task worthy of Perseus.

**9**

To *zazen* by bicycle. Coffee with friends, then to school: the final lesson with the illustrious Ids de Vries:

*Als je te veel schrijft, gaat de kwaliteit achteraaf,* he says. It can be taken as advice: write too much and you'll leave quality behind. The lesson ends, and I give him some of my poems translated into English, courtesy of Kris Dijkstra. "Dijkstra?" Her surname is Frisian.

**JUEVES**

*Zazen.* School, our last day: diplomas given out, cake eaten. Each student receives a rose. The teacher Jacinta Raadschelders informs us that throughout the program, about 500 exams were given. Back at the *dojo*, I put my rose by the image of Bodhidharma taking off the *kesa*.

I set myself to the vile job of looking for a job. Through the window I see ships passing by: there's one called *Koophandel IV*, Commerce IV!

Reading *Che. El camino del fuego*, by Orlando Borrego, who worked with him in the Ministry of Industry. You can observe a Guevarian asymptote as if from a watchtower.

*Je n'ai pas l'etoffe de la vals viennoise.* Chopin, 1830.

The cold, and the perpetual humidity, cause my fractures to remember me. At night the temperature goes up, so windows can be opened. I go out to walk through the neighborhood. Elderly Turks are talking on the corner; I drink a couple of beers at the snack bar where two Moroccans consult their cell phones; a Dutch family unloads furniture from a pickup truck, blocking the way, etc. The night is cool. You can hear a flute.

### LUNES

I rise at 8. *Zazen*, and I leave to go to the CWI: *Centrum voor Werk en Inkomen*, work and income, according to the prerogative of the recent graduate, *inburgerizado nieuwkommer*. Mukti Abdusalam, the young woman who receives me politely, indicates that www.werk.nl is the next door on which to knock. Like a Playstation game called Work Force, knock and it will open for you, send your resumé and it will put you into the database.

### MIERCOLES 16

*Zazen*. I stay at the *dojo*. Pious readings from Pater Hugo Lasalle, a Jesuit priest: Christians discover Zen.

A German Jesuit, Lasalle served in Hiroshima after the bomb. In *zazen* he discovered "the key to the spirit." The Japanese spirit, he clarifies.

In Zen, he says, the spirit goes to meet God, goes to the very limit of its own possibilities.

Deshimaru was not entirely pleased with this idea.

Since the XVI century the Jesuits had been in Xipango, causing, to say it in passing, all kinds of messes. A portrait of one of these missionaries appears, by the way, in the stained-glass windows of the false-Gothic cathedral on Reina Street, in Havana: burial with Japanese.

From the Japanese, Lasalle received citizenship and a name: Makibi Enomiya. In the vicinity of Tokyo, in a mountainous forest, he founded a Zen *dojo*. 1970.

I work on a new application letter, in which the applicant lists his reasons for working at Mondial Assistance: Do you like to work with groups and help people? Is it a good challenge for you to improve your Dutch and use other languages: *Engels, Frans, Spaans*? Send your application, and within ten days, etc. In this apocalypse, we cats slam our tails in the door!

### Jueves

At night I go to meet up at Café Volta: The Open Stanza. Megan invited me to perform some poems and songs. As agreed, I arrive at 7:30 to test the audio and the *cajón*. There's also an English bard who tests his voice and first verse to see how they sound. I sit down for a beer: poets get free entry and two complimentary beers. When my turn comes, I do four poems, and three songs with the *cajón*. I finish with a ballad by Kimbo: Ocean Wing.

The ambiance is favorable. As always, the troops offer good lyricism and cabaret. Summary of the program: the outrageous host; a quartet of melodic/poetic jazz called Soup, with a lady who sings to the contrabass, drums, sax, and piano; a Dutch *dichter*; Tsead, a Frisian poet with a beautiful, almost Scandinavian sound; the British bard; and a DJ. The *cajón* behaved well.

### Viernes

Negative reply from Mondial Assistance.

Contact with C. Aguilera for an event in Graz, next October. I send out applications: La Puerta & Jomadu: translation bureaus in Hispaniol.

Until noon I work on a painting: NAIF. Portrait of a kitchen knife. Then Cristina kidnaps me to go to Volendam, an ancient fishing village. *Nu niet meer*, not any longer: European regulations render the existence of the small fisherman pointless. These coastal towns depend more and more on tourism, and the pleasure yacht gradually takes the place of the power-boat. The bridges are short and ingenious, bridges with counterweights, occasionally drawbridges if it becomes necessary for something larger than a rowboat to go through.

Dril Brug is a bridge like this, green and solid, with a date: 1976, and in the inset is a weeping willow, dry and yellow.

On the shore of the gigantic harbor is a tiny house with windows all around: the Praathuis, a house for talking. Not a café or a bar, but simply a little house made for conversation. Although there's no poster, none is needed. Men are the soloists here. The women talk in the store, for example the seafood market, where we taste the local *haring*. It's excellent, practically flaking apart on the white bread, and the archaic flavor of the pickle is right on point. Outside it's cold and drizzling. As much as possible, you stay with your back to it when walking and look forward with a certain dignity. Otherwise it weighs you down. Cristina tells me that her family taught her to do this when she was a girl. In these towns I truly feel far from home, lost in space and time. So that is Volendam, and its people are friendly.

<hr />

Lately, every time I go through Max Euweplein, I dream about staging the Euwe/Capablanca match. The one from Amsterdam in 1930.

<hr />

The perfect man is the immovable cause. *The Hermit's Treatise.*

<hr />

When I was living in my original self and my eternal essence, there was no God for me.

I wanted to be who I was, and the one I wanted to be, I was.

Through my own free will I emerged and changed into what I am.

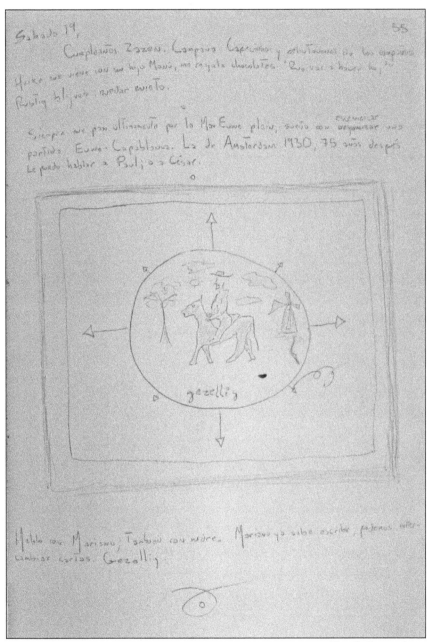

*"Gezellig" journal page*

I had no need to change myself into anything; if I had wanted to do so, I would not become a creature.

So God can't know, can't want, can't do anything without me.

With God I've created myself and all things, and my hand holds up the skies and the earth and all creatures …

Without me, nothing exists.

Brother of the Free Spirit. Brabant, XIV century.

And in Brabant, five centuries later, Van Gogh would be born.

I make a phone call to the builder from Cleves, Ralph Peters. We talk about this floating life. I remind him that he's the one who taught me, there in Tuscany, to clean my tools every afternoon after the workday ends. Let's meet up, he says.

**MARTES**

Emails: translations into the Spanish. Kris Dijkstra; Kent Johnson. Dream & Charcoal: *Sueño y Carbón*. I write this translation.

> *Y entonces ella dijo: he ido hacia la luz y me hice hermosa.*
> *Y entonces ella dijo: he tomado un par de alas y las pegué a las diversas retro-partes de mi cuerpo.*
> *Y entonces ella dijo: todos los invitados están volviendo adonde estaban y entonces hablan.*
> *A lo cual ella dijo: sin mango para agarrarla, cómo puedes reconocer mi desnudez?*
> *A lo cual ella replico: sin nada es cuando mueren todas las cosas.*
> *Que es cuando ella sostuvo una loca batalla con las ramitas.*

*Que es cuando el carbón pasó de su cuerpo al mío.*
*Que es como ella ascendió hasta los cielos, cegando a los peatones.*
*Que es como nuestra unión fue traspuesta a un garabato oscuro.*
*Que devino la hija llamando, mi nombre para despertarme.*

⚜

Jomadu responds: I send resumé

Nothing.

### MIERCOLES 23

*Zazen* with *quatre chats*. It's snowing. We go through the Jordaan, the nine little streets and three noble canals: Lords' Canal, Emperor's Canal, Prince's Canal, with its library and steamy gatherings.

Answer from La Puerta: *helaas, niet. Misschien in de toekomst*, etc. The future.

### JUEVES

Summing up millenarianisms, and the *ad libitum* conversations with Gaspar Guevara, *adviseur* on these and other topics, for him friendly ones. I discuss them with him.

"*Deus le volt*! King Tafur and his sacred cardsharps: a gentleman making rules who switched sides. In sum, from Provence to Syria and Palestine, they are the same faces."

"Long hair, bare feet, I remember Cuba's revolutionaries. Trading my beer for your *vin*."

"Agreed: King Tafur has the emblem of Saint Spear, coincidentally typical of Saint Andrew, patron saint of Amsterdam ..."

"By which you mean?"

"Saint Andrew appeared to a farmer in Provence, I mean. And, is this Jerusalem! Mokum, garden of the North …"

"*Nsallah malekum.*"

"*Malekum nsallah*: The King thinks he believes in God and obeys the rituals, but at the same time he's calling Muslims 'sons of bitches,' 'the race of Cain,' so there it is."

"Millenarian is hate, the poet said, and all the hype about a second Charlemagne: Changó gonna come."

"Don't forget the four lines of the *copla*:  When Bolivar was born
Venezuela sent up a shout
Thinking the one who came out
Was the very Christ reborn"

"And?"

"Crossroads, geopolitical *coplas. Miroir des simples ames.*"

"I'm not copying you, brother."

"Don't bother. Even Gardel hopes for the second coming."

"'*Volver con la frente marchita.*' Weariness: In the field I cleared, they let weeds grow freely, as Father Varela used to say. Spiritual matrimony is possible in weeds too."

"Salute! Hate among the religious is the thorn stabbing humanity's evolutionary spine."

"Long live Spinoza, who perfected lenses to improve our vision. Between heresy and sin, man remains subject to man, and there's no wolf who can fit through the eye of the needle. If you finish your beer quickly, I'll take you deep into the port so that you can see the spoils of divine Amsterdam."

"What are you talking about?"

"Boats that don't move anymore, residences for the latest sailors. Anabaptists of asphalt, flint, and indigenous hemp."

"Slovakia is a great example of what can happen when people are set free": Bush meets Putin in Bratislava.

## VRIJDAG 2

I work on translations of poems by Merik Van der Torren, and I read *Dylan Thomas* by Karel Wasch. In the afternoon, I go to the lesson in Sabar with Lamine. In the same place as always, he shows me the basics:

> *Ngadef*
> How are you, in Woloff:
> *Pa'da pan pan*
> *Pa'da pan pan*

which I execute with a drumstick made out of a wooden coat hanger: Right hand does syncopation, left hand rests. He brings his drumstick from Senegal: "Special place, special tree, special time." Maybe for me too: Amsterdam, coat hanger, February.

> Everyone keeps talking about my drink
> but nobody is talking about my thirst
> Everyone says I'm too attached to this drink
> but nobody mentions the attachment that's got me
> My thirst
> Everyone talks about my love for the drink
> Nobody talks about the love thirst has for me
> My thirst.

—According to a poem by CAESAR,
homeless in Amsterdam

243

The canal froze. Seagulls play above it. They perch, they walk. If you stop looking for a moment, they all disappear. Finally a boat named Zaandam breaks the ice, and the seagulls return, curious. Three barges pass by:
Casa Nova
Co Trans
and the ever-present Vincent, with a frog as its figurehead.

I revise my draft of "Science, Poetry & Religion," as it was given at the *Universitá di Milano*. The visions: *The Papalagi*, Erasmus, Robert Duncan on science, *Paradiso* and the *Tao of Physics*. Dante's Canto XVII:

> *lo naturale e sempre sanza errore*

From the Nahuatl: No one has a permanent home on earth. Only flowers and songs! From the Zen poets to Calderón: Life is dream. Mediterranean synthesis, Cuba and the night, like a poetry radio program, like a renga:

| | |
|---|---|
| Introductions to poetry | poetical means |
| Philosophy | *cadavre* exquisite & science fiction |
| Myth | the seasons and the cardinal points |
| epopeia & science | the diary & the navigation logbook |

### JUEVES 3 MARZO

Elan Languages answers: *Formulier Nieuwe Vertaler, woordprijs vermelden.* Price per word: 15 cts.

*Vrieze punt: sneuw.* The coldest night in March in recorded history: -19°.

### VRIJDAG 4

I take the slow trolley toward the station at Sloterdijk for the state examination in *Lezen-Luisteren*. Neither easy nor hard. In the evening, under the snow, I take my soul to Lamine for rhythmic training. *Sabar, djembé, cajón.* Perfect! Lamine asks me to sing some songs "from your land":

*Nsusu Ndamba*
*Yo mismo Palo Yaya*
*Cuenda Ndokito*
*Erisi Baluande*

### ZATERDAG 5

Z. From the *dojo* to another site for the *Staats Exam*, in the *Centrum*, a building at the *Universiteit: Spuistraat. Schrijven en Spreken, maar ...* This is not writing or speaking, just reacting, taking notes, even commenting: *bespreken.* They'll know writing, these teachers of clocks and machines, in this theater of a police academy: "*Dames en heren, jullie hebben nog vijfteen minuten.*" The voice of a presenter of burials. Recap: writing better than I expected; speaking, worse. Bullshit, the transmitter doesn't betray, being able to say something into the microphone, intimate and cordial, is exciting. Casual, sort of like a blues song. Babel Bauhaus.

Disposable dictatorship: notes on a transitional model of government. Reflections based on Dutch & Scandinavian Politics and the current actualization of dictatorial models in Asia and Latin America.

*Toerental:* revolutions per second.

### MIÉRCOLES

*Zazen.* Alga returns from Argentina. She laughs at my beard. She says I look like a *zwerver*, a beggar. "Thank you." As for the "beggar's mentality": wanting to possess something superfluous. Something that's out of reach or out of one's way. Even to go so far as turning away from it, in order to achieve the thing one dreams about, and to end up begging for alms from life, after abandoning the fundamental terrain of existence.

And so, Gaspar, we'll meet at Barney's, with Christophe. He will understand our dialogue, even in *lingua franca*, since an Italianate Breton dominates our jargon. The music sticks. Gaspar breathes the *chilong* like a natural. Aerodynamic servers come and go like soundwaves: Don Miguel tries everything they have and blends it, improvising: *bulerías* and provençalisms.

Christophe: Therefore, to have few desires?

Gaspar: *Shoyoku*, says the Buddhist. I was in Nepal. A volute under the influence.

Me: Where did you get that reference from?

Gaspar: Don't underestimate the gypsies. To have few desires, not like you begging now for work and money you didn't need in Cuba. Volute in the face.

Christophe: In Assisi there's a temple eager for …

Gaspar: Don't interrupt. Have few desires. New volute.

The documentary *Benigno* in Nederland 3: directed by Marlou van der Berge & Lisa Arias: the story of an illiterate farmer who became a hero as a guerrilla fighter, but who spends his final days as a disillusioned emigrant in Paris. Benigno with his frayed French: "*Un té, sivuplé.*" Benigno with the useless guerrilla radio. Benigno looking for a job as a plasterer." *C'est très calme maintenant, monsieur, désolée.*"

6:50 p.m. I take the sabar and sticks, the winter *cajón*, and I go to Lamine's to practice *le rhythme*. *Padan padanpanpanpan*: Lamine has nowhere to stay and nowhere to work. At the end I invite him over to have a coffee and use the telephone. "You have to keep the rhythm, otherwise you lose your heart here."

**SÁBADO**

Baby-sitteraggio with Elia. Sometimes we go to the park at the Noorder Kerk, where the prince's canal comes to the corner at its end, or its beginning. Relaxed. Elia loves "la lotta." Also cartwheels, stories, and gibberish. Whenever it's sunny, we go to the park.

New information from Cordula Quadt about a small translation bureau in Leiden *dat op Spaans is gespecialiseerd.* Fine, but *op dit moment is het vrij stil.* A euphemism: *stil.* I remember Benigno looking for work in Paris: "*C'est très calme.*" *Très calme*! For whom?

*Lost in Babel* is a website of useful things for translators. For example, it has dictionaries. From one specializing in anthropology:

> Sampling error: In population genetics, the transmission of a nonrepresentative sample of the gene pool over space and time due to chance (!) See also founder principle & genetic drift. www.webpersonal.net/dmarques/resources/index.htm.

Today there's no sun. From 1:30 to 6:60, Elia and I swordfight and watch movies. Too many, perhaps, says mom.

Elia speaks Italian with me, with his mother and mother's family; French with his father; and in asylum, Dutch. Thanks to Walt Disney, he picked up some words in English. He has not yet turned four. He's strong as a Breton and says *toujours* he will be *un cavaliere.* With the mask, or without it. With his pink phosphorescent sword in hand, which he uses to give great whacks. *Attento*, Elia!

The good thing about this occupation of caring for children is that you get therapy and they even pay you. It's really a stipend for learning about kids.

Den Hague has a clockwork orange feel about it, the Fritz Lang capitol. Ministerial and timid. Spinoza's sepulcher. Looking through the arcade of the glass & steel bulk of the Ministry of Living and Environment, the staircase of the train station opens theatrically. Behind it, towers on other ministries give it an imperial touch. It's an ampitheater for Batman.

Van Gogh, who made his first forays into the shelter offered by art sales and the Haagse school here—how would he feel now between these glass walls? I drink a terrible coffee and wait for Cristina. Who descends and invites me into the bulk. Mr. Kafka works in the office, but the sculpture at the entry has a different feel: man and horse made from discarded wood. Old furniture transformed into one eternal joint, man and steed.

After a stroll through the friendly offices in search of Jeroen Van der Sluis, all three of us leave at the hurried pace of functionaries at lunchtime. In Scallywags, Richard's *restorantito* (Richard is an admirer of Lady D.), we have coffee with chocolate tart amd talk about Game Theory. I don't want to be didactic, Mr. Nash, but is this exactly what happens: what happens happens, and it happens to us all.

We go out into the wind. An elderly bearded man looks at me and spits, "*Snotneus*." Snotnose. This even though I have a beard. Or precisely because I have a beard. "He might be a Merlin," Cristina points out.

**DINSDAG 15**

To Leiden, to Leiden! Today is the talk called "Exiles and Insiles in Cuban Poetry," referring not only to those living outside but those who feel exiled within. Prats Sariol gives the talk for the Hispanic and American Department. Prats surprises me by remembering Mariano, "A very nice, intelligent and ... quick boy," whom he met in la Víbora. He gives me a few clues: to Multatuli, who published *Max Havelaar* in Cuba in 1985, *een tendensromaans*. He also mentions an extensive anthology of Dutch poetry, not very well translated. I manage to forget the title and publisher.

Around fifty students. On the board: Proust, *à la recherche* ... "The only literature in the Spanish language—it makes more sense to talk about literature by languages and not by countries—that maintains the paradox between exile and insile, like turbulence, like a virus, is Cuban literature." And here he turns to Proust, revives the topic of diaspora, the inside/outside division that is "absolutely external to literature. This virus is extralinguistic and extraliterary."

He refers to the absurdity of the question, "Are you a Cuban from Cuba?" as if asking a Dutch person, "Are you a Dutch person from Holland?" I remember that conversation with Huigen Leeflang about De Kooning, Dutchman of New York.

"What matters," he says, "is the book's publication date, not the author's age. And don't erase Proust from the board, because it's bad luck." (Laughter) I forgot now why Proust was there, but the speaker brings up a comparison with a poem by Gastón Baquero. "Marcel Proust Sails Past in Corinth Bay." And he memorizes generations: The *Orígenes* group, Lezama, Cintio, Fina, Gastón, Eliseo. Young people from the Cayo: Roberto Fdez Retamar, Fayad, Baragaño, Francisco de Oráa y Padilla. The conversationalists. The others. The youngest ones: 1960–1970. Characteristic of these four generations is critical eclecticism. Colloquialism and sonnet, the *décima* and orality, *rajando la leña están*.

> *Olé!*
> *confluye la incertidumbre*
> *muy raro el palo, el poema, el joven*
> *poema sobre poemas:*
> *incertidumbre en Francia,*
> *parece en Rusia también*
> *la miscelánea, la miscella y el miscuglio*

[*Olé!*
uncertainty converges
strange stick, strange poem, strange youth
a poem about poems:
uncertainty in France,
in Russia too it seems
miscellany, miscella and *miscuglio*]

Let's see, then, the poems …

From *Fuera de juego* (*Thrown Out of the Game*) he cites

> *Se pasa el dia entero cavilando*
> *ese malhumorado del verano*
> *siempre le sedujeron las catástrofes*
> *canta, entre dientes, la Guantanamera*
> *sonrie, abre la boca.*
> *Despídanlo, ese no tiene aquí*
> *nada que hacer.*

> [He spends the whole day pondering
> surly in the summertime
> catastrophes always seduced him
> through his teeth he sings "Guantanamera"
> he smiles, he opens his mouth.
> Send him away. Here there's nothing
> for him to do.]

which I cite *ad libitum*, abridged version. "This is a decisive book," he says. "I'm not going to erase Proust. With this book there's a canon-agon relationship, to use the categories of Harold Bloom." Bilingual poem:

> canon agon
> harold boom
> *cagón* pluto
> *puto plutón*

"When literary critics use the prefixes 'pre' or 'post,' it means they don't know." Joseph Proust *dixit*. It's over. The students applaud. Poetry: a rhizome in the Jurassic Park of Literature. We go out for a walk through the city of Leiden: Prats, his wife, and two Dutch students who act as our guides: The Romans got this far.

&

After I say goodbye to Proust Sariol, I return to Camino, a large bar-restaurant where professors go. Topics to discuss, the house red wine that isn't so outstanding, the Romantic novel of XIX America, the modern city: imposed and supposed, left and right. Avatars of theory: the Leviathan, the *bon sauvage, Das Übermensch*, from each one according to his job to each one according to his much-ado-about-nothing, and finally Guevara's new man. Theoretical vicissitude of the left: its incongruence with practice.

I return to A'dam by the railroad coda: reality is a field of signs, a force field; knowing the nature and meaning of these is the same as ordering them via one's consciousness.

## MIÉRCOLES

Joel Humbler passes me a text to translate, French to English, from Bio Protekt System: *"une vraie solution fiable et peu onereuse face a la pollution magnetique que nous subissons tous quotidiennement."* 13 illustrated pages in uneven technical language.

Before I leave the *dojo*, Julia Strijland proposes baby-sitteraggio to me twice a week. Two midday times with her children. This afternoon at 3, we get together so that I can meet the older child, Luciano, who is going to play *voetbal* on the grounds of the Amsterdamsche Football Club Ajax: *Ajax toekomst*, the future of Ajax.

The children play on a field divided into four sections, with eight teams. In the interstices the specialists, gray-haired soccer players, take notes. Then they send a note home: "Dear Luciano, you have been accepted for an *opleiding*, education, in the mythical fields, Ajax's fields of glory." Or, "Sorry, Luciano …" Either way, the kids play *voetbal*, and their elders drink beer in the stands. For a moment it's spring.

⊛

Irving, the Visual Arts student who has chosen me as a tutor from Havana, sends me his works. Also his resumé and a photo: Irving smiles while chopping carrots. The drawings are subtle, childlike. I begin my translation for Bio Protekt System. It's about offering a protective advice that attaches to computers, mobile phones, televisions, power lines, etc. The basic scientific theory centers on the difference between biocompatible and bioincompatible electromagnetic waves. Indisputable, unavoidable, impassable, and translatable.

⊛

Topics for a definition of Cuban irreality: —Refutation of commonplaces:

> What will happen in Cuba when Fidel Castro dies? Ask the 99.9% of people who, when talking about Cuba, hop around with futuristic fantasies. Erasure from the great chalkboard; their reflections depart from the present and past perfect tenses, with no *hubieras*: no grammar signaling hypotheticals, regrets, or uncertainties about the past.

> Cuba, an underdeveloped country: this misconception is key. Other evils peel outward from it: the temptation to help, in solidarity or not, that masks one's own participation in the problem. Cuba, the potential utopia. A positive variation on the prior issue. Latin Americanism is the metastasis of nationalism. As you can very well see today in Europe, those nationalist waters drag all this mud along with them.

In the era of the spirit, there are no chosen peoples. No clusters of them either.

In the afternoon I go to an art space, Zal 100, to read my versions of poems by Merik Van der Torren. He's already there, with a face like Silenus. Then Cristina arrives, a surprise to me since she didn't think she could come. He invites us to have a beer. This place offers shelter, cheap food and drink, and wholesale art to the city's pariahs. An Amsterdam-style artists' café. More than twenty poets energize the evening. An aquarium of colorful figures hangs from the ceiling. The kitchen is off to the left with its usual racket, the podium in the center. An oval of drinker-smokers encircles it. The performers are diverse. With guitar, flute, or background music; reading or declaiming; Dylan style (Bob or Thomas); Broadway or language poetry. A mother with her daughter, an adolescent with a pipe, the ex-hippie and the *clochard* with a tattooed face and heavy metal outfit, the truck driver with his gold and emerald cross: white thrash.

Merik and I take turns reading a poem, alternating Dutch and Spanish; in this context we seem very elegant. After we finish, a colleague suggests that we could read again, this time line by line. Days later, talking with Ricardo Cuadros at the Mellow Yellow, he refers to a reading he did at the same place: the poem and the translation in unison, babel. Merik, *a la prochaine*. "*A la prochaine*," he says, shaking our hands.

At ten a.m. I go to Alga's place to work in her garden. The job involves a wooden portico in three pieces. I work with Nacho, who defines himself as *porteño-correntino*, someone partly from a port city in the Southern Cone and partly from the province of Corrientes. These pieces weigh about 50 kilos each. The top is lighter: one foot fitted to the brick cabin by the entryway, the other buried in the garden between the pine and the magnolia. We eat lunch with intervention from Alga's sister, who makes paper and artisan books.

From there I go to De Balie for the launch of a book about Cuba. But I'm already impatient with the first speaker: it opens with a video clip from *Reporters sans frontieres*: a German tourist tries to get through Cuba's customs offices with a newspaper unnoticed under his arm. The metal detector goes off; the customs official, with the face of a bandit straight out of *The Treasure of the Sierra Madre*, snatches the booty. Moral of the story: remember, genteel tourist, that Cuba is a dictatorship without freedom of the press, where independent journalists get thrown into jail. This is the theme of this event. The history of tobacco gets told in many ways, and today I don't feel like hearing any of them.

ZONDAG

*Voy a dormir al dormitorio Apeiron*
wees onschuldig,
ongeduldig, *inocente*
*e impaciente.*
*La figura del héroe durmiente*
*Arturo o Charlemagne*
*tan cara como el champagne*
*al folklore del medioevo*
*me voy a poner el huevo*
*en el dormitorio Apeiron*
*hasta el final de los tiempos*
*cuando las tiranías*
*impacientes e inocentes*
*fluyan en la alcantarilla*
*del teatro callejero*
wees onschuldig, ongeduldig
*sano esplendor y placebo*
*en el dormitorio Apeiron*

[I fall sleep in the bedroom,
a Greek Apeiron,
*wees onschuldig,*
*ongeduldig*, innocent
and impatient.
The figure of the sleeping hero
Arthur or Charlemagne
valuable as champagne
to medieval folklore
I'll place the egg
in my Apeiron bedroom
until the very end of time
when impatient and
innocent tyrannies
may flow through the sewer
of street theater
*wees onschuldig, ongeduldig*
healthy splendor and placebo
in Apeiron, my bedroom]

Within two weeks, the temperature in the Low Countries has ranged from -19 to +19 degrees.

### Maandag 21

Thomas Muntzer, the "eternal student." Not just for studying philosophy and theology, Greek and Hebrew, German mysticism, but rather because "he was never a pure intellectual." His studies were meant to resolve "a serious personal problem." In Prague in 1521, with the help of an interpreter, he made this prediction: *Harvest time is come, so God himself entrusted its gathering to me. I have seized my scythe. Because my thoughts are anchored in the truth, and my lips, hands, feet, body, life curse the unbelievers.* He was expelled from the city.

BPS trans.: Guy de Moroque-Slucki offers a permanent magnetic field, specific and oriented to certain wave forms. Using sensitive crystallography, one can evaluate and visualize the impact of electrical fields on living matter: the vitality and dynamism in processes of cellular growth, the quality of cellular structure. That is to say, the form and amplitude of actions of matter's formative forces. Briefly summarized: the influence of biologically incompatible radiation from, say, a mobile phone can be verified and eventually reversed by way of a BPS pill.

And I face the funny situation of using a computer to translate a text that denounces the computer's maleficent radiation, and the radiation from almost all the equipment adorning our modern conviencencies, convienodernity, modernsnottty, modernshitty.

The linguistic assimilation of the state to "apparatus," with the dismal connotations that word conjures, reveals its condition as an unnatural entity. The Leviathan, for its part, is a beast of nature, but it retains its structure as a Chimera.

> And the North is a Chimera, pure bullshit!
> And they say there you can live
> like a pasha.
>
> Venezuelan song.

I go to baby-sitting: Goodbye Ballonetje, the road has curved! There goes a revolutionary from the Upper Rhine.

According to Cohn, in the Medieval period, the priest transmuted into a salaried preacher was the most common sort of prophet. The ancient religious jargon, today replaced by democratic and economic jargon, offers a new preacher with a millenarianism whose apocalypse we can observe at ease, sitting in front of the television. Nothing is supernatural.

*Fey*: adj. 1. Interested in or believing in the supernatural. 2. Clairvoyant, visionary. 3.Chiefly Scot. Fated to die, doomed. 4. Chiefly Scot. In a state of high spirits. Feyness. n. *The Collins Dictionary & Thesaurus.*

Baby-sitting: ridiculous term. Middays and evenings with Julia's children. I explain the Italian meaning of their paternal surname, Balestra: an artillery weapon called the ballista. But the word also has uses in printing, seafaring and mechanics: *muelle di balestra*, for example. On Tuesdays, like today, I have to pick up the kids from school, and I take Ana to music school, where I play *voetbal* with Luciano in the patio as we wait. I eat dinner with the family. Luciano reads an article for school about "the miracle of Amsterdam." An engraving from 1518 displays the city's ancient name: Amstelredam.

Oh, Amstelredam, mercantile aquarium, society of societies, market of markets, Chinese box of commercial introspection. All that is air vanishes into solidity. What would become of you without the crow's vigil, what would become of you, city, without your birds.

All important decisions have one thing in common: they're made at the right time. A Kenyan is sent by his mother to buy a dress in the city. Instead he buys a pair of Nike shoes. The Kenyan will become world marathon champion.

From a television commercial.

> the Dutch paradox
> when there's a wall, there's a way
> when there's a way, there's a landscape

*Zazen*. Only Julia. She tells me about the impossibility of giving Spanish classes.

Thanks to Cordula Quadt, a link: www.utrecht.cervantes.es/direccionbiblio_1_2_39_6.htm It leads to a collection from the Cervantes Institute library, founded by Spain's Ministry of Labor for Spanish immigrants in Utrecht.

Telephone conversation with Ken about the demolition job in the office at Wenckebachweg: bring a book and a meter. Take photographs, ideally with a digital camera. Good impression. Prepare for the issue of debris: container. Plastic floor protection. Don't give the price up front. As a last resort, say 15 to 17 €. *per uur*. I can use his tools, eventually with the name of his company: *Built by Design*!

"Not if it's a supporting wall!" says he. Description of the wall. Position of wall with respect to the front of the building: "With your back to the street …"

> What lies behind us and what lies before us
> are tiny matters compared to what lies
> within us.
>
> EMERSON. On a Sleepytime teabag

### GOEDE VRIJDAG 25

To Wenckebachweg at 4, demolition research. Unsuccessful. Passing the Mondriaan Tower and the Bijlmer prison, I find the street but not the number. *Toch leuk*! that in search of work I've found prison gates. The zone is notable for other reasons: the contrast between Mondriaan Tower, an upperclass beacon, and the prison, symbol of the underside. Between the two lies the home of Amsterdam's Hell Angels, folkloric types fallen into disgrace with the *politie*. Too much settling of scores, too many scores unsettled. So much swimming just to die upon the shore.

The enlightened bicycle carries me back home on an ungodly evening of high, damp winds. There alongside the canal, with its flat-bottomed boats.

I dream about a prison without guards, where the prisoners are the officers of their own transformation; where prisoners' wives can live next to the walls of the jail and receive visits from their husbands every night; where you work, study, and practice *zazen*. Our Lady of Mount Carmel, New World, and making a new man out of a criminal. "It's the least this primitive civilization can do," an old prisoner tells me, "when it hasn't learned how to fix crime and punishment, and the jails are the cloaca where civilization hides its own ignorance."

> *las flores que besé*
> *las calles que dejé*
> *lalalalilalilalilalalá*
>
> [the flowers I kissed
> the streets I left
> lalalaleelaleelaleelalalah]

Walking down Havana's Vapor Street toward the ocean, mumbling like Juan Formell: that's how I wake up.

⚜

Walking along Adelaarsweg, the eagle's road, you arrive in a neighborhood adorned with the names of birds: pelican's street, kingfisher's street, an old working-class neighborhood. Some houses display their date of construction: 1922, 1923. Pluvier Straat, plover's street.

"My grandparents lived here," Cristina remembers, and we retreat by a step. A little plaza opens up. It has a mural of every kind of bird co-existing with humans, which certainly happens here. Seagulls and pelicans abound, as well as forest or semi-urban birds, like the crow, or that white and bluish-black gentleman who has the flexible structure of the mockingbird and is arrogant as a musketeer, and whose name I don't know. Some corvid? Or that wild pigeon who crosses the canal, to collect twigs for the nest it's building on an apartment balcony.

Not far away, near the traffic circle, some men from the neighborhood are talking. They're workers, maybe on the river. One of them, tattooed and with a rough-looking face, shows us where the old stadium of Volewijkers is. Cristina's grandfather played there years ago.

### Lunes de Pascuas, 28.

The air like gauze, the light like a flame from alcohol; stationary seagull on the tower of the building on the opposite side of the canal. In one sitting I read García Marquez's last novel, *Memoria de mis putas tristes* (*Memories of My Melancholy Whores*). A piece originating the same way as all his books, as is his custom, entertaining. Is there something unfair about the writer tirelessly repeating himself, exercising—as the author says of his prostitutes—"the impudence of the trade"?

Kimberley, daughter of the upstairs neighbor, arrives impromptu, stays for a while, plays the flute & drum, drinks tea & crackers, draws some dolphins. Wants to come back to show more of her drawing, and teaches this song,

> *Ik ken een liedje dat de mensen irriteert*
> *de mensen irriteert, de mensen irriteert*
> *ik ken een liedje dat de mensen irriteert*
> *en de liedje gaat goed zo.*
>
> *Yo me sé una cancioncita que a la gente irrita*
> *que a la gente irrita, que a la gente irrita*
> *yo me sé una cancioncita que a la gente irrita*
> *la cancioncita dice así.*

I know, I'm a little song that bothers people
that bothers people, that bothers people
I know, I'm a little song that bothers people
for the song says this is true.

It can be irritating, or not, depending on your mood. In my case, I go to sleep for 12 hours.

BPS, finished; pick up bike from the repair shop: 7 e. next time. I can do it myself. At 2 I go baby-sitting. At 7:30, I light up the Barcelona pipe, toss two letters into the mail, and write to my acquaintance Martijn Blok: *Ik hoop*, hip hop, etc. I prepare for Spanish lessons, *Spaanse Les*:

The course moves freely / it is not free: free is not for free. Each student has common tasks and specific ones according to individual level, but they work together with a goal: to enter into contact with the language. *Het Spaanse* … I select four sources to begin: an informational edition about the island of Cuba (Mo Veld found it discarded in the street); an issue of *Mandorla* magazine from which I'll take some poems; Norberto Codina's anthology *Siglo Pasado*, and Danilo Manera's *Suonare sogni a Cuba*, for its photos. Let's add a little music: rumba, Silvio Rodriguez, Camarón. Grammar for the start of class, music for its end; images between, interspersed, like a work of marquetry by Gaudí whose final product is the Spanish language. Like the Parc Guells or "Guantanamera." All in all, friend Gaspar, you're the one I can tell about these things. In the tapas bar, Lacosta.

"You see, I'm a taxi driver for children, a bit of a waiter when serving them lunch, and something of a tourist at the end of the day."

"How is that."

Gaspar, lacking a *shilong*, grips his San Miguel beer.

"The navigation plan is to pick up the children from school, take them on my bike to the Copernicusstraat …"

"Where's that?"

"It's a district on the east side, full of scientists: Archimedes, Newton …"

"Got it, got it, and all three of you are on one bicycle."

He scrutinizes me like a bear.

"Not always, unless the kids forgot their bikes. We also take a soccer ball, to kill time kicking it around."

"Does that work?"

"Not today. The older one gets bored and says he doesn't like being at the school. I tell him that it's about getting outdoors, but he refutes my argument: 'It's the schoolyard. *De schooplein.*'"

"In what language do you talk to them?"

"Sometimes Spanish, sometimes Dutch. It depends."

"Depends on what?"

Tonight is his night to talk and ask too much.

"On the situation, the weather, and I guess on me."

"That's just it. How are you going to set up Spanish classes if you can't even motivate a couple of kids who are even half-Argentine, to top it all off. OK, go on."

"The boy asks me to take him home to empty his piggy bank. He wants to buy a book on Linnaeusstraat."

"More scientists."

"Yes. I tell him I'm not a taxi driver but I take him there and back anyway, and when his sister finishes her workout, it's her brother's turn to go to *voetbal*, so I have to get him to the stadium."

"Well, at least *on s'ennouillera pas*, as De Gaulle would say.

I tell him that at the end of the day, as I was taking Ana to her father's house, she decided that it would be better for us to walk. And so we found a box of books by the curb. She chose a fish book, and I took one that I've been thinking about lately: *Tracy's Tiger*.

"You got lucky," Ana tells me. And it's true. Since we watched an episode of *X Files* together, where a boy has such a powerful imagination that he succeeds in turning his thoughts into reality, I've been wanting to talk to Cristina about Tracy's tiger. And here it is. Thanks to Ana, who wanted to walk, so tomorrow I'm giving my bicycle a vacation.

⚮

I start to read *Tracy's Tiger*. To each his own.

### DONDERDAG 31 MAART

From Jeroen's balcony you can see the Dutch school. Zacharias the bartender smokes a cigarette on the patio while he talks with a student; inside the computer labs, the students hibernate in their headphones. It's 10:05 a.m. I finish at 12. Record time, and I walk over to De Balie. I invite Ricardo Cuadros to a change in habitat, and we move over to the Mellow Yellow. He tells me about his experience on Chile's Monte Grande. On its peak, they say, there's a stone Indian lying down and looking up toward the cosmos. Next to him, a stone hare whispers about things happening down in the valley.

Today Ricardo delivered an introduction to Alonso Ercilla's epic poem about the conquest of Chile, *La Araucana*, written in "*ottava rima*—can you imagine that?"

⚮

Thomas Tracy resembles that Summerhill student who went to apply for a job with a famous company after finishing school. "When I saw him come in and greet me with no fear of my status whatsoever, I realized that he was a Summerhill graduate," says the head of the company. In *Tracy's Tiger* this is Otto Seyfang:

"Do you know who I am?"

"No, sir," Tracy said. "Who are you?"

"Otto Seyfang."

"Do you know who I am?" Tracy said.

"Who are you?"

"Thomas Tracy."

**MARTES 5**

Redheaded spring, Asymptote: *A straight line that is closely approached by a curve so that the distance between them decreases to zero as the distance from origin increases to infinity.*

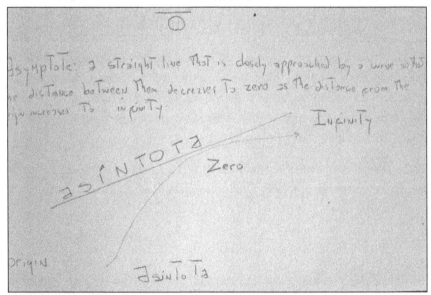

"Asymptote" journal page

*Jaguar*

*cara cosa Cuba frac actor*
*querer quiosco*
*kilo, cero cigarro*
*zaguan zorro zumo*
*paz juzgar*
*jugarjaguar*

[Jaguar

cameo canto Cuba frack actor
craving kiosk
kilo, zero cigarette
zigzag fox juice
peaceful judging
jumpingjaguar]

I show Rashid, who is doing it for the first time, the *guenmai* ceremony. He gets nervous, which usually happens, and freezes in front of the *tatami* mat like a paralyzed bird. In the end everything works out.

Sometimes I'd like to substitute what I lived with what I wrote. Some portions of happiness appear amid the junk, the worthless parts of every-day life among which illusions are born only to die right away, like mosquitos or butterflies.

Why does spring cause impatience? What motor drives it? You remember you were writing about the door leaning against a wall in the furnace room: Impatience is driven by motors, but it wasn't possible to write that anywhere else. I've got a tiger, Tracy thought …

265

The following Saturday, Tracy quit his job at Otto Seyfang's and went back to San Francisco. Impatience is driven by motors, and it has direction: Saint Francis, who also undertook just acts of impatience. Science unequalled, unequalled science: do you know the poem? Tracy said. Tiger, tiger, burning bright …

From March 21 to April 20, the ruminant jumps out the window. A billy-goat, but also a noble animal. After all: Bloodstained Ares, as Homer said.

Taxi driver, cook: pesto pasta: not for Luciano, he's allergic. Thus the goat is not a ram; that would be the macho male, but also *Ariete*, as he is called in Italian: *ariete agitatore, ardere. Ardere adrede, maschio de la pecora in cui il Sole transita dal marzo al aprile. Antica macchina d'assedio per sfondare mura, nella forma più semplice. Voilà!* Knocking down walls in the *più semplice* way. Warship stocked with an *ariete*, a battering ram. "His handlebars were the horns of a goat," like El Flaco in Piazzola's lyrics to "The White Bicycle": "It's not about arriving / it's about going on."

### JUEVES

I go along the Kerkstraat, microcosm, and although it doesn't have canals—remarkable!—in the middle, it begins and ends with canals. From the Leidsegracht to the bridge over the Amstel: the Magerebrug, or narrow bridge. If you continue to the right, you'll find the Royal Carré Theater, where the Buena Vista Social Club played in Europe for the first time.

First Spanish class in the house on Oosterparkstraat: a nicer day, thirteen degrees. I improvise. All of the papers I prepared are still in the *dojo*, locked for afternoon *zazen*. Why poetry, Theodore Adorno used to say? Well, because we've forgotten our handouts.

> Alphabet, vowels: phonetic introduction.
> The verbs *ser* and *estar*, in dialogue.
> Analysis of preposition, adverb,

prefixes and suffixes. An exercise about Cuba:
pick out the verbs.

*Bois ton sang, Beaumanoire.*

We had said already that in the curves of the canals, the most peculiar
places turn up. The space opened after a curve: perhaps the unknown.
Honeysuckles?

Lady Salsa

> The Hottest Sensation from Cuba: 20 perfectly formed dancers
> moving like they are having the best sex of their lives.

Sex, Rum & Revolution: Pacha Mama smoking tobacco. As a backdrop,
the Cuban flag.

28 April–22 Mei. THEATER FABRIEK. Amsterdam.

*Bendito sea el dinero*
*que nos libera de las obligaciones*
*del amor.*
*La enseñanza de la lengua*
*desprovista de la enseñanza de la poesía*
*es un infundio de lugares comunes.*
God doth with us
As we with torches do:
Light them, not for themselves.
*Shakespeare: la tinta, aquí hay malayerba*
*y hay que chapearla,*
*paciencia, colibrí*

*así como cierras la puerta al vendedor*
*de seguros, de billetes de lotería,*
*o al sonsonete que uno leyó en un libro*
*ofreciendo un hermoso futuro a domicilio:*
*pensioen, hypoteken, financeering,*
*la muerte a plazos y a veces ni siquiera.*
*Asimismo abres otras puertas.* Beatti maledetti.

[Blessed be the money
that liberates us from love's
obligations.
The teaching of a language
without the teaching of its poetry
is a pack of lies told in platitudes.
*God doth with us*
*As we with torches do:*
*Light them, not for themselves.*
Shakespeare: ink, here is a weed
and you must clear it away,
be patient, hummingbird,
like when you close the door to a salesman
peddling insurance, or lottery tickets,
or to the singsong someone read in a book
offering a beautiful future, straight to your home:
*pensioen, hypoteken, financeering,*
death by installments and sometimes not even.
Similarly, you open other doors. *Beatti maledetti.*]

The secret of the asymptote is not to accelerate transit toward the final objective of a perfect society, but to observe the approach happening between lines: evolution of consciousness and evolution of productive powers. Aren't they the same? Hardly.

I continue on to the bank to deposit money for my flight to Cuba. The employees are already converting last night's coins. The noise in their machine is like water. Running water.

An invitation arrives: to participate in the next state *Spreken* exam. My other three tracks are approved. All that's left is speaking in Dutch. Paul Loomans the other day: "Omar says so little that one wonders why he even studied Dutch."

### 30 DE ABRIL. QUEEN'S DAY IN HOLLAND.
### AND CRISTINA'S BIRTHDAY.

At midday we get a coffee in Café Alverna and go on to the Jordaan. In some of the alleyways you can barely walk. Next to the Prince's Canal, an orchestra made up of Hollanders plays salsa. Two girls on a *tablao* dance flamenco at the fair, while a Russian sings in baritone and drinks vodka. On a corner, for just 1 e. you can get a *goddelijke massage*, a divine massage. Some offer blessings for 1.50. Everything is for sale, everything's being purchased: it's the spring street market. We cross the Vondelpark.

Things that abound in homes are for sale at ridiculous prices: records, books, clothes and shoes, pieces of computers, crafts, and relics. Children take the opportunity to sell their possessions. When evening falls, whatever didn't get sold gets thrown out.

Next to the dumpster I find a damp copy of *Ulysses*. Superstition aside, why read *Ulysses* now? Clearly, it's not every day that you find *Ulysses* by the dumpster. Ten years ago I interrupted my reading of this novel, after deciding it was too sumptuary. An academic duty, improve your fucking English, have you read? Oh, no! *Ulysses*: masterwork, firework; I set it out to dry.

> When one reads these strange pages of one long gone
> One feels that one is at one with one who once ...

Joyce sounds like Gollum.

In Alverna I bump into Ricardo Cuadros. Almost an hour in the café without spotting each other. Absorbed, far from the door, reading *Ulysses*, I didn't see him arrive, nor did he recognize me from behind. I was already leaving when I discovered him sitting before a cappuccino. Then we talk: Ricardo tells me about this father, who ruptured his eardrum years ago with a hard slap. They reconciled after Francisco, a friend from the Chilean mountains, would ask: "Have you asked what your ear was doing at the height of the furious hand?"

Seven countries are now designated, by the U. S government, as state sponsors of terrorism: North Korea, Syria, Sudan, Iran, Iraq, Libya and Cuba.

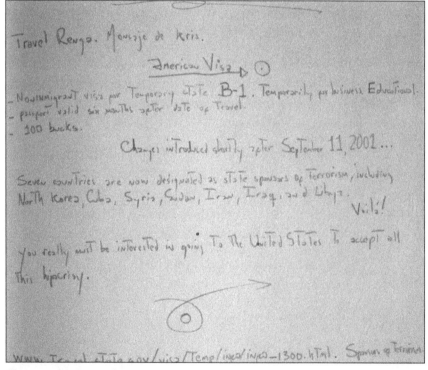

*"Seven countries" journal page*

I finally repair the bicycle with the help of our Georgian neighbor. He finds me by the door to a building among nuts and tools. He's a professional. Once he worked in a *fietswinkel*.

I take care of the Balestra children for 4 hours.

Spanish lesson that night, the fifth one:

- "Veinte años" ("Twenty Years"), by María Teresa Vera.
- Verbs for second conjugation.
- Formation of adverbs. The preterite tense of verbs, litera -rily.
- The poem "Romance de la niña niña" ("The Girl-girl's Romance"), from Julio Ortega's anthology, which Ricardo loaned to me. They translate it, as an exercise, into Dutch.

They've already translated Silvio's "Sueño con serpientes" (I Dream about Serpents), and we analyzed the verb "plantear," which can mean things like "to lay out" or "to contemplate." We worked with Silvio's sentence, "Llego a su estómago / y planteo con un verso una verdad" (I arrive in its stomach and with a verse, I pose a truth).

You travel with a box, says Charlotte, a student. It's an error, a misreading, but it makes sense to me.

Song in English.

### IT'S IN THE FOOD

The life that you live
the air that you breathe
it's in the food you eat
it's in the food
the face that you kiss
the animal you miss

it's in the food you eat
it's in the food
the water you collect
the chief you respect
it's in the food you eat
it's in the food
the lies that you say
the game that you play
it's in the food you eat
it's in the food
the rain you don't see
the bird, you and me
it's in the food you eat
it's in the food
the book that you read
the root of your greed
it's in the food you eat
    it's in the food
the forest you take
the noise that you make
it's in the food you eat
    it's in the food
the face in the crowd
the pain of the cow
it's in the food you eat.

Dreams.

El Zurdo dream: El Zurdo, "Lefty," appears in Central Havana. San Leopoldo, tranquil and picturesque. We examine an old photo of the arcades, from Belascoaín to the port, decorated with Hindu motifs. Sculptures: Shiva makes love to the revolutionary women. I give El Zurdo a copy of the magazine *Espiga*. El Zurdo is always and forever The Tiger, and also, as he says, Son of the Sea.

Varadero dream: I land on a beautiful beach with crystalline blue waters. Tourist area. *Weltklas*, but also there are very humble Cuban families. The buildings to the left recall architecture in Den Haague: solid towers of glass and steel. 'Specially the Hilton going up in the center of the group, under a slightly murky sky. It's not fear, it's not laziness: I hesitate before jumping into the sea. It's about not being 100% in the here and now. I realize that I'm in Varadero.

Marlén dream: Marlén and César take me out to wander through Europe. The train runs through an immense arm of the sea. In my right hand, I clutch grams of dirt. From my native land. The grams trickle out, disturbing an elegant lady passenger. I'm standing up, I turn and look through the amphibious train's panoramic windows. Open and blue, with olive groves and edifices on the left side. Cubans travel on the train.

El Mono, "The Monkey" dream: Going to the Fondo on a modern train, maybe the same one. A group of Africans. Also a monkey completely dressed in clothing. I can't accept it, but there's no doubt: the monkey talks to me, I don't understand. I get closer and the monkey speaks into my ear. In English, he tells me to relax. Take it easy. Everything is allright. The Africans are happy too: they're students. Professorial, I remind them that the African teams—Cameroon, Nigeria, Senegal—didn't place in the top three in the latest World Cups for soccer. They ignore me, they laugh, they don't care. They're happy. I conclude by saying: Africa represents important things for humanity, for our development. They're startled but keep on laughing.

La Playa, "The Beach" dream: Nude beach, presumably in Greece. Joris, my brother Félix and I are sunbathing nude. *C'est la vie*, so it is written: we three worlds will lie naked in the sun, Cuba, Europe and Greece, and what do you call that world I came from? The Sun? We're not collectors but travelers. Félix says, to that effect: Folk Theorem. In English I write:

> The equilibrium's outcome in an infinitely
> repeated game coincides with feasible and
> strongly individual rational outcomes

of the one-slot game
on which it is based.

I call my sister on the phone. It's not a dream: I tell her that next week I'm starting a class in Dutch painting: painting a cafeteria in the neighborhood. She laughs.

※

Cristina suggests to Paul that during *zazen* he could say something about the Buddha's birthday. Paul responds: "*Ik ben niet een gelofeer.*" A believer, no. That's how it is. In Zen people come together who are religious and not, believers and not. During my stay in Europe I find that the ones who declare themselves to be believers and religious are the exception.

※

Cristina, after waking up:

"*Ongelooflijk!* Incredible. Now I realize that I have no Islamic friends."

"Do you have a friend who has Islamic friends?"

"No, I'm shocked, I've been living in a whitepeople world."

We all live in cages; Zen cages too, *boudhist* cages. And it's a marvel to get outside of them.
*Lunes*

> *Hombrenuevo y clon*
> *podredumbre del huevo*
> *llega y pon*
> *servidumbre del golem*
> *componte canallón*
> *de la* tekne.
> Übermensch *corredor*
> *bienes raíces*

real state of the art *en oclusión*
get a life, get a life
*de creación*
*relaciones de cromosoma al pecho*
*cimarrón*
*de la* tekne.
*Hombrenuevo y clon*
la vie en rose *del universo en producción*
*tarzan, rimbaud, frankestein en el balcón*
*de la* tekne
*guirnalda en el blasón*
*del hombrenuevo y clon*
save as save as Revolution
save as *Revolución*.


[The New-Man and the clone
the corruption of the egg
arrive and construct
the golem's servitude
a path to clean up his act
from *tekne*.
*Übermensch* passage
real estate
*real state of the art* in occlusion
*get a life, get a life*
of creation
relations from chromosome to chest
runaway
from *tekne*.
New-Man and clone
*la vie en rose* of the universe in production
tarzan, rimbaud, frankenstein on the balcony
of *tekne*

wreath on the coat of arms
for the New-Man and clone
save as save as Revolution
save as *Revolución*.]

z. I serve *guenmai*. 12: Balestras. The Wild Logical Guess.

Notes for an anthology of contemporary Cuban poetry:

> The Bardic tone: Homeland, family, "my mother," not "the
> mother," the friends, not "my friends," (like in the Beatles). The
> Persuaded Past Participle: I have seen, etc. The British influence:
> Borges, Keats maybe. And in an affected first person from the
> French: I have understood. The skeptical *déjà vu*, the anguished
> vibrant *laissez faire*.

> Sociological Waltz, the figure changes: the sociopolitical rhythm,
> politics of associates, Cubanism and a bible from the slum: the
> island, the island, will we talk about the topic of the island?

Cristina returns from the zoo. She saw the seahorses and greeted the
gorilla: "Your brother."

At 7, *ser* and *estar* in various tenses. Poem: *La niña niña se hamaca, en la
proa del bajel.*

9:30, Gary's Muffins. First painting session with Christophe de la Porte
in the café on the Kinkerstraat: wide brush, narrow brush, roller; white
and yellow. We finish at three. When we're done we stop at Touchée for
a beer. I'm pretty much *touché* with the beauty of an Indonesian patron,
with her long legs, and I become aware of what it's like to routinely desire
what you don't have. Desire / despair. Christophe seems calmer about this
matter, and the Indonesian woman is looking at him with desire / despair.

I find Lamine on the corner.

"Are you playing music now?"

"No man, ain't playing nothing now."

"Just with your woman."

"That's it."

Afghan president optimistic on drug war

Charges for the Amsterdam-Havana flight, 807 €. and 21 cents

If one keeps busy, says the *I Ching*, dying earlier or later matters not to Man

Maria Mullisch pays me for 3 and a half hours of cleaning, and I have a beer at The Rookies

Madonna owns a flat in the Bijlderdijk Kade, but she's never there; quite a place here, Madonna, to look at the rushing clouds and fool moon. But you don't care if they have made a big parking lot.

No trees, only carousel.

## Viernes

Cristina invites me to Zandvoort, the beach. *Magnifique.*

> *Señor de su tiempo, dueño de su memoria*
> *todo le supo a muerte en la distancia*
> *sólo el sol, el cegador, vino a salvarle*

> [Lord of his time, keeper of his memory
> everything spoke to him of death in the distance
> only the sun, the sun who blinds, came to save him]

and the frozen fish, and the ladies with their boobs drooping like banners, and the children with their dogs with their owners with their balls with their protective windsurfing helmets for dancing to the swing of the waves, with their scenes of conflict, with fried fish every afternoon.

### DOMINGO

When in Limbholanda the sun comes out, it's paradise.

At night in The Sugarfactory, an old candy facility converted into soul for a heathen city, I read a few poems in English, courtesy of the kindness of lady K.

An ensemble accompanies the night. Floris, a funky NorthernEuro group with a beautiful, plump singer who has almond eyes and double-bass hips.

Black coffee, spiritual, hummingbird, falling on the ground I slip of the tongue back home.

### MARTES

The French just voted *Non* to the Constitution. Now it is the Hollanders' turn.

On the corner at the Coffee Company, I meet Lamine again. The African's life is rough; he only works to pay his debts and is not *inburger*ized, not filtered into the structure of *samenleving* that includes school and a trade. Thank you. Man does not live from art alone, they tell him.

### MIERCOLES 1RO DE JUNIO

You're going to turn yourself into a lone wolf! Asklepios was right. The Dutch say No to the European Constitution, such a pretty face that launched a thousand ships.

The U. S. confirms that urine touched Koran at Guantánamo. Associated Press. Artistic revolution emerges in China. *The Chicago Tribune*. Work on translation of Stéphane's documentary. *Mondo*:

Disciple: "I want to know, as a Zen nun, which attitude to take about work."

Master: "I don't know. I never worked."

Dream:

*Lezama aferra con ambas manos el dedo meñique del gigante*
*y es finalmente transportado a Hungria,*
his house transformed into a modern art museum:
big blue rotating canvases,
reproductions of Leonardo's machingegni
*chromed* toilettes. *Would you like to buy it?*
*Would you like to see it?*

[With both hands Lezama clings to the giant's pinky finger
and at last he is transported to Hungary,
his house transformed into a modern art museum:
big blue rotating canvases,
reproductions of Leonardo's machingegni
chromed *toilettes*. Would you like to buy it?
Would you like to see it?]

## LUNES 13

The frigid summer continues. Berlusconi, abstentionism, *Corriere della Sera, destra, sinistra e centro sinistra*. Discovery Channel: "until technology makes the sea transparent." A boat passes through the canal: *Je suis*.

# The Intellectual and Power in Cuba

(An intervention I read at the Havanna Virtuell event featuring Cuban poets and writers in the city of Graz, Austria, on October 21–22, 2005.)

1. Consider my passport. The personal data line where you define your "profession" lists "writer." Though I'm not trying to mimic Mayakovsky, I can't forget the taste, the euphoria of that poem we learned in school: I'm a poet, I serve the power of the people. In real life I limit myself to verifying just one fact: the Republic of Cuba recognizes my condition as a writer. This has two secondary effects. One, that my mother is proud. The other, that police at Customs ask me, "What do you write?" "Poetry," I answer. On a certain occasion, a certain policeman took it farther than the others. The incident took place at JFK airport in New York some weeks after September 11: he asked, "What kind of poetry?"

"Philosophical poetry."

"What is philosophical poetry?" he insisted, putting me in an awkward situation. I don't remember what I answered. I don't know what poetry is, much less what philosophical poetry would be, or even philosophy, *bios kubernitis*, governor of life, as the ancient Greeks said. Despite the difficulty of the question I must have given a satisfactory answer in the face of power incarnate. It's not lost on me that a good many truths are told in order to get out of tight spots, then forgotten. You'll ask what relationship the interrogation by a New York airport officer has to the theme in question. First, the dialogue between poetry and power is always the same, latitude and circumstance aside. Second, the situation of a poet confronted by power in Cuba is not disconnected from his situation when confronted by power in the United States of North America. This point, which might seem to a European intellectual like a mere theoretical sleight of hand, has been a constant reality for more than a century on our lands. Don't worry—this time I'm not going to quote José Martí. I proceed with the interrogation: the uniform persisted, "Your name is Omar. Are you Arab?"

"Not that I know of."

"Then are you a Muslim?" Good question: in the sense of being "abandoned of God," be God whatever he is—Tao, Buddha, cosmos—we are all *muslim*. However, not wanting these theological considerations to aggravate my status as a poet originating from a nation now considered "terrorist," I said no.

"Then why is your name Omar?"

"In honor of the great poet Omar el Khayamm—Persian, not Arab—my mother gave me his name."

Persian or Arab, Cuban, atheist or believer: poet, always suspect to power constituted in uniform. So far though, in one place or another, that power has—after some interrogation—let me go on down my road in peace.

2. Every time I come back to Cuba, I return with intensity to the fundamental political condition: daily life. I feel an imperative to organize political discourse, and poetic discourse, not around criticism of power incarnate but around observation of the way of life of the people, beginning with mine. I understand this observation to ennoble humans in their existence and prepare them to modify reality. Their reality. In this process I am not the passive object of some power external to me, telling me what I should see and how, what I should or should not change and in what way. Not as long as I'm a poet, here and there, lord of my own reality. Naïve? Romantic? Pushkin said it, that he was neither safe nor completely defenseless in the face of power: the poet should be a little stupid. But it's not this basic and immemorial stupidity of the

human-poet that blinds or denigrates. In it reside ideals, the sediment of our eternal life, and these are eternally realizable.

Now what, etymologically speaking, is criticism without crisis? Let's welcome this crisis of systems, discourses, powers that in the end is the crisis of an entire civilization and its model of consciousness. Without crisis not even poetry would be given to us today; not even reflection; not even philosophy. Who will throw the first stone at it? Today, obviously, it has come to be considered a normal act to throw stones, invectives, bombs. He who criticizes today should also know how to plant seeds for flowers. And if necessary, to throw them. This would be the greatest act of power.

3. I pause a moment on this point. Maybe it will be said that I have tried to use rhetoric to evade the matter of the relationship between the intellectual and power in Cuba? Not by a long shot. I have firsthand knowledge of censorship and other extreme resources of political therapy. They can't dissuade the poet who has devoted his energies to spying on a higher state of consciousness. Having made the poet hostage to reality is not the fault or privilege of any specific system. Even when all systems, by their nature of being systems, may have in some moment been attributed the doubtful merit of subjugating all nature, and therefore human nature and the root of poetry, it has in reality been the poet, in his or her purest impulse and at the four cardinal points of the world, who has decided to subjugate him- or herself, to remain among men, chanting. The force of this choice is what has caused the poet to subsist among the persecuted and the silenced to the present day: we who will watch the sun move across the other side of the mountain tomorrow.

4. I go out for a walk. Yes, I know. It's the devastated city you've all seen on the pages of *Le Monde Diplomatique* and in Wim Wenders' *Buena Vista Social Club*. I leave my son at the door of the renovated school, formerly a store for goods decommissioned by the state. According to the state, my son's future is guaranteed. According to my instincts as a father and a poet, his present is no more or less uncertain than that of all inhabitants of this planet in turmoil, our everyday volcano. The price of the *noni*, or Indian mulberry, a prodigious fruit said to possess 101 curative properties, is 5 pesos per bundle in the state market and 7 pesos at the herbalist's store. The young women I bump into on the road to central Havana look as beautiful and healthy as ever, "like precious pearls, the adornment of dream ..." On the Malecón a typical scene of *latin socialism*: one man in charge of the excavator, working; 19 men observing. They're not bystanders. They're workers and bosses on the job. These gesticulate, those remain absorbed in contemplation. One even stretches his body along the wall, rests his head on a colleague's thigh, and smokes a cigarette. Marx and Lafargue, father and son-in-law, eternally reconciled: the right to work and the right to rest in dialectical unity.

For their part, those people from think tanks of the Christian and materialist West who have determined Cuba, among other non-hegemonic nations, to be a poor country, profess not only an extreme and fundamentalist materialism but also a limited vision, one impoverished in turn in the spirit-matter of development and movement. Because spirit-matter is not just object, its liberty is not only free will, and its realization is not only gratification.

5. Who said that all reality was rational: an ideologue in the service of a party or a poet in the service of publicity? In the propaganda of capitalist society the call to an individualist *carpe diem* is paramount: *be yourself*. And even, as I have observed in the Amsterdam airport, *be a tiger*. Don't let others consume for you. Here and now, consume anything, so long as the one consuming it is **you**. *Get a life*. In the most austere society through which Cubans have ever lived, propaganda attempts to activate other regions of consciousness. For example: ideas cannot be defeated, ideas are immortal, etcetera. *Platon dixit, Marx dixit*. There is, furthermore, a word in which commercial and political propaganda coincide: ***revolution***. And still another word into which all ideological, economic, mystic, and sumptuary messages and values flow: energy. Supreme mystery of our unreality.

As long as I'm an individual, a poet, and in a certain way an idiot—following the Hellenic interpretation of an independent individual—I find both calls sympathetic and stimulating. Full of grace, yes, and empty of meaning. Grace and meaning: here is one of the points around which the intellectual can take action in the face of power and the social matrix. I propose combinations. Such as: *Be yourself*, ideas are immortal. Naturally one knows that to dialogue directly with power, one must have better tools than the mere verbal and conceptual ingenuity that underlies all philosophical poetry. But at the end of the day we won't lack for work or for *materia prima*: how do we go back and fill these pairings with meaning if not by using contraries, by using the badly applied concepts that we inherited from our decomposed civilization: messianism and productivity, savings and dignity, future and death, honesty and democracy, revolution and consumption. Revolution: today they name you in advertisements at the four corners of the world: alleluia!

# 4. THE TABLE TALL AS YOUR HAND

3.5 hours to travel to Greece from Amsterdam.

**WEDNESDAY 6**

Wake up in Athína, Ayía Paraskeví, 10 a.m. Breakfast. Cemetery. Oikos Karpousilos, to visit the remains of the Karpousilos family, Christina's ancestors. Cemetery located in Dimos Vyronos, or Byron's neighborhood. In Greece many places bear his name, and until recently, a brand of cigarettes too. *O Lordos Vyronos* died of fever in Misolonghi as he insisted, in vain, on the organization of a small Independence army to fight against the Turks. His death, nonetheless, served to attract attention from other nations and European groups. They say this led, in the long term, to the British naval presence in Greek waters. Then to the confrontation, said to be chance, with the Turkish fleet, which was left in a bad way, thus weakening their dominion and facilitating a gradual liberation. Thus the veneration of the romantic and frustrated warrior.

4 p.m. Visit to the priest. Babas Kiprianos and two devotees who live with him. The Babas takes Christina's hand, caresses it as he speaks in psalmody, and does not let go. He is elderly.

Then to the Klifada neighborhood to pick up Yaya, grandma Olga.

At night, again in Ayías Paraskeví, conversation with Babis, a Cypriot, friend of Grigoris and the family.

He says, if you want to come to live in Greece, see if you have a place to live. Then find little job. Then you can learn Greek fast. Learning how to talk, he emphasizes, to write is *dískolos*. Difficult.

Then we talk about the Greek language, how three letters were lost. Ancient alphabet, 27 letters equaling 3 × 9. God's number. 999, now you know why. *Ennead.*

*Le droit a la paresse*. Eating, siesta. At 6 a walk. Center-university-Plaka. Acropolis. I mean the mountain, not the monument you see from afar, 500 meters as the bird flies. A theater group performs an ancient work. All women, *gynekés*, only the director and the two musicians, drum and flute, are men. Then to the Psiris neighborhood to hear *bouzukia*. That is, a duo with guitar and *bouzuki*, who sing Attic standards. Something like the salsa and soup found in Havana's tourist neighborhoods.

**FRIDAY 8TH**

Nothing relevant but a three-hour nap, a walk through the area. There are quite a few trees and steep streets; tossed on the sidewalk I find two cup holders with reproductions of ancient Greek ceramics. Curiously, Made in Amsterdam.

There's a bookstore, a lighting store, a sports center under delayed construction, its usual exposed concrete bristling with iron bars. Ambulatory vendors sell fruits of the earth, especially melons, but also sets of plastic tables and chairs. They go around on loaded motor scooters and hawk their wares with megaphones. Out past the freeway you can see the mountain.

Bombings in London claim 50 dead. Disaster.

**SÁBATO (AS IN THE ITALIAN) 9TH**

Yayá is not well: to hospital, *nosokomeío*. The word "*nosocomio*" is no longer used in Spanish, and yet I remember having seen it in a story by Mario Benedetti. The *Dictionary of the Spanish Language* retains *nosología*, as "division of medicine with the object of describing, differentiating, and classifying illnesses." At night we go to the *platía*, or neighborhood plaza. Activity by the KKE, communists. Then a rock band. The television reports a hurricane in Cuba: *tifónas*. 10 dead.

To the *nosokomeío* to visit Yayá. Typical hospital, buildings of three or four floors in the middle of a park with trees. Not at all different than the type of hospitals seen in Havana like Calixto García, Covadonga or la Dependiente. The buildings are newer, from the 50s, but the atmosphere is identical. From the balconies you can see the same chain of mountains that flanks Ayía Paraskeví.

Then to the sea, *thálassa*: *Porto*.

After the visit to Yayá Olga, Internet Café: expensive: currently 2. 70. K. D. goes on translating poems from *Algo de lo sagrado*. *Thálassa*. Open. 10 p.m. Athanassios comes, the bubble bursts. We talk, I show him the soundbox.

At 8:30 we go out to buy chicken, *kotopoulo*, for grandmother. Then on to the house on Mekina Street, in the Elisias neighborhood, more central. Where Christina's father Grigoris once lived. Marvelous routine I came to know on the earlier trip, *spanakopita* (like a spinach and cheese empanada), *platía*, greetings to the two neighborhood carpenters. Then to the university zone, *panepistimío*. Back to the house: "Tourists!," says Uncle Yura.

I accompany him to Piraeus. Another *nosokomeío*, this one more modern. From the street you see the ships in port. Meeting with the *maniatiki*, or natives of the Mani región, famous in ancient times for its bellicose character. Today more calm. They're relatives by way of one of Cristina's aunts, an ex-cabaret singer, married to one Astelios, man of the sea. Sly and educated. He has been to Cuba on his boat. His mother, another yayá facing troubles, is admitted here. They stage the most marvelous miniature theater. The husband of the dying woman, himself a miniature, with a little hat and cane, erupts out of the elevator like a walking loudspeaker. I don't understand Greek, but based on the dramatization, I think he wants them to tell him whether his wife is dying or not. "They must tell him the truth!" His daughters calm him, of course, with pure lies. The son-in-law, and really all of the men, impassive. A full minute of phonetic power and expression. The wife will not die for now.

Back in taxi to Athína. "Are you Greek?," says the taxi driver. "I'm from Cuba." "Cuba? Which Cuba? Fidel Castro?." "*Mono* Cuba. Only one Cuba, just as there's only one Hellada," say i. "Well, yes, there's only one Pakistan also," enigmatic taxi driver. At home, we watch *elenikó film*: *Political cuisine*. A story of a family, divided by the war between Turks and Greeks, and reunited by food. *Orea*.

### *Tetárti* OR FOURTH DAY. WEDNESDAY 13TH

Reading *Rough Guide. Greece*. Internet Point. Multilingual poem.

> *Kristokinético*
> Christ in chains!
> *elkómenos khristos*
> Christ in chains!
> *elkómenos khristos*
> why! *ay*
> *un kristo encadenado*
> *kristo en cruz*
> *y no hay* why!
> *un kristo en movimiento*
> *kristokinético*
> *salvo tal vez*
> *en la película*
> *kristokinética*
> *de Passolini*

*ay! tal vez, tal vez*
*katalavenis?*
people kill you if you
forget yourself
kill you if you don't.

Another in English.

the rough guide to Greece
there are
sheer drops
from the rock face
and unguarded cisterns
so.
  descend
    before dusk
and if you have young children
keep them close

Christ's heart is like a grain of coffee in his abdomen

On the ancient frescoes of Ayíos Oros, Monte Athos. 2030 meters at its peak.

Siesta!

Around 9 p.m. Cristina and I leave on the metro for Sindagma to meet up with Athanassios (the Athens metro is beautiful), who drives us to a singular place. A café-theater, hidden in a dark alley, behind the door of a normal-looking house, *kanoniká*, which creates no suspicions as to what lies inside: a bar, that is to say a bar of brick and ceramic tile, a patio, and a hall with stage and tables. Empty. Just one man inside who seems to live there as caretaker. Certain places in the city (I had seen something similar in the Psirri neighborhood on my previous visit) don't open during the summer tourist season, when the artists go off to the provinces or wherever, returning in the winter. That's why friends here insist that you have to visit Athens in the winter.

I take out my drum box at Athanassios' request and sing a song. "*Glikó foné*," says Athanassios. The man agrees but says nothing. We go to Psirri, where we talk in a corner café until 4 a.m. Athanassios tells his abrupt, philosophical stories, a little uncouth. He has a gray beard, expressive hands. He speaks of a decline in knowledge of Greece, how today the meaning of things in Heraclitus has been twisted, how traveling through mountains one still heard until a few years ago the feeling and sense of ancient Greek, how he thinks he has found the true meaning of *pólemos* at the moment when Heraclitus elevates it to a "supreme law." "It's not war," he says. "The *pólemos* of old was a little votive shrine placed at the entrance of homes, and what Heraclitus says is that the home is the foundation of everything else." He also takes on the famous phrase of the dying Christ, which he considers a message to Apollo. We leave the closing café, all three peripatetic, and the session extends until dawn.

## THURSDAY, *Pénti* OR FIFTH DAY

I reread Pithagóras (*Iámblikos*), but the ridiculous sense of reading abstruse things from the Greek past in the land of the Hellenes itself causes me to interrupt the reading. Those who write here do not know what they're talking about, except secondhand. Their contact with the Pythagorean method is, to say the least, oblique. So I leave the book forgotten on some shelf, cross the highway at last and scale the smooth mountain: *Imitos*. The mountain is always right.

I gather wild oregano, very light, thyme, and an aromatic herb unknown to me (a neighbor informs me later that it's *dendrolíbano*: rosemary, a more wiry rosemary than the one with which I was familiar). Also two small pieces of marble, rectangular, of ancient appearance, and another one that is large, oblong, which I place on end over an anthill. The energy of the mountain here, a serious thing. I return before the sundown can advance too far.

Very important: it rains after midday: heavy downpour.

In its place, the bird. I clean the house with a vacuum. The machine overheats and stops, the bag isn't full, nor is the pipe blocked. I take it as a sign; I won't clean other people's homes with machines any more. Ready for *zazen*, the chirp is heard. I feel no nostalgia for Amsterdam or my former life. There.

At naptime I can't sleep; I go off to the mountain and find the dog. It's accompanied by a bearded man with a staff and a *próblema* on his left leg. "*Yasu, yasu.*" On the way back I try out a new footpath, get lost, find my way. I have walked in an ellipse.

I look up the meaning of *sophrosyne* (wisdom) in the encyclopedia that the lodgers at this house left by the trash: *autoierarjía, enkratía, anoría.* Debate between self-control, *autokiriarjía,* and dominion over oneself. Athanassios explains to us later that *sophrosyne* is an agreement between project and realization, between determination and act. With a gesture of his broad hands he indicates that if we want to square off our life, we should make it square; if we want it to be rounded, then round.

I look up the meaning of *agathós* in a Greek-French dictionary: *bon,* brave, naïf. At night we go out with niece Olga to find Jurryt, in the same place at Psirri. Terrace, good food, *musikí.* The same duo, tonight mostly playing *rebétika.* We return at two.

**Sábato 16**

To the mountain. Internet. Flowers. In the afternoon, another meeting with Athanassios next to the Acropolis.

*Jurryt van de Vooren, Athanassios Sikelianos, and Cristina in Greece.*

### SUNDAY 17TH

Athanassios drives us to Rafina, to Danae's home. Also there are a musician named Vassili and another gentleman. Danae is a singer, translator of Neruda and Racine; she lived in Chile for several years. Her songs sound like Lecuona in Greek. 92 years old, she doesn't like to have her own photograph taken but to take pictures of her visitors with the Polaroid. In good health.

Afterwards we converse on a promontory. Athanassios assures me that Rafina is the best of the areas surrounding Athens: 30 minutes from Ayías Paraskeví and with crossings toward the islands, Mykonos and others. Athanassios talks about the two types of education: the majority who learn to say Yes, yes teacher, yes God, yes government; the minority who learn to command those who always say yes. The rest is fantasy, he says.

292

### Monday 18th

I fast, read *The King Must Die* by Mary Renault, who rewrote the *istoría* of Theseus: a slave in Crete, dancer and acrobat, destroyer of worlds, variation on Shiva.

### Tuesday, Tríti, third day

I continue my reading and go at midday to the house on *odós* Mekina, Mekina Street. Cleaning and ceremony. Everything is as the dead man left it. I ask Grigoris to borrow *Prospero's Cell*, by Durrell. I return.

Cristina goes to the *nosokomío* where her grandmother agonizes. At sundown, *zazen*; I return half-naked. At night the moon is full, or nearly so. 40 degrees. The rabbit of the house follows me everywhere.

### Wednesday 20th

*Nosokomío.* I return and cook pasta. Siesta. Then we go to a bananapalm corner next to the neighborhood *platía*, a sort of café with postmodernity gone native, where they sell colorful drinks; nickel-plated architecture in the middle of a patio of Attic farmers; the waitresses are lovely, the music is okay: the Greeks also have their salsa, their elevator music and heavy metal records. *Diskobólos.* A beer, three cigarettes, lawyers for the devil, or is the devil your lawyer?

### Thursday 21st

As agreed, Cristina and I travel to *odós* Xiroyanis (pronouncing the X as in Mexico), in the Ilisias district two steps from the house of the deceased Grigoris. First we drink a coffee with Yura: he says it's better for me. *Skepsis*, he says, *skepsis*. We arrive and there's no light: three floors. "You're strong." Unpacking and cleaning. I proceed with my readings and short siesta, one hour maximum. Jurryt arrives from the Cyclades, Serifos; I think about Mariano. It's the island of Perseus. Jurryt drives me to the corner internet café, just 50 cents, which he offers. Possibly the cheapest in the Mediterranean.

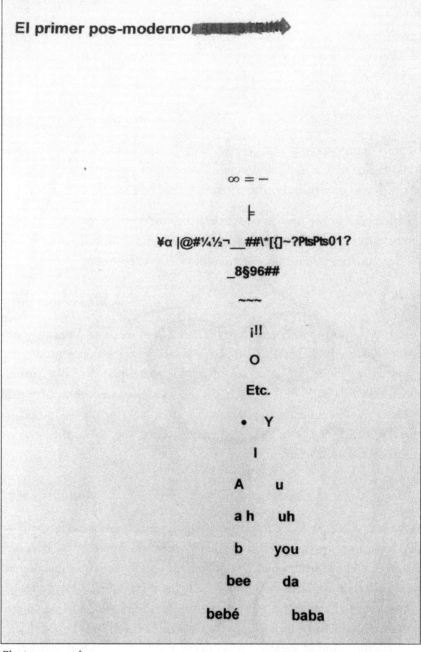

$$\infty = -$$

$$\models$$

¥α |@#¼½¬__##\*[{]~?PtsPts01?

_8§96##

~~~

¡!!

O

Etc.

• Y

I

A          u

a h          uh

b          you

bee          da

bebé          baba

*El primer pos-moderno*

"I was a king and a king's heir, I thought as the ship cast her moorings. Now I'm a slave": Mary Renault, *The King Must Die*. "She was a big ship." In English, as in Dutch, ships are feminine. She,

> She was a big ship
> slow to find the cranes
> crane dance is my life
> rice & beans is my beautiful
> mother earth, le droit a la paresse
>   "like the phoenicians who always come dancing
> and singing into harbor"
> *los que comparten el pan, es decir*
> *compañeros y ya que no podemos ser*
> *más que eso, intentemos*
> *no ser menos.*
> Small dog, big bark
> *perro pequeño, corteza gruesa*
> *ladrido amargo, sólo corteza*
> *corteza amarga que no canela*
> *estilo* skilos, *hueso pelado*
> *en luna llena.*
>
> [She was a big ship
> slow to find the cranes
> crane dance is my life
> rice & beans is my beautiful
> mother earth, *le droit a la paresse*
> "like the phoenicians who always come dancing
> and singing into harbor"
> those who share bread, that is,
> companions and since we can be nothing
> more than that, let's try
> to be no less.

Small dog, big bark
little dog, thick skin
mean barking, just skin
mean skin no nice spices
*skilos* style, bare bone
under full moon.]

**FRIDAY, PARASKEVÍ 22**

Jurryt heading back to Amsterdam; sounds decisive about the end of his Athenian dream: he won't be back in summer, or for the same reasons. "I've had enough of Athens," he says. Funny how I feel the same as him, but about Amsterdam. I feel at home here, but for the people: people are people. "But I'm not people anymore," says Athanassios.

*Tipota alási*, say the Athenians. *Panta rei*, says Heraclitus.

Likavitos, 9: 30 p.m, going down the esplanade in search of nuts, I encounter Athanassios with raised cigar in hand. "*Telepathía*," we smile. "*Ise kalá?*" "*Kalá.*"

Then the three of us talk, sharing a coffee more expensive than ignorance. Ideas, who could remember every word. He speaks about Greece and its ambiguous present. Without bitterness, but the question has its seriousness: what's the principal source of our income? It's not the olive, or tobacco, cheese, wine, shipping, not even tourism. It's betting. And in the meantime, the priest is robbing the earth again. Of that we speak. We'll meet after the *diakopés*, the break. Mother Athena, free me from this pipe, which turns my heart to a torpedo.

**SÁBATO**

Internet, *nosokomío*, *to spiti*: home, final siesta. Silence, *perimenes*, a wait, Ares Enyalios will come. Dionysus planted the vine in Naros, Ciclades.

Visit to the *nosokomío*; good bye grandmother.

At 10 p.m, departure from Pireas.

Empty boat, Knossos Palace red & white. No Euro, no tourist.

At dawn the ship rattles off, *epileptiká* on the way to Crete. What is this, Poseidon? We arrive at Heraklion at 6:30. The driver swaggering and pleasant; still the mountainous, fast trip makes one sick.

We make a stop for coffee. On the other side of the highway are enormous hundred-year-old olive trees, columns of marble thrown wherever. Culture. We arrive at Lendas, southern coast. The first encounter on the beach: Koneehee, a traveler from Alaska who offers mocha to drink; we stay in his store until *mezzogiorno*.

Cristina wants to rent a room: siesta. Sea, tavern, *Chan chan, c'est la mode.* But that's not what I came for.

## MONDAY, DÉUTERA 25

Swimming, like *padsimadi*, king of stale breads: when the bread goes stale, you put it in water and bake it again. It's like eating rocks made of bread. With tomato, garlic, olive oil—but you also dip it into other dishes. It gets hot and softens up. There's a little corner store here; the wine of the country people is good, and so are the oil and the *rakí*, an aguardiente that turns the imagination upside down. Like *padsimadi*, I look at the stars …

"A landscape for resolutions and partitions," says Zarian in Durrell's book, "a landscape which precipitates the inward crisis of lives as yet not fully worked out."

## WEDNESDAY 27

The feather. Owl.

Gypsy melody that I forget, like others. She walks in front of me like Orpheus; I am Euridyce. We find ourselves on the sand, in front of the rock that rises in the middle of the cove. Then we put up the tent. First night.

Melon, *karpouzi*. Eating melon and reading that copy of *Ulysses*, picked up by the trash in rainy Amsterdam. The eagle glides over the area. Jupiter. A white bird dissolves into the white light. We all dissolve, sooner or later. In the afternoon I play the drum box. Night falls, stars come out. I sing: a girl approaches and asks to listen. Then her friend approaches: "It's nice," broken English. They're Austrians. Stephanie & Tania.

Here the drum box has a more metallic timbre. I sing the same three songs as always.

Afterwards I go to Nikos' restaurant, where Christina and Henk are having dinner together. He offers me a taste of his fish: *dorada*. And beer, then *rakí*. Nikos, the owner, likes to play with words: *eharistop*! When serving the *rakí* he asks, What will you? He writes on the menu board, mixing English with German and Dutch. They're his best clients. With Henk you can talk about art and other things. The stars are spectacular.

**FRIDAY**

We have Greek neighbors. They clash with the rest of the cosmopolitan population. They put out little chairs and tables, bring a hoop, a pail and shovel. Beach ball. Dressed for summer—along this stretch of beach, almost all of us walk around nude. I pull the copy of *Ulysses* apart: all the better to read you. I myself had bound it. Now it's time to concentrate on the reading, and even the spine is annoying. In the end I get bored. It's not the first time: several years ago the same thing happened. Arriving at page 250, I ask myself why I'm reading so much. I leave it on a tree root: what good luck for a book. Seven hundred pages to say so little. A master of literature is not the same as a master of language, much less of thought. The ants will take care of it.

I go out for a walk and run into a couple, a Greek man and Andalusian woman. Two lovely children: Ganesh and Sarasvati. They've spent some time in India and still come and go today. There they buy merchandise to sell here: fabrics, clothing, handbags, and other Indian items. His name is Alexandrós, and he invites me to get together for a beer in Odisseas, a tavern. Her name is Ana.

Late in the day I take the drum box out of its case. Spectator: a Greek girl, one of the neighbors. Sad eyes, if you so desire, but she knows how to watch.

At midnight, we share pizza with Henk, who heads out. Alexis doesn't arrive "in an hour at the tavern." Christina warns that for a Greek, an hour can mean any time.

Here in Crete, one doesn't do much. There was someone who measured time and space by cigarettes: "Two cigarettes away from here." And during eras of scarcity, they smoked leaves from banana trees and other things. As we're leaving, we turn around and the Greek arrives. Christina goes off to bed. We stay to talk. He's a *sadhu* in crisis: "I've come back to earth," he says, "which might be a mistake." But he really means it.

We continue in a place called *Diskos*, a sort of rustic discotheque. One smokes and drinks, rock and roll: "I'm coming back to earth!"

We return at dawn by the steep shortcut.

The meeting leaves an impression on me. While walking around Europe I haven't often met up with people who live with their feet on the earth and their gaze intense. For a moment I glimpse reality, my reality. Europe is an aging pall. The right thing is to return to Cuba in order to dig my hands into matter and raise the imagination's sails. Today, Sábato, I spend the day alone, taking a break from myself and my desires. Meditating. Sophrosyne, the word alone calms me like a goddess. Late in the afternoon, another bath in the sea, and I follow the trill from Lendas' country house to a tourist restaurant, El Greco. Nothing from the other world. We say goodbye to Hans, fireman from Antwerp.

Visit to the lion's mountain. Actually a large crag from which you contemplate the entire zone. To the left is the little town of Lendas, to the right the strip of beach and the structures called Diskos. In front, the sea, and to one's back, rugged mountains with olive trees and stones. I go back and we set up a sunshade, then meet Alexis and Ana in their migratory shop.

They're seen haggling with a German couple. 75. From the German (because he believes that haggling is appropriate and nice), 65. 70 from Alexis; the German insists 65; 68, the German still insists. "I've come down twice, and you still insist! 67." *Datsi.* "If you hadn't haggled so much, I would have given you a bag for your purchases!" She stays with the children, and Alexis joins us for dinner at the tavern of old Odyseas after disposing of, as he calls it, "the rest of the day" faltering under age and heat. We talk about the wind: *meltemi, boriña, boreas. Kirie Boreas*, as the singer Tsarandonis says, Mr. Boreas, northern wind. We eat surrounded by stars, spaghetti, salad, bread, and a bit of *rakí*.

"If you want to come to Greece, I invite you to join us in the mountains."

He's got a dream. Small community: school for children & natural life. Who knows the future: *kataklismós* or paralysis, I mean, paradise.

### MONDAY AUGUST 1: PEACEFUL

Christina speaks with Charis about a didjiridou, which he's playing by the sea; I can see them from here. He's kind and she can always make good conversation. And forget breakfast. In late afternoon, we eat in another country village called Sifis. We talk and drink rakí with Charis and a girl named Dimitra. I bring the drum box and sing two songs: *Pajarito* y *Ala de mar*, Little bird and wing of the sea.

*Mes ton potamó tou Ná* (by the river Ná)
*ine yemato Ligariá* (a lot of plants)
*pu pernane ta pankiá* (punks)
*ke tis kapnisum ta kladiá* (smoke the leaves)
*ma ke I mikroastí* (the bourgeois)
*tin pernun ya hasishiú dendri* (confuse the hashish tree)
(Refrain)
*Ligariá, ligaría,*
*se pernane ya Foudiá* (mistake it for cannabis)
*An vrezis poté sto Ná* (if you ever go)
*min se verdepsi I Ligariá* (don't get confused)
*ine dendro liyeró* (supple tree)
*ma ogi taxidiotikó* (but not travelling)
*ke an thes onirá gliká* (if you want sweet dreams)
*na protimás kanavouriá* (choose cannabis)

Alexis and I put this song together facing the sea, which seethes today with jellyfish, *tsuchtras* (I get stung twice). The song is about the *Ligariá* bush, which is called *vencedor* (victor) in Cuba and resembles *Indica cannabis* in more than one way. So much so that the punks, like the good bourgeoisie, smoke it in vain. For the body of the song Alexis has chosen a *rebetiká* tempo, whereas for the chorus he prefers a more dynamic mode, from Cretan festival music. I tell him that if I were to do a Cuban version, I'd choose a *chachachá* tempo, and for the chorus, *palo*.

A Spanish rendition would open:

*Junto al río tenaz con su verdor*
*crecen muchas matas de Vencedor*
*confundiendo su forma y su color*
*se las fuman con especial ardor,* etc.

Then I go out to swim in the bay, over which a great crag presides. I'd like to climb it but can't. The natives warn me that it's dangerous because the currents are changeable as the wind. "You swim too much," Charis tells me when I show up in front of his cabana of stone and reeds. He just plays the didjiridou and occasionally rinses his body at the shore. He tells me that the name of this bay is *Ditikós*, from the west, *dísi*. En Cretan, they call the place *Diskos*.

Then with Sifis, Nikos and Alexis to Odysseas tavern to drink and smoke. The aged Odysseas, family patriarch, used to play the Cretan lyre, but now he's very old and the lyre hangs from one of the walls, worn out. I'm going to sleep and dream of Havana: witnessing the capitalist resurgence I say to my colleagues: so much swimming in order to die upon the shore!

### WEDNESDAY 3RD

I start with *zazen* on a stone wrapped in a pair of pants from India. Then off to swim; with the drum box I try out a possible versión of Ligariá. Lunch: *tomata, anguri* (pepino), *padsimadi*. We go quickly to town, run into Alexis & family, agree to versify in Sifí. We drink a few beers with them and a pianist from Hannover. Alexis invites me to play drum box in his migratory stand, but I don't go. I'm suffering from a social overdose, I tell Christina: I stay out under the stars. I sleep until she gets back. Wake up with an ancient feeling, like someone coming "from an old peninsula": Anatolia.

### THURSDAY 4

Perfect. I wake at dawn, smoke a cigarette, Black Dog comes by with greetings. I do *zazen*. And return to life. To the sea: I find Evil Water, *psuchtra*, which stings in three places: arm, left leg, and cock. *Kalimera, Alexis*. We talk and drink *chaí*, but first he has offered *ellenikó kafé*. Then we go to the old temple of Asklepios. Say hallo to Asklepios from me!, says Alexis.

The temple is a ruin, well preserved, with a floor of mosaics representing dolphins, an ancient olive tree, and a little orthodox church astutely erected to take advantage of the energy at the site.

As is my custom, I sit down under the olive tree to listen to the voice of the leaves:

You have to break your inner circle of stubbornness by moving toward a more natural kind of life: sea, mountain. In the city you'll also find your place if you let your inner nature free; this can transform your surroundings into a natural place.

Abandon the protecting hedge, anything that reminds you of jail, a holy place, cross, sacrifice, suffering, pain, orders, rules, uniform.

> Don't be a priest inside your land
> or marry outside of her.

Take a look at Miyamoto Musashi again: The activities of the Samurai.

> Music
> Building
> Sword. Real sword, not metaphorical.
> Translation, in the broadest sense. Messenger, healer. Traveler, ambassador.

### FRIDAY 5TH AUGUST

*Aletheia? Ne.* Hop, we're in Monkey Town. The sea was getting rough: jellyfish and south wind, unlike the Libyan kind: cool. Go first to Miamou (a variation on *maimoú*, monkey); we ride in Alexandros's van. Stop there for good *raki* and conversation. Maybe, Alexandros says, the reason they gave this village its name is the pithecanthropus bones they discovered here. *Píthikos.* Never mind, we ride to Mires, stop for water. I talk with a man milking his goat:

> *Milais elleniká*; do you speak Greek?
> *Oji*, no.
> *Pou es etci* ; Where do you come from, Romania?
> *Oji*, Cuba.

Cuba! *Pou dulevis* conf.; where do you work?
*Hollandía.*
Aah … problems with immigrants here, too many.

We move on, from Mires to Matala.

Famous caves, built in the stone. Chambers, beds, corridors, balcony, if you will, terrace, rocks. Climb. Roman cemetery, they say, hideout for those diseased with *lepra*. Especially noticed during the Seventies because of the hippies' use of the place as a shelter … We eat and sleep on the beach, sea is kind of rough, find a *kombolói* on the sand, in the morning. Looks like a rosary, brown plastic beads, like resin. But not prayers, swinging in the hand, spinning around one finger the wheel of life. Good for not smoking.

During coffee 2 German ladies come plus a Greek old-timer. *Moira,* we move to Mires.

Destination, market. Alexandros and Ana run the shop, Cristina looks for food, I play the flute and part of the time the drums. Wake up a sleeping vendor. The children play and listen. The sale= 70 €. Pick up everything and go for one last *souvláki ké birra*. Good bye, *andío*, Alexandros and family, we'll write about the weather: cloudy, rainy, windy, sunny.

One bus to Heraklion, one ship, 10 p.m., to Athína. *Kaló taxidi, bon voyage.* Actually, at dawn, Pireas. Subway to Monastiráki. Syntagma neighborhood, bus, home. Time to rest.

We sleep, wake up as other sleep. Siesta? Tired, no, a calm in the body that has left nature to come to the godless city. Polis, never said better. Nature here as well.

Quiet neighborhood of the masses missing neither bird nor cat. I clean the house in Xiroyanis street and go on to that of Grigoris. Here I feel at home, whatever may happen.

On FM 93.6 I listen to good music and they talk about Cuba. It's Sunday, August 7th. 8 p.m. and still with daylight. You can write, read or talk on the terrace, facing a building, above the street that is 8 meters wide. In the afternoons a couple of youths, university students, are talking next to a window. They drink coffee continuously, smoke until noon. She's black, he's white, like that song. Sometimes no one's there.

Here things are left unwritten. We go to Psirri. A month in Greece and I'm already rotting, another month and they'll have to hunt for us with dogs, which certainly ...

### MONDAY 8TH

Repose. Breathing, oh Kriti, island of the south, land of the body-spirit.

### TUESDAY 9TH

The marmalade at the little market is incredibly expensive.

*Etniki trapeza,* community bank. *Trapeza* is also table. Omonia neighborhood, noon. What are we doing? Changing itineraries, pushing the departure back from the 10th to the 29th. Olympic Airways.

Back to the *nosokomío,* visiting grandmother. She dies tomorrow.

She suffers no more at the hands of doctors.

### 10TH

Marjoram, Merlin prescribes, and exercise. We go: Hospital-Ayía Paraskeví- Mekina.

### 11TH

*Spanakopita* dreams: *spanako-pita,* spinach-pie. Clean up Yayá's garden. Speak to the plants, water the soil, sweep, throw away old things, dusty memories, forget and go away. Nothing more. In the afternoon Christina and I go for a walk through the neighborhood. At dusk, we go to Ayía Paraskevi. Babis Kharalambos talks about the difference between *dulevos,* work from *dulos*, slave; and *ergasía* from *ergos*: work as undertaking something for the others.

The first, job; the second, deed. It's a heroic view of work, like the Works of Herakles: cleaning, hunting, battling, killing; not much creation though. Herakles, they say, was in this case sort of an employee of a certain king. But later, he undertook his own creations, which were sometimes similar to his previous jobs. He says: "The first only works to get money for himself. He's not responsible for the process nor its final results. The second, artist, creator, *graphos, musikí, kaliteknés,* creates mainly for others." Yura says that today there's not much difference in Greece.

### FRIDAT 12TH

Funeral. Dimos Vyrona, or the Byron district.

The mourners nearly make you cry. Ah, earth that returns to earth, Yayá. *Kafeneion kai taberna: psári, krasí, psomí.* Fish, wine and bread. Hellos and goodbyes. Aunt Mary invites us to the sea, *sto thalassa,* a neighborhood on the coast: Nea Makri. "Only one family, Cristina, only one family." We eat supper near the beach, *psári* and *skordaliá* that you can make with potato or bread: 7 cloves of garlic per half kilo. Vinegar and oil.

### SÁBATO

*Kalimera. Ellenikó kafé. Monasteri Ayios Efraim. Megalo* martyr, tortured by the barbarians. In this case, Turks. Miracle worker. I take my shirt off in the sun. We go to the sea. I read the novel *Che's Suicide* by Petros Markaros. A detective novel.

### SUNDAY 14TH

I sleep outside. Ocean. Back to Mekina street. At night we take a walk through Omonia and the perpetual Psirri district. A sad night. Today there was an airline disaster: Olympic Airlines, 125 dead. Mystery.

Panayía. Old tune.

*Mi nuevo vicio, dormir*
*mi religión respirar*
*mi necesidad comer*
*y mi obligación cagar.*
*La montaña mi jardín*
*mi cuarto de baño, el mar*
*de pasaporte un jazmín*
*y mi partido un panal*
*de l'avispa el aguijón*
*de la mariposa el baile*
*en los labios la canción*
*y la canción en el aire*
*dios una lluvia de abril*
*tus ojos amanecer*
*mi privilegio morir*
*mi capricho renacer*

[Sleeping, my new vice
breathing, my religion
eating, my necessity
shitting, my obligation.
My garden the mountain
my bathroom the sea
jasmine my passport
honeycomb the game for me.
From wasp the sting
dance from butterfly
on my lips a song to sing
and the song hangs in the sky
god a rain in april

in your eyes the dawn
dying is my privilege
my whim, to be reborn.]

Reading *De zelfmoord van Che*, by Markaros, whose title has no relationship to the rest of the book and seems to be a gimmick. A series of distinguished Greek citizens commits suicide before television cameras. As if incited by the recommendations of a political sect. The superintendent, typical anti-hero, sallies forth to navigate the turbid waters of the polis. We'll see.

At night we go out: in the historical and tourist district of Plaka, an excellent gathering: Spyros and his daughter Nora, *misí misí,* half and half, like Cristina, Dutch mother and Hellenic father. They run a craft shop: curiosities, old postcards. He gives me a princely jew's-harp from Tanzania. His concepts for *oikonomía*: lower the prices, neutralize taxes, split the benefit, profit that brings everyone like dogs to the hand of a lunatic. In sum, capitalism: *malakíes. Malákas*: jerk. *Oxford Learner's Pocket Dictionary* by D. N. Stavropoulos.

We go on with wine, a black dog comes to visit us, one of the city dogs. We listen to *músiki* from Ioaninna, *Lesbos kai Mytilene* (*kai*, pronounced "kay"). Infinite music from Eládas, each island a country, every mountain a kingdom. At dawn, we circle the old city painting the walls. I leave the sign of four winds. We eat pita.

**TUESDAY 16TH, ΑΙΣΧΥΛΟΣ**

Aeschilus or Skilos, dogpoet. Dog: *skílos. Orestíada*, in an English version.

Your chaotic skills
your eyes like sunrise
from the first minute
say "I love you"
correct me
if i'm wrong

Some people talk about women's emancipation. Others talk about the emancipation of man from his dependence on the woman. *Kimeras.*

Read in *Prospero's Cell,* by Durrell:

> Count D: "Therefore if you come to me, like Zarian, and
> ask me why I am not writing down these discoveries, I can
> only reply that that is not what I mean by philosophy. I am
> enduring, and that is enough."

Night. Athina is enough. I read the *Oresteia.*

17TH

Success is now humanity's god

Coephori

I rock the boat. Then Jarálambos invites us to Nea Makri. Swimming with the family. We eat at his home: *makaronia me oktopodia.* Macaroni with octopus. *Jorta,* vegetables, excellent. *Brian* or *turulú turulú,* a baked dish based on eggplant and other vegetables. Ke *joriátiki,* a peasant salad or Greek salad: tomato, cucumber, feta cheese, everything cubed, olives with their abundant corresponding oil, onions. Then fruit, with cheese from Chipre. Long conversation until midnight.

18TH

New suit, new plumage: new trip. Hushed or loud voice: a question of taste, says Athanassios. *Palinuro.*

> No mother gave me birth. Therefore
> the father's claim and male supremacy in all things,
> save to give myself in marriage,
> wins my whole heart's loyalty.

Athene. Eumenides.

Apollon Loxías: God of words.

*Traketeo lunar*
*vive la luna!*
noisy star
*embarcación*
*de cuyo nombre olvidas*
*hasta el último trazo.*

[Rattling moon
the moon lives on!
noisy star
vessel
whose name you forget
even its last trace.]

We've gone to the market in the Ilisias district: *etnikí ágora*. Greetings to the carpenter. Would you like his job? Announcement from the city: Seeking wood sculptor. *Kaliteknés*.

Siesta. Three musicians pass by in a daytime serenade. They saved my day, says Christina. And mine.

"Alexandros, drunk!" shouted Ana at the aforementioned, who without putting hands to the rudder, described and wrote history in gestures. Monkey's Pass, in rugged Crete. Raki, ouzo, with calligraphy there are no fixes, the hand trembles. Like a tulip of ash my cigarette peters out. Those conversations in Greek that you can hear from the street. On the patio the pigeon with her hollow sound, which the children love. The icon observes me with a guilty smile.

**19TH**

*Foreign footballers, tightrope walkers,*
*poets and authors*
*will be subject to a special residence status*
*if they wish to come to Greece.*

12 month residence permit. Working contract. 150 € . *Athens News*. 12 August 2005.

In the morning, Yura comes to look for us to go to the cemetery, *koim-itirion*, place of rest. Dimos Vyronas, where seven days ago the second farewell ceremony was held for Olga. Incense, candles and *sítari*.

*Sítari* is a kind of sweet crumb wich they pass around with raisins, pis-tachio-*fistíki*, clove … cinnamon, to be shared. The Papas psalmody, a rushed farewell. *Evaristó Papuli:* thanks, *Naste kalá,* he responds. Be well, he disappears.

Glyfada, with Zía Magda. The landscape of our thought, according to Durrell, landscape as a form of metaphysics. Beyond, *meta- físi,* nature. Our metaphysical landscape is Greek, *elénikós*; according to Martí one breathed a Greek breeze there. Referring to the seminary of San Carlos. They say the Acropolis is open tonight for the full moon.

We eat at Jaralambos' home. Seashells on the island of Cypros, *karaolos, salingári* in Attic Greek. We drink *ouzo chipriota*: Isidoros, like my grand-father: gift from Isis.

And the Cypriot cheese: *jalumé.* Gummy.

### SÁBATO 20

We go to the ocean: little beach, *anijtó piélagos.* Zesi, a small strand on a wide gulf; limpid water, rocky shore. Facing the island of Evia, moun-tains like feminine bodies, round, smooth, naked, spattered with pine and olive trees. At the top, modern windmills. On the road home I find a song:

    *Keté——— keté——— keté——— keté*

*Dekapende*, fifteen. It depends.

Jarálambos comes to guide us to the mountain called Imitos. From the top he shows us the city. The modes of green, the structure. The mountains inside: Likavitós, Akrópolis, Filopapo and Turkovuniá. The ones outside: Imitos, Pendelis and Parnases. We return from the peak to a nearby tavern. On the way, he shows us the abandoned stone monastery where Atanasios spent fifteen days, with no sustenance other than the mountain itself. He recounts his Pythagorean vision of the world in numbers, letters, sounds. Why we see the green in a plant only thanks to the number of electromagnetic vibrations that arrive at the eye; why the o micron, with a small o, represents the 360 degrees of the circle; why the planets sing; and so on. He has already taken us to the *koimitirion* of Athens, with its legends in marble:

> *Matheodoxía*, he explains, for nothing, something dead people don't need anymore.
>
> *Spondí*: offering libations to the dead. *Omeospondía*: federation. Shared belief. *Ikos*: house.
>
> *Nomía*: rules of the house: *oikonomía*.

Jarálambos, sporadic philosopher. An amateur. At night Cristina and I go to Akrópolis from the peak of neighboring rock. We look out over the city again. And the moon, waning somewhat, takes its leave of us. A black dog sleeps next to the abyss. I could stay here forever. Cristina smiles.

## MONDAY 22ND

Resting my skeleton here, reading *Opus 100* by Asimov, save for a brief Internet break, resting the bough.

In the morning Jarálambos takes us to Nea Makri. Splendid day. We continue the conversation about cognates. According to Asimov, a million seconds equal eleven and a half days.

> 97 calories per square cm per minute: solar constant.
> Why the idiot? Dostoyevsky, and others. *Idios*, oneself. *Idiótis*,
> citizen of one's self. *Idiotelia*: selfishness. Self-interest.
> *Autarkía* and *autárkis*: self-sufficient.
> Asshole: *ilízios*.

Siesta. I dream that I'm wandering through Jerusalem with two bottles of ouzo.

New visit to Spiros and Nora: he does my portrait. I do his, just a caricature. We go on with our dreams. Nora paints a Cuban scene, a rumba. Perfect rhythm and emotion. Not to speak of color. We say goodbye next to the Acropolis.

## THURSDAY 25TH

I clean the house with a hose. Read Asimov. Life is dream. We go to Nora and Spiros' store, where there is *polí oreo raki*. A very good aguardiente.

## FRIDAY 26

At night we go to Ayía Paraskeví, eat pizza, receive presents. Tomorrow we're going to Delphi. A certain Asklepios has killed off the cigarette, they say. The serpent gives us health, like the oracle, with the leaves of dafní or laurel. But maybe some other herb or substance, to lend an ear to Robert Graves.

But tomorrow we're not going to Delphi. Instead we're going to Glyfada. Table talk with the merchant captain Stelios. No, Cuba is not a satellite, Stelios. He talks to me about his colleague in Havana, one Kiriakos who repairs ships.

We take the Katexaki subway to Monasteráki, final return.

The past serene, packing baggage. I'm nothing more than an ordinary Jaraghiosis. Siesta. Dinner with Babys: "In the winter, it's better."

### MONDAY 29

Airport. *Aeroliménas.*

Greece has exported 51, 807 words to the world
from Abyss and Alphabet to Zodiac and Zone
and kept one for itself
MYTHOS
HELLENIC  LAGER  BEER

In the check-in line, 8 in the morning.

### 27 OCTOBER, HAVANA.

Have arrived here; I don't count the days that separate me from, don't count the days. Talking yesterday with Reina, a project emerged: an introduction to Dutch writing given on three consecutive dates in November,

Winter has come with the hurricane. Off to seek shelter soon!

*Je m'*meet up with Enrique Sainz at l'UNEAC. For the magazine we plan a small dossier of Dutch material: contemporary poetry, Nanne Timmer and her teaching experience in Leiden.

Separately: a selection of Dylan Thomas: 15 poems.

### 1ST OF NOVEMBER, TO MY READERS, THE STRANGERS.

Poems as biography of D. Thomas

*Estos poemas, con todas sus crudezas, dudas y confusiones se escribieron por amor al hombre y en alabanza de Dios y yo seria un tremendo comemierda si así no fuera.*

(These poems, with all their crudities, doubts, and confusions, are written for the love of Man and in praise of God, and I'd be a damn' fool if they weren't.)

—D.T. in the introductory note to his *Collected Poems* (New Directions, 2003).

Poet and tightrope walker, an angel and an acrobat, *sobre el despeñadero de las rocas* ("on a breakneck of rocks"). From the beaches of gulls and bagpipers, where the shells "hablan siete mares" ("speak seven seas"), to the eternal cities of error, from Laugharne to New York, from the bracken-covered hill to the heroin bar. And from there to the sky.

*Un proceso en l'intemperie del corazón*
(translation of "A process in the weather of the heart," by Dylan Thomas)

*Un proceso en l'intemperie del corazón*
*Vuelve húmedo lo seco; el dorado proyectil*
*Se huracana en la tumba friolenta.*
*Una intemperie en el barrio de las venas*
*Vuelve la noche día; la sangre en sus soles*
*Enciende el gusano viviente.*

*Un proceso en el ojo premoniciona*
*La ceguera en los huesos; y la matriz*
*Puja una muerte cuando la vida se derrama.*

*Una oscuridad en l'intemperie del ojo*
*Es la mitad de su luz; el escrutado mar*
*Rompe en tierra sin ángulos.*
*La semilla que hace del lomo monte*
*Bifurca la mitad de su fruto; y medio fruto cae*
*Lento en un viento dormido.*

*Una intemperie en la carne y el hueso*
*Es húmeda y seca; lo rápido y lo muerto*
*Se mueven como dos fantasmas ante el ojo.*

*Un proceso en l'intemperie del mundo*
*Vuelve fantasma al fantasma; cada niño de madre*
*Está sentado en doble sombra.*
*Un proceso sopla la luna en el sol,*
*Arranca las chapuceras cortinas de la piel;*
*Y el corazón rinde sus muertos.*

The medical metaphor, scatological, for birth and death. Dylan was born on the 27th of October in 1914. His father Jack, a teacher in the public school, found his name in the *Mabinogion*, a collection of Welsh legends: Dylan, son of the waves. The Dutch astrologer and writer Duco van Weerle gives his reading of the poet's chart:

> This is not at all the typical horoscope of the artist; but Dylan
> Thomas shows in his creative disposition, beyond a mere
> egocentric self-expression, the social application of his abilities.
> With its strong constituent presence of water, he drains the
> sources of collective emotions and learns therefore how to
> tell stories in fascinating ways [...] A "speakmaker" (sic), a
> troubadour who leads the clan's evenings, but who follows
> his path the next day in search of a new audience to enchant.
> He enjoys the attention but does not desire to be an object of
> appropriation.
>
> Scorpion with ascendant Gemini and culminating with the
> Moon in Aquarius, therefore: of deep waters, of difficult
> personality, changeable, and simultaneously a lovable speaker
> and a jovial, sociable presence.

Jealous of his liberty and independence, Van Weerle adds, Dylan offers little ground or terrain on which to pigeonhole or question him. A freethinker enamored of words. Taken from the biography by Karel Wasch, poet of South Amsterdam.

News: Negotiated for next week the transfer of Mariano to the Pepito Mendoza school in Cayo Hueso. "A lovely neighborhood and with agreeable people," according to Pello the Afrokán.

### TUESDAY 2ND

Continuing to translate Dylan. Irving comes by with some antibiotics for my mother, Christina calls. The sun appears at 4 in the afternoon. A fresh sun, but the dark moves in quickly, as in Holland. This light—is it a flaw in perception?

### THURSDAY

The Rimbaud of Cwmdonkin Drive; what the poet has to say about himself: a maritime sketch, necessarily.

Waiting for Enrique Sainz at the door of UNEAC, the National Writers' Union, to discuss these things. The sun comes back out, a welcome balm: *non ti allargare*, the sun seems to say in the voice of Marcus Aurelius: life is not an empire to be constructed, there's nothing to conquer.

Enrique doesn't show—typical UNEAC rhythm.

### SUNDAY

A marine tobacco for the weekly entry: "From Sunday to Sunday!" This week I started to go to the *dojo* in Havana. After sitting *zazen*, the ceremony for Patricia's death: she dies young and beautiful. There are no tears.

One senses the presence of the master and the harmony between "the new arrivals" and "the veterans."

On Monday it rains, rains, but still Mariano and I go out to take a walk down the Prado and Malecón. On Tuesday, after leaving Mariano at school, I cross the Cerro neighborhood by the canal, where I eat bread and yucca and soda for breakfast on a street corner; the neighborhood's smooth dewy surface gives it the quality of a pearl. Not very clean, not very dirty: an equilibrium of nature and construct, country and city, mountain and alleys: Macedonia, Florencia, Buenos Aires, Zaragoza.

Time weighing a bit heavily, I translate poems: life-breaths, as the Greeks understood them.

Walking through the streets of Cerro, Santos Suarez, Centro Habana, Las Cañas, you notice the presence of the numbers game, called *charada* or *bolita*. *Kábala, tómbola, tíbiri tábara.*

Pythagoras said, life is number. Thursday I go out walking, but only after offering my salutations in the false-gothic church on Reina Street to Jesus and his father Joseph: I ask of the gods that they permit me to ask nothing of them (Pessoa). The prayer that may be less a petition than a report: here, again, one facing the other, *qu'est q'on fait maintenant?* For the moment I find the Koran on a streetside bookseller's table; after haggling: 75 pesos.

I also buy a pair of running shoes: 7.90 pesos in the national convertible currency. The two clerks whom I ask about the value of my change make it all very mysterious. Serious expressions, "I don't know, I don't know." By contrast, another clerk –loquatious– treats me to all of the information in luxurious detail, with figures I don't know how to appreciate or staunch. Code of silence meets logorrhea, as General Gómez said.

I cross Jesús María to visit the good Sigfredo: he offers gingered coffee; we discuss the Greek's current situation, and that of the Vieja Trova: Seferis, Sappho and María Teresa Vera.

Sophrosyne.

Speaking of ginger, when I get back to my neighborhood, the carpenter R. asks whether I can get him Viagra in Holland. I explain that I'm not going back north right now. I recommend celery, with which he's not familiar. And the ginger? No results, he says. I remember a Japanese proverb noted by Santoka in his diary: never lend your money to the man who doesn't get hard in the morning.

Since the CD and cassette player are broken, I rediscover the radio: did you know sir that as a young man Shakespeare stole deer to feed his family? Shakespeare: Robin Hood. Last night I dreamt of a deer who ate out of my hands.

On Saturday following *zazen* I go out with Mariano to las Cañas to visit Grandpa. *Lapsus mentis*: paying the taxi, weighed down with bags, I lose my wallet with 80 pesos and my ID card. The *lapsus mentis*, which spreads into my misuse of my hands, is a short-circuit caused by an overload of thought: while I do what I do in the here and now, I'm thinking about what I'll be doing later. The cart gets before the ox, the milk jug breaks the pitcher, Elsa the Intelligent loses her mind: *first things first*. Principle underlying all magic.

*Donc*, working on the "Dutch Studies"; the relation between Cuba and Holland across time-spaces: Piet Heijn and Joris Ivens, the letters to Theo Van Gogh (translated from the French by Francisco de Oráa with a prologue by Fayad Jamis), De Kooning's Havana nocturne, Capablanca and Max Eeuwe, Anne Frank and the Dutch buses that drive around Cuba with their signs made in Rotterdam, Delft, Nassausingel or just *Geen Dienst*: out of service.

As for the rest, notable dialogue with Tata Lázaro about the dichotomy between Oggun and Shangó, Sarabanda and Siete Rayos.

### MONDAY 7TH

I must not sing songs in class
I must not sing songs in class
I must not sing songs in class
I must not sing songs in class
I must not sing songs in class
I must not sing songs in class

I must not sing songs in class
I must not sing songs in class
I must not sing songs in class
I must not sing songs in class
I must not sing songs in class
I must not sing songs in class
I must not sing songs in class

Mariano's homework-punishment from school.

## TUESDAY 8

Among the advantages o'listening to the radio: *Rítmicas*, by Amadeo
Roldán. Dylan translation: I went translating along from one line to
the next, *enjoy the word ocean*, riding a motorcycle of Ariel 14-pt font.
Metallica: *and nothing else matters, never care for what they know*. The Paris
Opera paying homage to Nicolás Guillén: Concha María, supermulatta.
*Metaforiki*: relocation. In the end I go out on the balcony: no one waits
for me there, only a star.

## WEDNESDAY 9

I just wanted to drink a beer. Exhaustion with this tropicapitalism, an
old prostitute who returns to the land where years ago she might have
been a celebrated hetaera, and she must start again from zero. Capitalism,
old whore, how you resist death, how you adopt cute and silky masks.
A single hour of streets in the city center, money exchange office, music
store with the monotonous rash of folkloric music, San Bernardo salsa,
dive bar stretched to casbah *supermarket* where the waitress doesn't know
which beer is the best: "I don't drink!" As if a virgin in a brothel were
telling a client, "I don't know, I don't fornicate." A beer and you learn
that in the desert there are still virgins: desert, paradise of the clown and
prophet, drink before the storefronts of the merchants, nomads and sed-
entary fugitives flood the Mediterranean plain. *Take it easy*, *rebetika*, l'eth-
ics eclectic and celtic, polyphyletic litany, leaving Aristotle in the dust

with his poetics. The China tea rose, the Cretan pipe, Oggún's rumba, but first the implements.

First day d'school for Mariano in Cayo Hueso. I go back to *The Odyssey*; translation of prose by Luis Segala y Estalella; or to the *Koran*, in the English version by N.J. Dawod. Translator in a translated world, I translate Dutch poets for *Unión* magazine, a day of breathing deeply.

> *I'm going to speak to you, o guest, with great sincerity. My mother affirms that I am that one's son, and I know nothing else; and no one ever learned his lineage on his own.*
>
> TELEMACHUS. *The Odyssey.* Canto 1.214

Sunday sunrise, Cubanology, What is the drug that verse contains? Incontinence, insomnia: navigation in unexpected waters; eddies, sandbars, breakwaters. The poet acts as pilot, but purely for drifting.

Mariano gets through his first week in the new school—and gets his first scolding. According to the teacher "he's enjoying himself too much." I say nothing: how can you enjoy yourself too much? The "Romance of the Naughty Girl" by Raúl Ferrer should be posted at the doorways to the schools like a Lutheran manifesto. And his nephew's musical rendition sung to start the day.

I organize my living like a martial arts show: exercises, long walks, races, meditations, koans (with salesclerks and in markets), readings for the devout: the *Koran* and the *Odyssey*; industrial arts, sweeping, collecting pieces of driftwood, a humble servant. Today, for example, I recover six tarred pieces at the coast: tree trunk, board, plank, strip, beam, and tie. As Robinson noticed: all things exist on the island; the hard part is carrying them around. Wheelbarrow. Sometimes buying the thing. Market. Charles III: consumes as if the world were going to end. Maybe it's true;

apocalypses at three to the kilo, four confused layers of so much crap: little plastic Christmas trees, fake Chinese porcelain, and very few tools.

Last night we watched *Cinderella Man*, the story of James Braddock, Irish gladiator: Russell Crowe in the perennial role of the hopeless centurion, stevedore and duende, derelict exemplar, hope of the poor d'esprit: *heavy-weight with beautiful mind. Greek in the Irish sea the ageless voice*: Proletariat of all the nations: off to your labor! Get into the ring, onto the dock, out there in the art world.

Today I re-encountered *Bury My Heart at Wounded Knee*. I read the history of Geronimo, "*the last Apache chief*," again. On November 3 1883, the Supreme Court of the United States ruled that "*every American Indian is, by birth, alien and dependent*." Based on this logic, we're all American Indians.

Last Friday a small bird got into the house; apparently a songbird escaped from its cubicle. It doesn't know what to do with freedom; I think it finally went back to its apartment. Havana prepares for its next birthday: 486, and there's a storm of *habaneras* on the radio and an irradiation of stormy *habaneras* on the streets. There are rumbas that are boleros.

## SUNDAY 20

5 a.m. the moon like a coin, perhaps a drachma. Angel of circumference: an imagined fact based on real histories.

## MONDAY 21

German class on television. University for Everyone.

Germans from the North and from the East, Elba, Weser-Rhine, North Sea: five tribes.

Translation of the Bible to the Gothic. Song of Hildebrand and Song of the Nibelung. 8th Century

Invention of the press: Gutenberg & Luther: Everybody's Bible. S. XVI.

90 million speak German as a first language: Germany, Austria, Switzerland, northern Italy, Luxembourg, Lichtenstein, etc.

Germans in Cuba: anti-Fascists in the 40s. Humboldt Circle of Democrats, 1946; addressed by Heinrich Mann and Leon Feutzschwanger.

6 themes: family, housing, food and drink, school, free time and work.

Proverbs and songs.

Havana's German House, 1862; The German Beneficent Society, 1819.

There is no Frenchman without vino, nor German without casino
JOSÉ MARTÍ, 1884.

*Auf Wiedersehen.*

⚜

*History of Western Philosophy*, by Russell. What better place to encounter Bergson? For though Bergson may pass as a serious savior, his study is pure comedy and there's nothing wrong with that. It wasn't one of Borges' favorite texts for nothing. Nor is it an accident that Bergson would appear sandwiched between Marx and William James, two of the founders of our psychology, or named in the ancient mode, ideology. Russell notes that the attempt to classify French philosophy is improbable, *since it cuts across all the recognized divisions.* This first aspect of disobedient resistance to classification should have called l'attention of Deshimaru; nothing less than the Bergsonian hope of placing l'intuition before the intellect in the fundamental attempt at comprehension; *the intellect is characterized by a natural inability to understand life.* Russell himself describes, with typical irony, the intellect as a carving knife that slices a chicken imagining that it was always already divided into parts. *Not bad, Russell!*

If duration is the true substance of reality, and if duration expresses itself above all in memory, *at the intersection of mind and matter*, then memory has, according to Bergson, a quality that is penetrating, vertical. Yang. This recalls the practice of certain Amazonian Indians, described by Strauss in *Triste Tropiques*, of memorizing long directories of elements (for example, a shopping list) because the exercise of memory is equivalent to the conservation of virility. Is writing then—and more specifically the writing of diaries—absolute yin? An exercise of femininity, Penelope's chore. Let's go one further: *things and states are merely visions, taken up by our mind, of becoming. There are no things, there are only actions.* The void is to phenomena as phenomena are to the voice. Only instinct, Bergson says, is knowledge at a distance. And this Pauline substance of the things to come is to the intelligence as sight is to touch, a companion meaning. *Faith, Dr. Ku*; outside it rains, the result of some cold front or movement of the atmospheric spirit. We are free when our acts grow out of the totality of our person, though in truth this moment of activity is rare. What is the identification, according to Bergson, between person and ego, between being and personality? For the time being, his tools of definition are poetic: like the perfume of deep jungle, Deshimaru used to say. Russell confesses that *the number of similes for life to be found in his works exceeds the number in any poet known to me.* The comparison, a favorite metaphor for Martí. This does not concede, however, too much value to Bergson as a *philosophe* in Russell's eyes, but probably it does in the eyes of Deshimaru, for whom l'action without any object other than l'action itself contains heightened value.

&

*Lugar recordado*
*espíritu fugado.*

A place remembered lives on
Its spirit gone.

MARIANO's rhyme

I dream about master Stephane. Tall shadow, kind eagle; Havana future, chaotic and happy. Mass *zazen*, sitting open to face the sea; the people come and go, Stephane shows them the posture, they follow their path.

Pauline is here, and the children of the future. An air of Maitreya.

Total and informal, l'education.

"Is L'abana yours now?" Pierre asked in an email. I'm still timid and cautious. To every lunatic his karma; the cycle d'discussions "Dutch Studies" has been initiated now at the Torre de Letras, thanks to Reina M. The translations for *Unión*, completed. The house quiet. The weather is favorable; here they say it's wintry. As Eddy Martin said on TV last night, good for playing ball.

Mrs. Fina García Marruz telephones in the morning just to offer, she says, "a patriotic greeting in the style of Martí." Perhaps the reason this day has an intimate, insurgent pulse; it's also because I complete my reading of *Diary of a Mambí*, by Piedra Martel, at midday.

Wd be excessive to comment on the etymology of the term *mambí*, or to recall that of the name *Martel*. *Piedra* and *martillo*: stone and hammer: *Oggun mambi mambi*.

In the afternoon I go to pick up my son at school and he says, while passing the statue of Maceo, that in his imagination Panchito Gómez Toro fought at the Moncada Barracks. "In my imagination," he emphasizes. How could anyone refute that? He asks me to buy him a juicebox because his head aches; he clarifies that it's not a headache like older people get, nor did it result from getting hit on the head. This is about a juicebox, the pain that a juicebox can create inside one's head, as one thinks about that juicebox while we're leaving school. Out in the fresh sea air he forgets the juice.

Thanks to Mariano, I've reconciled myself to ballet. A few nights ago a friend of his mother's invites him to a performance of "Swan Lake." They sit up in the box seats. They sneak me in too, and I slip from balcony to balcony, from the president's box where the great Alicia herself will sit dressed in red, to other lofty but less honored places. This thing has its virtues. Mariano watches the two-and-a-half hour function without an instant of boredom and dances his way out. He says not that he will become a ballet dancer, but that he already is. And that he wanted to be one before. "Before, when?" I ask, thinking of his age—seven. "When I was three." "And why didn't you tell me then?" "Because I still didn't know how to talk very well." *Reasoning.* The performance was magnificent— which I state out of pure ignorance, since I know nothing about ballet and don't care to learn. But having moved from one location to another throughout the theater with no ticket or invitation, I've observed the subject to my satisfaction: dance, theater and audience. Even the dancers who, between curtains, strip off their slippers and, resembling shadows from Degas, watch their colleagues as they dance; curled up, the dancers take on the absolutely informal air of statues composed with thread.

⚜

Having seen the word in a TV movie, Mariano asks me what *poise* means. We look it up in a pocket dictionary: elegance, equilibrium. I think this was why we went to the ballet.

⚜

*Mortal decisions*: all decisions are mortal. Divine, too: *deicisions.* Thus the veneration of Odysseus, "fecund with schemes," whom I may have judged too lightly while reading the ninth canto with his narration to Alcinous—where good and evil become confused. Past, present and future are flexible too.

*Perez apartment bookshelf and blackboard*

327

*Mariano/Spiderman*

*"Portrait" line drawing*

*Omar and Mariano, 2017*

*"Sisyphus" print*

KRISTIN DYKSTRA

## 1. A Book of Days

Poet, essayist, and translator Omar Pérez López (b. 1964, Havana, Cuba) began writing in a notebook in 2002 while living temporarily in Europe. The notebook is the origin of *Cubanology*, this book of days.

The journey Pérez documents began as a short professional visit. It shifted into something less defined after Pérez fell in love with a woman named Christina. One of his daily entries suggests what the notebook chronicles in general, fusing everyday life into travel: "A memory of a flight, a journey, *jour*" (August 14, 2004).

*Cubanology* does not recall a luxurious stay in Europe. Based in Amsterdam for much of this period, Pérez sought ways to eke out a living from scattered jobs in translation, editing, domestic work, and childcare. He wondered whether his stay might lead to a long-term change, actual immigration to Europe.

Unlike some migrants from this time period who sought support among others from their home country, Pérez did not approach his situation by looking for a diasporic Cuban or Latin American community during resettlement in Europe. Still, his notes on the journey include telling details about everyday experiences—and common paperwork—that migrants to Europe encountered in this historical moment.

During the years he portrays in *Cubanology*, Pérez occasionally returns to the island for visits and updates to bureaucratic documents. In keeping with travel writing traditions, his returns prompt questions about his Cuban home, as well as meditations about where he really belongs and why.

Zen Buddhism played an important role throughout this period of his life. In Cuba Pérez had previously met a visiting French Zen master, Stephane Thibaut, who led sessions in Havana as one of his many outreach programs to Latin America. When he was a young man, Thibaut trained for many years with Taisen Deshimaru, who reappears in Pérez's later written transmissions. Thibaut followed that apprenticeship with a study of Japanese Soto Zen traditions. Afterwards he synthesized these influences into his own approach to Buddhism, leading a *sangha* (a Buddhist community of practitioners) that he characterizes as "international."[1] Taking on an identity as the monk Kosen, Thibaut framed himself in "the lineage of the great iconoclastic masters, free from any yoke, liberated from every dogma." Readers familiar with Zen traditions may find in *Cubanology* departures from customs familiar to them. For example, Pérez refers to Zen centers in Amsterdam and Havana as *dojos*, a term not used in all circles. Thibaut openly asserts that his style is "always disconcerting."

Pérez situates himself as a learner throughout the diary. This self-portrait as a disciple enhances his long-term interests in how everyday habits tie into wisdom. In an essay that Pérez wrote about Taisen Deshimaru, a piece that he also incorporates into *Cubanology*, Zen tradition suggests "a direct and daily contact with the process of coming to knowledge." Deshimaru's writing even suggests to Pérez the importance of the travelogue to global understanding.

Pérez did eventually become ordained as a monk, but he tends to emphasize the importance of thought over titles and other formalities. One of the most consistent activities he records in *Cubanology* is *zazen*: meditation in a sitting lotus position, understood as a process for modifying one's own mind. His meditation processes fold into questions running throughout the diary: Is transformation of my mind possible? How does meditation affect everyday life? Can ancient traditions associated with China and Japan be meaningfully integrated into my local present? What kind of life bridges contemporary Cuba to Holland? To Greece?

For a genre that seems to be focused so heavily on the self, and even the dramas of the mind's quietest recesses, *Cubanology*'s diaristic form allows for reversals: attention to anything and everything outside the self. Andrew Schelling observes, "The journal as a regular writing practice shifts the focus of writing from that old Occidental head trip 'who are you'—to 'when' and 'where' are you."[2]

---

[1] Descriptions taken from Master Kosen's website, "Zen Deshimaru" (http://www.zen-deshimaru.com/en/zen/monk-kosen, accessed on 21 July 2017 and 8 January 2018).

[2] *Wild Form, Savage Grammar: Poetry, Ecology, Asia.* Albuquerque: La Alameda Press, 2003.

Schelling elaborates, "Attention relocates on an out-there world: history, geopolitical observations, bioregional specifics like flora & fauna & weather currents, other peoples' customs, foreign vocabularies, and the indelible impact of capital on the twenty-first century." This is a terrific description of moments that happen all across *Cubanology*. The book of days swivels between external details and a carefully parsed expression of interiority, a record of thoughts and images that external stimuli prompt inside the writer's head.

## 2. The Words and the Way

Once there was a real, original, handwritten version of this journal. Now it is lost. I received a digital transcription of it from Pérez in 2008, who had typed up his notes. He wasn't sure at the time that the journal would ever appear in book form, so the transcription was an experiment in writing process.

Two years later we looked through the original, handwritten diary in Havana. I had started translating the digital file and took some photographs, which show that he had made diagrams and sketches alongside words as he wrote. Unfortunately, the physical notebook disappeared after this moment in 2010 and before I completed my translation, along with nearly all of the original visual elements. This translated edition of *Cubanology* relies on Pérez's digital file and visuals from more varied sources.

He composed much of the original journal in Spanish. My translation shifts this anchor language into English to reach those readers who don't read Spanish. However, the overall issue of language is slippery throughout the entire book of days, and this translation aims to capture something of that quality.

First, Pérez took a conscious interest in traversing what he calls the "translated worlds" of the visitor, the temporary resident, and the potential immigrant. He interacted with people from many nations and experimented with multilingualism throughout his book of days. He reflected on values and ways of life connected into this diversity. Describing this book as "multicultural" is no empty gesture.

Second, Pérez used the flexibility of this genre (book of days, writer's diary, traveler's journal) to blend systemic elements with celebratory anarchy. Sometimes he marks words as foreign, italicized, contextualized—he shows us that he even studies and defines words in classroom settings, where he will be tested (*biep!*). Day by day Pérez was required to demonstrate an increasing mastery of languages. To disregard his degree of multilingual competence is to misunderstand the demands placed on emigrants that he so successfully depicts.

In contrast to what we might call that "disciplined" relation to language, Pérez occasionally uses words more rebelliously, writing across languages but dropping these formatting signals for the reader. On a parallel and more conceptual level, he displays suspicion of exerting too much control over his travels amongst languages, preferring the freedoms of playfulness and imagination.

While "translating" *Cubanology*, I encountered Dutch, Greek, Italian, French and more, as well as the dominant language of Spanish—and in a secondary relation to Spanish, chunks of English. I chose to leave Pérez's use of languages other than Spanish or English mostly untouched, recognizing that his depictions of informal socializing, classroom learning, and an embrace of amateurism and play combine within a strong conceptual slant. They all make it problematic to go very far with corrections aimed at expertise and perfection.

Pérez has not published the journal in Spanish, so he had not edited details with a book-length consistency in mind. How then to strike a balance between order and disorder in the translation?

I decided not to write out numbers in words, given the informality of the journal. As for degrees of foreignness, I circulated excerpts to test readers and heard a strong preference for italics with languages other than English. But should this reaction be resisted? It would be possible to push readers to another level of difficulty by abandoning those markers of linguistic difference entirely, and that challenge would have a conceptual validity for *Cubanology*, as I'll discuss below. In this case, though, recognizing that some degree of clarification could help with striking a balance, I opted for a relatively consistent italicization within the body of each daily entry.

In a general way, I standardized the bizarre muddle of fonts and spacing in which the document had come to me. These issues resulted more from technology glitches than choices by Pérez. In order to gesture towards his plays across order and disorder, however, I left additional signs that *Cubanology* remains informal, multilingual, and not fully controlled.

I decided not to use italics where Pérez records days of the week, one of the places where he consistently plays with switching languages without marking their difference. I left his multilingual wordplay in translations of his poems, since he clearly intends certain pieces to exist as multilingual artifacts. In a few cases, the pieces are so thoroughly multilingual that I gave no translation at all. Where loan words make it unclear whether or not italics are needed in English, I decided to follow the mood of the original notebook. In entries where Spanish is essential to the meaning of his remarks (particularly for his poems, his brief poetry translations in progress, and moments when he reflects on details of the Spanish language), I include some of his original Spanish passages with the English translation. I did not standardize all of his varied spellings of people's names, the most important of them Christina/Cristina; and where he used accents in names, I left them. Loan words traveling across languages occupy the most questionable space because they are not recognized by all speakers universally, regardless of what authorities have decided. In the absence of absolute borderlines I followed my subjective sense of what might or might not be familiar, dictionaries be damned.

These formatting decisions were more difficult than usual because of conceptual echoes throughout the notebook. The relation between multilingualism and knowledge expands in importance across *Cubanology*. In an early entry (February 12, 2003), Pérez incorporates his essay, "Deshimaru and His Books." Here a multiplication of languages is practical, but it is also philosophical. Taisen Deshimaru represents the possibility for

> a true *lingua franca* of philosophy. Here one must understand the term as a direct and daily contact with the process of coming to knowledge. The *kusen* (from *ku*, the mouth, and *sen*, the teaching) was originally delivered in an English peculiar to

Deshimaru, called *Zenglish*, rich with expressions from Sanskrit, Chinese, and Japanese, plus French or German.

Pérez highlights Deshimaru's pursuit of "a venture of the greatest human and intellectual interest: creating an exchange between two cultures." For both of them, Deshimaru and Pérez, the relation between two cultures unfurls into something exceeding the bounds of even bifocality, or the "dual frame of reference through which expatriates constantly compare their home and host countries."[3] *Zenglish* and *Cubanology* become landscapes of multiplying languages, aspirational terrains dotted with the structures of knowledge they might ideally bear. Each terrain gestures toward a new, polycultural world.

Preserving *Cubanology*'s unresolved contradiction between linguistic control and disorder leads to a third dilemma for the translator. A polycultural world (real or ideal) brings people together who would not already understand each other's cultural codes. While the process of mingling leads to sharing of knowledge, social heterogeneity also involves moments of unintelligibility. If some degree of unintelligibility will never get resolved even as we navigate disparate cultural codes, then surviving without total translation is an important skill.

These oscillations between intelligibility and unintelligibility lead to questions about how much knowledge language can bear within a translated utopian visionary text. In practical terms, these questions imply a sub-question of how much context the translator should add to the translation, where words may drop essential context in their new language. To pursue the concepts of *Cubanology* into English translation, then, is to ask why and where context can be included or ignored.

The parsed nature of the writing in *Cubanology* means that its author often presents a word in minimalist fashion, not with explanation. Pérez

---

[3] This definition is Jorge Duany's paraphrase of a formulation from Steven Vertovec in *Blurred Borders: Transnational Migration between the Hispanic Caribbean and the United States* (Chapel Hill: The U of NC Press, 2011, 2). While *Cubanology* passes beyond this dual model, Duany's study remains relevant. He asserts the importance of phenomena such as the "intense cultural process of hybridization" and the emergence of transnational imaginaries resulting from emigration (228).

poises his words against silence. Coupled with the realistic significance of partial intelligibility that I have noted above, his style argues against adding any context at all. Anyone who looks back at the famous notebooks of the Cuban writer José Martí (1853–1895) will realize that when an author using the notebook form does not try to fill all its spaces of mystery with explanation, the lure of incomplete understanding can draw readers back to meditate on the writing more than once. The translator's entrance as a Cubanologist and explicator can infringe on precise experiences of unintelligibility and mystery evoked by the author. The world of his book of days should not be over-interpreted.

But stopping at this realization leaves considerations for the translator incomplete. *Cubanology* not only fuses the Americas with Europe but registers curiosity about traveling influences and objects from Asia and Africa. For example, Pérez drops details about different kinds of drums, which he builds and plays with migrants to Europe from other parts of the world. I contacted Pérez numerous times to clarify references because he invokes such an immense range of cultural literacies while on the move—in this example, registering cadences from different parts of the world.

He generously responded to my questions. These bits of information were useful but still did not answer all possible questions. I saw that brief fragments of context go a long way to help others take up the notebook's challenges, allowing for glimmers of understanding where there might be none at all. The glimmers can heighten the magic of mystery and white space, rather than just cancelling them out.

The next step was to decide how to give context while respecting the necessity of those silences framing words in what is, after all, a poet's journal. I experimented with adding some footnotes or endnotes, and we agreed that these strategies backfired. The notes projected an inappropriately academic armor that made the essential theme of "knowledge" in this book too inflexible. In fact, an academic veneer becomes ironic in light of the journal's philosophical dreams. Pérez explicitly validates writing that can teach while breaking from Western academic norms, a theme that arises in his notes on the legacies of figures such as Deshimaru.

After testing various strategies, I decided to place occasional, brief scraps of context into the flow of the journal's language. This strategy still bothers Pérez, as I believe it should, by pushing some near-pedagogical instants into the flow of the journal. But giving no context at all means abandoning other possibilities of the great polycultural adventure.

My approach is still based on a consideration of his principles, but from a translator's slant, an angle that will always be slightly unnatural to the author. When Pérez considers writing a novel, he writes in *Cubanology* that the purpose would not be to earn money, but to trace the pathway of a teaching (Saturday, August 14, 2004). If English-language readers are unable to comprehend too many moments throughout *Cubanology*, the pathway gets obscured. For example, specific terms from Zen practice recur throughout the notebook, requiring brief definition for anyone not part of the author's traditions to follow his activity. Something about the practice of meditation must be understood if the book is to point readers toward meditation's embodied wisdoms.

Other words needing context evoke details unique to a setting, for example to Cuba. I am placing a little of that material here in the afterword, while again avoiding temptations to be excessively comprehensive. This genre—notebook, diary, logbook, journal—attracts many readers with its intense grounding in daily experience, so I incorporate some details rather than just tracing general concepts.

Economic pressures and disparities are part of this notebook's foundation in lived experience. Currencies exist on unequal terms in the world, affecting the options available to travelers, and during the years of this journal, Cuba even had competing internal currencies as well as other economic features that are not universal. When Pérez jots a quick note about getting permission to pay an airport tax in Cuban currency, uninitiated readers could not know there was an airport *exit* tax at Havana's José Martí international airport, especially because they themselves may never have encountered similar taxes in their own travels. Noting the existence of an exit tax still does not even begin to communicate the economic message built into this moment. During this time Cuba had more than one currency in circulation, and Cuban nationals navigating between currencies were dealing with extreme imbalances in value. Paying a tax in the Cuban "convertible peso" (CUC), a bizarre monetary invention the state intended to circulate more on par with foreign currencies such as the Euro or US dollar, is vastly more expensive for Cuban nationals than paying in their conventional "national" currency.

Another bit of context best noted here involves his numerous vocabulary terms and cultural references pertaining to Afro-Cuban religious complexes, originally brought to the island by slaves from various parts of Africa and still practiced in contemporary Cuba. Distinctions between African diasporic traditions have been maintained on the island across generations, yet details from separate diasporic traditions cross divides in Cuban culture. Pérez does not present himself as any sort of leader or expert. Still he notes their presence.

The religion that is probably best-known internationally and has been studied seriously in Cuba since the 1940s is the Yoruba-influenced tradition of *La Regla de Ocha*, often called *Santería*.[4] Its pantheon of spiritual beings (*orishas*) includes figures mentioned by Pérez, such as Elegguá, Oshún, Shangó, Yemaya and more. Orishas have their own symbolic domains that can include aspects of the natural world, visual elements, legends, drum rhythms and other specifics. Ceremonies center on the *Ifá* oracle; Pérez spots an object from this tradition in a museum shortly after his arrival in Amsterdam. *Babalawos* are priests who interpret knowledge transmitted from the repository of Ifá, its history and culture. They write an annual letter of the year and release it to the public. In *Cubanology*, Pérez receives their predictions from one such letter on the first Tuesday of 2003.

The *Palo Monte* complex is associated with the Congos. Pérez sprinkles *Palo* terms across the notebook. A sample cluster appears in entries

---

[4] Due to the diffusion of Afro-Cuban religious complexes across arenas of everyday life and throughout island culture, it seems logical that explanations should not only rely on the world of academia, particularly given Pérez's interest in non-academic knowledge. Regardless, when considering how to write this summary I reviewed two academic sources offering English-language interpretations and translations: Stephan Palmié's *Wizards & Scientists* (Duke UP, 2002) and David Brown's *Santería Enthroned: Art, Ritual, and Innovation in an Afro-Cuban Religion* (U of Chicago, 2003).

from August 2004. The term *nganga* refers to an assemblage of symbolic objects and the container in which they are placed; meanwhile they can be anthropomorphized, so the translation "spirit vessel" captures more than one register of the word. Names for priests vary and include *Tata nganga*, "father of the nganga." In one entry Pérez manages to catch sight of the sign for Mama Chola, one of Palo's primary deities, and he tries to reproduce it. *Palo* dancing to which Pérez refers is part of this multidimensional culture. African sayings have been passed down in *Palo* culture too, such as one that Pérez includes (*Mal rayo parta talanquera congo*). Scholars have found their meanings to be preserved more through oral and ceremonial usage than formalized linguistic study. Phrases are understood in association with larger ideas or functions, rather than through their individual words. During our communications Pérez wrote something similar: "*Palo* verses are sometimes hard to translate; very often, whole phrases are [...] exclamations or imprecations with more emotional than intellectual meaning."[5]

Sometimes contextual issues point us outwards from Cuban culture rather than inwards. Another twist regarding the language of *Cubanology* comes from the author's own uses of English, which collide with my role in providing a translation into my (US-based) English. It's possible to argue that English has been present on the island in significant ways since the Spanish-American War, so English becomes part of "Cuban culture" up to a point.[6] But even before he began this journey, Pérez had more range in English than most Cubans living on the island. He had studied English in school and used it with visitors to the island for many years, and he was an accomplished literary translator before he began writing this journal. He then encountered English in many other contemporary forms during his European travels.

---

[5] Email from Omar Pérez to the author, 8 August 2017.

[6] For English-language readers who may not have encountered Gustavo Pérez Firmat's study, *The Cuban Condition: Translation and Identity in Modern Cuban Literature* (Cambridge UP), it may be a helpful starting point. Rather than presenting Cuban culture as some ossified object, Pérez Firmat explores culture as a ferment, as a site for translation, as a pushback against U.S. proximity and pressure, as a search for autonomy within histories of interrelation, and much more.

Sometimes English served as a *lingua franca* for interaction with people from all around the world. Pérez frequently spoke English with his girlfriend Christina, his fellow Buddhists, and other people he met in several nations—especially in Holland, where he had spent significant time in Amsterdam before traveling to Greece with Christina. In July 2004, he takes his English into Cuba. This moment inverts the relation between geographical origin and mother tongue: in the original book of days, the majority of his remarks describing his return visit to Havana (for Cristina, he writes) appear in English, not Spanish.

In my translation I've altered some of his English-language phrasing to maximize its effectiveness. Not long after a class discussion in Holland about an aesthetic movement, the New Objectivity, Pérez writes the following statement about choosing words carefully, apparently a reflection on his own words.

> You have to weigh every word; the ones that seem self-explanatory are, in truth, light. The ones that get heavy and multiply in the space-time tend toward the void, toward silence. One phrase too many ... They are already so many. (19 May 2004)

It is another reminder that a precise balance between words and silence matters, so the balance should be as effective as possible in the translation too.

Still I held off on transforming his English wholesale while merging it into mine. The textures of Pérez's English (sometimes in British spellings) are interesting. More to the point, they're conceptually twinned with his process of becoming an ever more multilingual, polycultural person. Scholars have made the important point that "weird Englishes" (Englishes "natural" to non-native speakers who acquire English around the world) capture realities of globalization as it is lived in the world today.[7] Estranged Englishes have their own authority. Their expressive power includes dissonance, which some readers will see as awkwardness: a contrast to the terms of a "fluency" perceived from any one geographical or majoritarian position, including my own.

---

[7] See especially *Weird English*, by Evelyn Nien-Ming Ch'ien (Cambridge: Harvard UP, 2004).

A fifth challenge regarding language: I have not even mentioned his creative wordplay. At times his creation of new words occurs across languages, and not only English and Spanish. So I too made up words, like "realviciousization," "deskritorio," "conveniodernity," "modernshitty," "thinkronicity," and more.

## 3. Among Systems, Against Systems

If this book is about anything, it is about throwing wrenches into the unsatisfactory systems that make you legible to others, while prying open gaps you can inhabit.

> Etymology of *repugnantia*: opposition or contradiction between two things; logics: repugnant terms> for an essay on the writer's condition: *La repugnante tarea d'escribir!* The repugnant labor of writing. (August 13, 2004)

To read any of Pérez's writing is to navigate the coexistence of differential things. He has a track record of focusing on opposition as he converts lived experiences into poetry, and in that entry, we can see that he is conscious of his strategy.

In *Cubanology*, this abstract opposition becomes visceral. His counterpoints give structure to tensions from everyday life. Consider the long, stressful process of choosing whether to live inside or outside Cuba, or choosing between languages for his self-expression (which implies having to choose between the audiences he could address).

Zen meditations appear to have enabled Pérez to use opposition more consciously in his writing, both by articulating oppositions and undoing them. Poet Jane Hirshfield observes, "Slipping the thought-construct of any form of duality and separation is one of the things at the center of Zen. At the center of the larger Buddhism that Zen is a subset of is the principle of lessening suffering, and the idea that the self, experienced clearly, is provisional and connected to others in every direction. All ideas can become barricades between people. Yet we are human beings, and keep having them."[8]

---

[8] Email from Jane Hirshfield to the author, 20 July 2017.

*Cubanology* reaches toward the strangeness of coexistence. Like much of Pérez' work it appears to disavow the strictures of national identity—Cubanness—but stubbornly returns to these contours too. At once playful and utterly serious, the study of a Cuban never relinquishes its grip on the island while afloat in the world. In the end, the writer's life could have taken a different turn, but it is thematically and formally appropriate that Pérez moves back to live in Havana at the end. Returning was his own choice.

The torqueing of nationalist rhetoric by Pérez and his construction of a more global, uncontrollably mixed cultural space is proper to his moment. In *Planet/Cuba: Art, Culture and the Future of the Island*, Rachel Price observes that the Cuban state revived nationalist rhetoric in the 1990s.[9] The nationalist reboot came in response to the collapse of the Soviet Union and the island's descent into the "Special Period," an extreme economic and social crisis that lasted until around 2006. The government reduced some of the Marxist-Leninist language in its Constitution, including internationalist discourse. More than one variant of national culture was encouraged, with an emphasis on local conditions. However, Price notes, as Cuba entered the twenty-first century the new emphasis on nationalism had become "asphyxiating" (6).

Pérez's singular take on the -ologies of Cubanness turns literary nationalism upon itself and inside out, responding to local and international pressures:

> Contemporary literature and art [...] may evince less an
> exhaustion with the socialist principles touted or debated
> in earlier works, and more an exhaustion with *cubanía* or
> "Cubanness" itself, and with the middlebrow realisms of
> the 1990s, which nonetheless continue to flourish in world-
> literature markets. (Price 6)

Through Price's commentary it becomes possible to understand why Pérez uses the journal to outline literary projects for himself, such as a

---

[9] NY: Verso, 2015.

novel and a work for theater, that do not resemble realist works circulating internationally.

Evelyn Nien-Ming Ch'ien reflects, "Implicit in the use of language is the search for an arena in which it is meaningful. Using language is a means of searching for a community, and when the community is intangible or inaccessible, or the immediate communities dissatisfy, language can become a tool to find a new one" (*Weird English* 38). I would take her point one step further to argue that Pérez uses language as a tool not only to "find" a new Cuba, but to call a new iteration of Cuba into being.

## 4. Essays and Poems

The notebook is shot through with references to artistry and craftmanship from beginning to end. *Cubanology*'s main character is a writer aware of international conversations about *techne* (in his spelling, *tekne*), the Greek term for methods and skills of creation. His reflections, the behind-the-scenes views of literature, mingle with literary texts that would normally take center stage in publication.

Pérez is a prizewinning essayist. Pieces that he has published elsewhere, such as "The Intellectual and Power in Cuba," appear whole or in part throughout *Cubanology*. In the informal notebook, one can read the essays against the textures of his daily life, a very different experience than reading the essays in isolation.

He also used material from the notebook to create his multilingual poetry collection *Lingua Franca*, published by Ediciones UNIÓN in Havana in 2009.[10] The book was met with some confusion in Havana, where so much contemporary literature is published with a more conventional use of Spanish. True, Spanish in Latin America is often infused with words from other sources, such as African diasporic terms, snatches of English, indigenous expressions, and (particularly in poetry) quotations

---

[10] Audio files and links to translations from *Lingua Franca* appear with some context in *Jacket2* magazine, as part of the "Intermedium" commentary series: <https://jacket2.org/commentary/xeno-audio>. PennSound hosts an author page for Pérez, presenting the *Lingua Franca* audio recordings without the project-specific context, but alongside a range of other audio and video resources: <http://writing.upenn.edu/pennsound/x/Perez-O.php>

from the French. *Lingua Franca* operates on a whole other scale of poly-lingualism, and as such, it was initially received by some as crossing the line: too weird.

As *Lingua Franca* drifts in and out of exile, linguistically, it is not sur-prising that its accompanying psychic shift would no longer conform to some frameworks of Cuban culture. However, if *Lingua Franca* and *Cubanology* do not align with singular notions of nation and language, or even with bilingual, bifocal formats explored by exiles and other diasporic Cubans who have settled in a second nation, they do something else that is still relevant on the community level. The essays, poems, and complete book of days give artistic performances of pressing, multidirectional real-ities for 21st century Cuba.

In 2008 Ruth Behar observed of Cubans living outside the island, "We have become one of the most intensely diasporic people within our con-temporary globalized world."[11] Cubans are not only living in the United States but in many nations around the world, where they use a variety of second and third languages that may not include English at all.

As a result, the concept of "Cuba" has become ever more portable and hybrid amongst writers spending significant time outside the island's geographical bounds. Unlike diasporic works circulating mostly abroad, *Lingua Franca* and *Cubanology* bring a diasporic drift back home, evoking psychic changes within Havana.

*Cubanology* reverses the itinerary mapped in a long history of travel stories from Europeans who encounter and colonize the Americas. Pérez explores European nations during his own new era kicking off the 21st century. Scholar Jafari Allen has proposed that it's useful to think of this moment as incorporating the "re-globalization" of Cuba: a series of changes triggered by the scramble for new international alignments in the wake of the Cold War and the resulting economic crisis for Cuba in the 1990s (3–4).[12] These changes force everyday questions about what

---

[11] *The Portable Island: Cubans at Home in the World*. Ed. Ruth Behar and Lucía Suárez. NY: Palgrave MacMillan, 2008.

[12] Allen, Jafari S. *¡Venceremos? The Erotics of Black Self-Making in Cuba*. Durham: Duke UP, 2011.

should be preserved and what must change in the future. Pérez's taut observations on European revolutions and capitalisms, with his notes on contemporary capitalism and socialism in the Cuban landscape, suggest volumes about how individuals experience periods of intense transition.

## 5. Returning

As *Cubanology* comes to a close, it reflects a process of partial reintegration into island life in Cuba's urban capital. Pérez portrays Havana through his daily activities, hinting at the identities to which they give form. Some of these activities are professional. As a translator and creative writer, Pérez deals with Havana's Torre de Letras (offering literary events) and its organizer, poet Reina María Rodríguez. He interacts with Cuba's Union of Writers and Artists (UNEAC). Then there are other roles suggested by everyday events: father to his son Mariano, carpenter, Zen practitioner. We might describe him as "a member of the citizenry" when he registers details such as the information broadcast on "University for Everyone," a TV show run by the government.

In many ways reintegration is a banal process. Yet for a translator in a translated world, it marks a complex and mythical state of becoming. It's no coincidence that highly symbolic figures like Odysseus and Telemachus wander through the notebook. Pérez economizes with his words, veiling emotions or suggesting their presence only through the placement of silences. Yet he references mythical, historical, and spiritual figures who suggest amplified emotions and conflicts. In the digital version he sent me in 2008, he had divided the book of days into chapters, suggesting a larger narrative arc of voyage and metamorphosis. His polycultural notebook, so deliberately entitled *Cubanology*, evokes connections that one Cuban has forged with others in all directions.

## List of Images

"Cubanology 1," with Sandra Ramy. Photographer: Arles. Havana, Cuba, 2000. Page 6

Omar Pérez in the Amsterdam *dojo*. Photographer: unknown. Amsterdam, Holland, 2004. Page 10

Cretan landscape. Photographer: Omar Pérez. Crete, Greece, 2002. Page 23

"Cubanology," opening page from handwritten journal by Omar Pérez. Photographer: Kristin Dykstra. Playa, Cuba, 2010. Page 25

Pérez desk diptych. Photographer: Sam Truitt. Havana, Cuba, 2016. Page 137

Pérez apartment view (rear). Photographer: Sam Truitt. Havana, Cuba, 2016. Page 170

"Dymaxion Map 2," line drawing by Omar Pérez. Photographer: Sam Truitt, Woodstock, NY, 2018. Page 183

"Amsterdam, 2004," page from handwritten journal by Omar Pérez. Photographer: Kristin Dykstra. Playa, Cuba, 2010. Page 195

"History of the Guerrilla Presence," page from handwritten journal by Omar Pérez. Photographer: Kristin Dykstra. Playa, Cuba, 2010. Page 198

Bijlmer Prison. Photographer: Omar Pérez. Amsterdam, Holland, 2004. Page 199

"Rijksmuseum," pages from handwritten journal by Omar Pérez. Photographer: Kristin Dykstra. Playa, Cuba, 2010. Pages 221–222

"Gezellig," pages from handwritten journal by Omar Pérez. Photographer: Kristin Dykstra. Playa, Cuba, 2010. Page 239

"Asíntota," page (detail) from handwritten journal by Omar Pérez. Photographer: Kristin Dykstra. Playa, Cuba, 2010. Page 264

"Seven countries are now designated," page (detail) from handwritten journal by Omar Pérez. Photographer: Kristin Dykstra. Playa, Cuba, 2010. Page 270

Jurryt van de Vooren and Athanasius Sikelianous with Cristina in Greece. Photographer: Omar Pérez. Athens, Greece, 2002. Page 292

"El primer pos-moderno," text, Omar Pérez, 1997. Photographer: Sam Truitt. Havana, Cuba, 2017. Page 294

Bookshelf in Pérez apartment. Photographer: Sam Truitt. Havana, Cuba, 2016. Page 327

Blackboard in Pérez apartment. Photographer: Sam Truitt. Havana, Cuba, 2016. Page 327

Mariano/Spiderman. Photographer: Lilia Rosa López. Havana, Cuba, 2003. Page 328

"Portrait," line drawing, Omar Pérez, 2007. Photographer: Sam Truitt. Havana, Cuba, 2017. Page 329

Omar and Mariano Pérez. Photographer: Georgina Hill. Havana, Cuba, 2017. Page 330

"Sisifo, Print 2," linoleum print, Omar Pérez, 2015. Photographer: Sam Truitt. Havana, Cuba, 2017. Page 331

Omar Pérez (author photo). Photographer: Kristin Dykstra. Havana, Cuba, 2013. Page 352

Kristin Dykstra (translator photo). Photographer: Anna Deeny. San Juan, PR, 2015. Page 354

## Acknowledgments

Excerpts from this translation of *Cubanology* previously appeared in several magazines, generally in earlier renditions. In some cases, that includes the embedded poetry and essays, presented on their own rather than in journal form. We are grateful to all of the editors and staff from these publications who supported the book in progress: *Asymptote*, *Mandorla*, *Jacket2* (within Kristin Dykstra's "Intermedium" commentary series as well as in poetry pages for Pérez), *Zen Monster*, *Fascicle*, and *Seedings*.

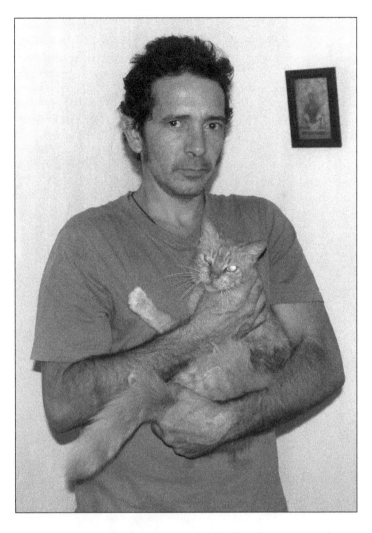

OMAR PÉREZ is an award-winning writer who has long pursued unexpected transformations. He won Cuba's 2010 Nicolás Guillén Prize for Poetry for *Crítica de la razón puta* (*Critique of Fuckup Reason*). His poetry collection *Algo de lo sagrado* (released in a bilingual edition from Factory School as *Something of the Sacred*) is often cited as one of the most significant works of his generation. A bilingual edition of his later book of poems, *Did You Hear About the Fighting*

*Cat? (Oíste hablar del gato de pelea?)*, was published by Shearsman Books in 2010. Critics have framed some of his work in relation to Latin America's "poesía civil" tradition. Pérez unsettles civic discourse with interference from Zen Buddhism, multilingualism, passages of children's verse and popular music, humor, and more. He is also a prizewinning essayist, a literary translator, an editor, and a carpenter. A charismatic presenter, Pérez has become increasingly committed to exploring interdisciplinary arts and performance, including collaborations with experimental dancers and musicians. In 2014 he was a Fellow with the University of Iowa's International Writing Program, and he has presented his work in many countries around the world.

## ABOUT THE TRANSLATOR

KRISTIN DYKSTRA writes about people, places, and culture, with a special interest in motions and intersections amongst the Americas. She is the translator of many book-length collections of Latin American literature, including a set of bilingual editions published by the University of Alabama Press in 2014–2016, featuring Cuban authors Reina María Rodríguez, Juan Carlos Flores, Angel Escobar, and Marcelo Morales. In 2018 Dykstra guest-edited a dossier dedicated to Flores (1962–2016) in *The Chicago Review*. With Kent Johnson, Dykstra is co-editor of *Materia Prima*, an anthology showcasing poetry by Amanda Berenguer (Uruguay) for Ugly Duckling Presse. She is principal translator of *The Winter Garden Photograph*, a collection by Rodríguez forthcoming with the same publisher.

CPSIA information can be obtained
at www.ICGtesting.com
Printed in the USA
LVHW092222241118
598171LV00006B/6/P